PROTEAN PREJUDICE

South Florida-Rochester-Saint Louis
Studies on Religion and the Social Order
EDITED BY

Jacob Neusner   William Scott Green   William M. Shea

PROTEAN PREJUDICE
Anti-Semitism in England's Age of Reason

by
Bernard Glassman

PROTEAN PREJUDICE

ANTI-SEMITISM IN ENGLAND'S AGE OF REASON

by
Bernard Glassman

Scholars Press
Atlanta, Georgia

Protean Prejudice
Anti-Semitism in England's
Age of Reason

by
Bernard Glassman

Published by Scholars Press
for the University of South Florida, University of Rochester,
and Saint Louis University

© 1998 University of South Florida

Funds for the publication of this volume were provided by

The Tyson and Naomi Midkiff Fund for Exellence
of the Department of Religious Studies at the University of South Florida

The Max Richter Foundation of Rhode Island

and

The Tisch Family Foundation of New York City

Library of Congress Cataloging in Publication Data
Glassman, Bernard, 1937–
    Protean prejudice : anti-Semitism in England's Age of Reason / by
Bernard Glassman.
        p.   cm. — (South Florida-Rochester-Saint Louis studies on
religion and the social order ; v. 20)
    Includes bibliographical references (p.   ) and index.
    ISBN 0-7885-0432-0 (cloth : acid-free paper)
    1. Antisemitism—Great Britain—History—18th century.
2. Judaism—Controversial literature—History and criticism.
3. Great Britain—Ethnic relations—History—18th century.
I. Title. II. Series.
DS146.G7G57   1998
305.892'4041'09033—dc21   97-4766
                                 CIP

Printed in the United States of America
on acid-free paper

To Sue

TABLE OF CONTENTS

Preface

The resurgence of anti-Semitism in the post-Holocaust era has rekindled interest in the study of this ancient scourge that refuses to disappear from human experience. Through the centuries, this virulent hatred has taken varied forms in a wide range of locals. Therefore, any in-depth study must, by necessity, be limited to one particular time and place. Certainly, eighteenth century England with its limited geographic area, its relatively small population, and its abundance of easily accessible research material, is a perfect setting for such a task. England's Age of Reason also presents some special situations rarely encountered in European Jewish history. In spite of a significant hatred against the Jewish people that was such an integral part of the folklore, literature, and the religious traditions of the English people, the Jewish community of the period was virtually unmolested. The negative attitudes towards the Jews, that had been nurtured through the centuries, were not translated into the severe persecutions that have been such a familiar dimension of Jewish history.

The absence of mob violence directed against the Jewish people is particularly significant since it will be shown that eighteenth century England, an age that is so often associated with reason, moderation, candor, and genteel manners, was, in reality, beset by deep underlying currents of religious tension as well as fears of foreign invasion and of domestic subversion and violence. The velvet glove, more often than not, covered a steel fist. Yet, neither the bursting of the "South Sea Bubble," the equivalent of a modern day stock market collapse, nor the threats to the Anglican Church and to the unique English way of life, could make the Jew the focus of serious national attention. Even during the brief public furor over the passage of the Naturalization Bill of 1753, virtually no serious physical actions were taken against either individual Jews or the Jewish community as a whole. Certainly, English Jewry enjoyed a much more secure existence than their co-religionists on the Continent.

At first glance, it might seem that this spirit of toleration can be attributed to the growing secularism and enlightenment of the period. However, virtually all those who were in the forefront of this new age of reason were hostile towards both Jews and Judaism. Although, in the case of the Deists, this hatred stemmed from a general hatred of all revealed religion, their anti-Semitic pronouncements were particularly vitriolic. Instead of combating medieval prejudices against the Jews, the Deists brought new charges that were based on their own "enlightened " value system. They added to the classical Jewish stereotype the elements of superstition, immoderate behavior, and a lack of both social graces and cultural productivity.[1]

It was traditional Christianity that supplied much of the ideological background for this period, and this faith continued to be an integral part of the lives of the great bulk of the English people. Although the sectarian conflicts of the prior century had cooled and groups like the Ranters and the Muggletonians were no longer on the scene, religious controversy was far from over. However, throughout the century, in spite of the differences that divided the various denominations, the theological image of the Jews as a people who had rejected Jesus and who could only be redeemed through conversion to "the true faith" persisted among all shades of Christian belief. This attitude was not affected by the scientific advances of the time. In fact, the new spirit of inquiry into the nature of the world was not divorced from the religious teachings of the past. The fledgling scientists of the period were deeply influenced by their Christian traditions; this new age of reason was in many ways a continuation rather than a break with past prejudices.

Throughout history, virtually every society has permitted an outlet for its aggressive impulses and deep-rooted frustrations to exist in a way that would not significantly harm the power structure. These scapegoats were not totally blameless, but they were persecuted far out of proportion to their real or imagined misdeeds. The Jewish people, from the time of Pharaoh, was the classic "other" who traditionally satisfied this need. In eighteenth century England, a host of such outcasts appeared on the scene that was far more numerous and much more of a tempting target for the wrath of the general populace than the Jews.

Stromberg points out, for example, that during this period Catholicism remained "as repugnant to the overwhelming majority of Englishmen as it had been ever since the sixteenth century; if anything, more so." [2] But Catholics were not the only objects of ridicule, fear, or

---

[1] Jacob Katz, "Misreading of Anti-Semitism," *Commentary* 76 (July, 1983):42.
[2] Roland N. Stromberg, *Religious Liberalism in Eighteenth Century England* (London: Oxford University Press, 1954), p.14.

disgust who drew attention away from the Jewish people. In this multi-religious and multi- ethnic society, it was now mostly the Quakers who were mocked for their distinctive garb and unique speech patterns. In popular imagination, the Gypsies and the Blacks were perceived to be more exotic and less trustworthy than the "tawny Jews," while the English Jacobins, in league with the French revolutionaries across the Channel, became the new international conspirators. Not only the Jews, but the Irish, the Scots, and the Huguenots were objects of scorn, ridicule, and jealousy for their clannishness; while sodomists were mercilessly harassed and threatened with death for practicing their "abominable acts." During this period, there was also an exaggerated fear of the growing influence of atheism. For many Englishmen, Masons, members of other secret societies as well as free thinkers of all shades of opinion, were perceived to be a greater threat to the Anglican Church than the Jewish people who at least maintained a religious tradition that was rooted in Scripture.

Elisabeth Young- Bruel has demonstrated that prejudice is not a singular phenomenon, but that it stems from a variety of different needs and varies in disparate social contexts.[3] As each of these "other" groups in the Age of Reason occupied the attention of the English people, and as prejudice, like the mythological Proteus, took new forms, the Jews were, to a significant degree, ignored. Only when they allowed themselves to become the focus of attention did they experience the sting of really painful anti-Semitic barbs. But even then, these attacks were mainly verbal in nature; they never approached the physical violence of the Gordon or Priestly Riots. As Allport points out, one scapegoat is sufficient to bring a closure to a period of distress.[4]

Thus, the Age of Reason's dark side, with its host of "others," provided a changing variety of channels for the hatreds and jealousies of the period. The equilibrium that resulted from the balancing out of these tensions was, in many ways, a blessing for the Jewish people. As Voltaire(1694-1778) notes, "If one religion were allowed in England, the government would very possibly become arbitrary; if there were but

---

[3]Elisabeth Young - Bruel, *The Anatomy of Prejudices* (Cambridge, Massachusetts: Harvard University Press, 1996).
[4]Gordon W. Allport, *The Nature of Prejudice* (New York: Doubleday & Company, 1958), p.248.

two, the people would cut one another's throats; but as there are such a multitude, they all live happily in peace."[5]

Ian Christie, in his book, Stress *and Stability,* theorizes why a revolution did not take place in eighteenth century England. He is correct when he notes that, "It is hard enough for a historian to assign causes for events. It is even harder – almost to the point of impossibility – to identify with confidence causes for the nonoccurrence of events" (p.2). This book will show how the protean nature of eighteenth century English prejudice was significantly, but certainly not entirely responsible for preventing the deeply ingrained hatred against both Jews and Judaism from being translated into violent acts of anti-Semitism. Though a great deal has been written about the philo-Semitism of the period, much of this supposed admiration for Jews and Judaism was primarily a means of converting a pariah group who, for centuries, had managed to withstand the forces of Christian persecution. In reality, the fear and distrust of the Jew, the classical "other," did not diminish. It stubbornly remained part of the spirit of the times; during the Age of Reason the venue had simply shifted.

Rather than repeat much of what has already been written about the Jewish community of eighteenth century England by such talented contemporary historians as Todd Endelman and David Katz, this book will focus on an overview of the prejudices directed against the "others" in the larger heterogeneous society of which the Jews were only a small part. Hopefully, many of the quotations taken from the periodicals, tracts, and sermons of the period will capture the spirit and the intensity of these festering hatreds that were directed to a wide variety of religious, ethnic, racial, social, and national groups. Historical works on anti-Semitism usually begin with a study of the Jewish community and the nature of its persecutors. Unfortunately, this approach, as important as it may be, tends to put this hatred into a vacuum. It removes anti-Semitism from the other major tensions in society which often influence its direction and virulence. Therefore, although scattered references are made to the Jewish community of England in the early sections of the book, it is not until Chapter Seven that I actually focus upon the Jews of the period.

Looking at the bigger picture of the Jewish experience, anti-Semitism, because of its intensity and longevity, is certainly a unique world-wide phenomenon that stands on its own in the realm of bigotry

---

[5]Voltaire. "Letter VI" in *Letters Concerning the English Nation* (London: 1733) p.45.

and hatred. Yet, as a study of this particular period of history will show, it has much in common with the experiences of various "others" in society as well. Hopefully, this book will encourage the study of the interrelationship and the protean nature of some of the prejudices that could only be touched upon in a very cursory manner.

My research in eighteenth century English anti-Semitism began while I served as rabbi of the Tifereth Israel Synagogue in New Bedford, Massachusetts. I am grateful to the members of the congregation who encouraged me in my work and contributed the funds for my research in England and Scotland. The Rockefeller Library at Brown University, the British Museum, the Scottish National library, the Harvard Widener and Divinity School Libraries, The Episcopal Divinity School Library, and the Library of the Jewish Theological Seminary, provided me with the initial material used in my research. It was at the Houghton Library at Harvard where the bulk of my original sources were located; where all the pieces of a challenging puzzle began to fit into place. I am grateful to a most competent staff who went out of their way to supply me with the religious tracts, pamphlets, sermon collections, and periodicals of the time that were so necessary for the completion of this task.

I would like to make special mention of Tom Amos, Head of the Houghton Library Reading Room during the 1995-96 academic year, who generously gave of his time to help me crystallize many of my ideas about the protean nature of prejudice and showed me the universal implications of my work. Jacob Neusner, a brilliant scholar and a devoted teacher, was a source of inspiration and encouragement when I first began to do research in Anglo-Jewish history. I thank him for the many kindnesses he extended to me during the final stages of writing this book. I am also grateful to the members of the British Study Group at Harvard's Center for European Studies who, by their own example of critical thinking and careful scholarship, demonstrated how to approach this complex topic. I was most fortunate to have had the opportunity to discuss my research with Thomas W. Perry. Decades ago, his book, *Public Opinion, Propaganda, and Politics in Eighteenth – Century England,* aroused my interest in this period of Anglo-Jewish history, and it raised questions which I am still trying to answer. His student, Amy Zaro, made several helpful suggestions that have been incorporated into the text of this book. In addition, Thomas Ford of Houghton Library proved to be both a competent proofreader and a most insightful critic of my work. Last, but not least, I would like to thank those faculty members and students of the Harvard and Episcopal Divinity Schools and of U Mass Dartmouth who showed an interest in my research and who encouraged me in the exploration of a complex subject. Our frank discussions on the nature of prejudice have convinced me that we are not doomed to repeat the mistakes of the past.

Bernard Glassman
Cambridge, Massachusetts

1

The Temper of the Times

When Britain first at Heaven's command
Arose from out of the azure main,
This was the charter of the land,
And guardian angels sang the strain;
'Rule Britannia, rule the waves;
Britons never will be slaves."[1]

The elegance of the sedan chair, however,
ought not lead us into overlooking the grimy
faces of those who often peered through its
glasses, or spattered it with mud in a riot, or died
on foreign battlefields to preserve the comforts of
its patrician owner.[2]

The Age of Reason is one of those nebulous labels that is placed upon a period of time and which, in reality, means very little. Under close scrutiny it fails to convey either the spirit or the substance of a complex age that was filled with contradictions and inconsistencies. There was no real unifying force in either the secular or the religious thought of the time, and, as a result, it was a period that is considered to be "rationalistic, sentimentalistic, optimistic and pessimistic, melancholy, necrophilic, contented with itself and fond of nature,"[3]

Although the Age of Reason is generally associated with the eighteenth century, some scholars believe that it actually began with John Locke's *Essay Concerning Human Understanding* (1690) or with Isaac Newton's *Principia* (1687).[4] Human thought rarely fits into neat

---

[1]James Thompson, *Rule Britannia, 1740*
[2]T. H. White, *The Age of Scandal* (Oxford: Oxford University Press, 1986), p. 106.
[3]George Boas, "In Search of the Age of Reason," in *Aspects of the Eighteenth Century*, ed. Earl R. Wasserman (Baltimore: The Johns Hopkins Press, 1965), p. 2.
[4]Harold Nicholson, *The Age of Reason (1700-1789)* (London: Constable & Co., 1960), p. 16.

chronological or intellectual categories, and this particular period was no exception. Along with the continuation of some of the more reasonable traditions of past generations, echoes of Puritan zeal condemning atheism, irreligion, and the desecration of the Sunday Sabbath could still be heard. It was an age of both scientific discovery and religious fervor when enlightened thinkers viewed natural happenings as supernatural warnings and signs; when statesmen spoke of divine support and displeasure. J.C.D. Clark warns of the dangers of being too hasty in diagnosing the supposed secularization of the period. "To a secular mind," he believes, "all things become secular."[5] In the words of John Redwood, it was " an age of enthusiasts against enthusiasm."[6]

In virtually every area of endeavor in this age, ideas, beliefs, and thought processes from the past continued to exert a strong influence upon all strata of the population. Along with the growing spirit of empiricism, the hallmark of eighteenth century intellectual life, there was also superstition, mysticism, a fascination with the occult, and the accumulated prejudices of past generations.

Throughout the countryside and in metropolitan centers as well, stories of fairies, ghosts, and goblins, passed down through the generations, were retold. Although the last execution for witchcraft took place in 1684, and the last indictment in 1717, as late as 1751, Thomas Colley was executed for his part in the brutal murder of an alleged witch. The persecution of suspected witches continued through the century and into the next. In rural areas, women suspected of having supernatural powers were harassed and dunked in horse ponds. In one such incident which took place in Somersetshire in 1731, the *Gentleman's Magazine* for January of that year reported that no less than 200 spectators gathered to witness the trial by water ordeal of an alleged witch (p. 29).

The belief in witchcraft, though on the decline, still attracted some very learned supporters, and in 1706 John Hancock (1671-1752), in one of his Boyle Lectures, defended it on the basis of both biblical and empirical evidence.[7] Later John Wesley (1703-1791) wholeheartedly accepted the reality of witchcraft; he criticized those who rejected it as being under the corrupting influence of the Deists. Along with Wesley, there were a host of clerics who believed that any denunciation of the reality of witches was a direct attack upon religious practice and belief.

---

[5]J.C.D. Clark, "Reconceptualizing Eighteenth-Century England," *British Journal for Eighteenth Century Studies* 15 (Autumn, 1992):138.
[6]John Redwood, *Reason, Ridicule and Religion: The Age of Enlightenment in England 1660-1750* (Cambridge, Massachusetts: Harvard University Press, 1976), p. 16.
[7]John Hancock, *Boyle Lectures 1691-1732* vol. 2 ed. Sampson Letsome (London: 1739), pp. 217-18.

Superstition was prevalent in all strata of English society. Samuel Johnson (1709-1784) was one of many educated gentlemen who was convinced that the royal touch was an effective cure for disease, and Tobias Smollett (1721-1771), a practicing physician, seriously believed that the application of the hand of a hanged man could cure skin tumors. Throughout the century, along with the new spirit of empirical research, pseudo-science and primitive religious beliefs continued to flourish. Edmund Halley (1656-1742), Isaac Newton (1642-1727), and William Whiston (1667-1752), shared a common belief that comets were instruments of divine intervention. The Bishop of London and dozens of other clergymen viewed the earthquakes that struck London in 1750 as God's punishment for the sins of the people.

The English people of this period have often been pictured as hard working, hard living, and plain speaking individuals who stoically accepted their lot in life. However, beneath this sober exterior there was cynicism, coarseness, and cruelty. Life was viewed as a very cheap commodity; even petty crimes committed by children were punishable by death. For many, solace was to be found in the cheap gin and spirits that, for the early part of the century, seemed to flood the country. One moralist, alarmed at the increase in ale-houses and "Strong Water Shops" noted: "that one half of the town seems to be set up to furnish out poison to destroy the other half."[8] Cock fighting, bear baiting, and public hangings were a great source of amusement. Another popular diversion was a tour of one of London's favorite attractions, the infamous Bethlehem Hospital, where the insane were mercilessly ridiculed by tens of thousands of yearly visitors. As Michael Deporte notes:

> Indeed it should not surprise us in an age where
> satire and lampoon flourished, where non conformity
> in religion or politics was bitterly resented and attacked,
> and where politeness was so highly esteemed, that the
> madman should exercise particular fascination as the
> ultimate departure from taste and good sense.[9]

Beneath the facade of fashion, elegance, and manners, the idealized image of upper class life, there was a darker side as well. The gentry were careful to behave in public with the proper decorum that was expected of people of their station. However, in private many indulged

---

[8]Richard Hooker, *The Weekly Miscellany* February 24, 1733. Although this is an obvious exaggeration, the *Penny London Post* of January 24,1726 claims that every fifth house in one of the largest parishes is a retail shop for "Geneva Water "and other spirits.
[9]Michael V. Deporte, *Nightmares and Hobbyhorses: Swift, Sterne, and Augustan Ideas of Madness* (San Marino, California: The Huntington Library, 1974), p. 3.

themselves in their secret societies, in their morbid fascination with death, and in their worship of Bacchus and Aphrodite.[10]

Both individual and collective violence was part of daily life, and mobs freely expressed the pent-up rage of the common people who found it impossible to express their grievances in any other way. In a society where any overstepping of the boundary lines between master and servant, squire and villager, husband and wife, father and child was considered to be an act of petty treason that was subject to the most ruthless suppression, resentment sometimes exploded in acts of desperate violence.[11] Riots were often spontaneous acts to express disapproval of high food prices, poor working conditions or threats to livelihood. Through them, the middle and lower classes could also defend their traditions, their church, and all that was dear to them from real and imaginary foes with little fear of prosecution.

Though much has been written about the changes that took place in English religious thought and practice during the Age of Reason, the great bulk of the English people were loyal to the legacies that had been handed down to them from what they had been taught was a glorious past. Because most of them believed that they possessed qualities that were far superior to those of any nation on the face of the earth and that their country embodied all that was good, noble, and virtuous, it was clearly in the best interests of the nation to leave things as they were. Furthermore, they believed that there was a special alliance between God and England ; no other nation was so blessed and so exalted by Divine Providence. The Established Church provided the solid religious foundations for the country's "fair and beautiful constitution" that allowed the English people to enjoy "the finest government under heaven."[12]This self-glorification justified the need to maintain the status quo and to keep those without property or who were not of the approved religion in their place. The English love of country also created an atmosphere where any thing foreign, different, or unchristian was viewed with suspicion and scorn.

The study of comparative religion that was popular during this age of travel and exploration was often a mirror of old prejudices rather than a search for greater toleration and understanding. The title of a work by William Hecford on this subject, *A Succinct Account of all the Religions, and Various Sects in Religion, that have prevailed in the World in All Nations and*

---

[10]Ronald Fuller, *Hell Fire Francis* (London: Chatio and Windus, 1939), p. 36.

[11]Harold Perkin, *Origins of Modern English Society* (London: Ark Paperbacks, 1985), p. 37.

[12]David Hempton, *Religion and Political Culture in Britain and Ireland: From the Glorious Revolution to the decline of Empire* (Cambridge: Cambridge UP, 1996), p. 13.

in All Ages, From the Earliest Account of Time to the Present Period, From the most Indisputable Tradition; Shewing Some of Their Gross Absurdities, Shocking Impieties, and Ridiculous Inconsistencies, reflects the popular prejudices directed against "other" religious traditions. The author's attitudes towards Judaism are particularly scathing. Although he leaves it to more competent scholars to determine how many of the ancient Jewish rituals were actually copied from the Egyptians, he is quite vociferous about modern Judaism. It is, he believes, "a manifest absurdity", a religion that is full of mysteries. Contemporary Jewish practices are "superstitious," and both the observance of the Sabbath and the laws of mourning offend his Christian sensibilities.(pp. 443-44).

Both directly and indirectly, this kind of thinking was reinforced by the Anglican Church, the bastion of the English way of life. Throughout the century, in spite of its crises, controversies, and challenges, it still remained the Church of England; the provider of social cohesion and the agent of benevolence and public morality.[13] Recent scholarship has shown that it was much more vibrant, efficient, and in tune with the needs of the people than was previously assumed to be true.[14]Yet, much remained basically unchanged. The fundamental doctrines that were taught by the Church of England in the seventeenth and eighteenth centuries had not been revised since the time of the Edwardian Reformation and the Elizabethan settlement. The *Book of Common Prayer,* the Catechism of 1549, as well as the Thirty-Nine articles of 1571 and the official homilies of 1547 and 1563 still retained their importance.[15] In *A Letter to A Friend Upon His Entrance On The Ministerial Office,* John Mason, (1706-1763) though an independent cleric, reflects the temper of the Anglican Church when he gives the following advice:

> Study moderation in all things....Extremes are always
> dangerous, often pernicious: none but persons of the

---

[13]E. R. Norman, *Church and Society in England 1770-1970* (Oxford: Clarendon Press, 1976), p. 15.

[14]One of the best examples of this new appreciation of the Anglican Church's role in eighteenth century England is John Walsh, Colin Haydon, Stephen Taylor, eds *The Church of England c. 1689-1833: From Toleration to Tractarianism* (Cambridge: Cambridge University Press, 1993). See also F.C. Mather, *High Church Prophet. Bishop Samuel Horsley (1733-1806) and the Caroline Tradition in the Later Georgian Church* (Oxford: Clarendon Press, 1992). Mather argues that even if the achievements of eighteenth century Anglican clerics may not have always equaled those of their predecessors, they nevertheless did a competent job of perpetuating their legacy.

[15]Ian Green "Anglicanism in Stuart and Hanoverian England," in *A History of Religion in Britain: Practice and Belief from Pre-Roman Times to the Present,* ed. Sheridan Gilley and W.J. Sheils (Cambridge, Massachusetts: Blackwell Publishers, 1994), p. 169.

strongest passions and weakest minds run into them.
Health, truth, wisdom, virtue, are all to be found in the
mean: Excess impairs or obscures them all (p. 7).
In order to be well established in the grounds of Christianity
and in the great principles of Christian liberty, you will do
well to converse with some of our best writers against the
Deists and Papists. But as for theological controversy in
general (especially considering the manner in which it is
too often conducted) you will find in it so great a mixture of vanity,
confidence, ill temper, wrong zeal. and fine-spun labour'd
trifles, as to have but few charms to attract a judicious, free,
benevolent mind (p. 25)....Beware of an innovating spirit,
or a love of novelty in religious principles. Tis a dangerous
affection; and hath drawn multitudes into scepticism on the
one hand, and the wildest enthusiasm on the other (p. 33).

Even though the eighteenth century was an age which Asa Briggs
believes marked the birth of a consumer society where "getting and
spending" and "having and enjoying" were very important, this did not
mean that traditional religion with its emphasis on the next world, was
not a vital element in English life.[16]Although it might be assumed that
the increasing emphasis on moderation and reason on behalf of the
leading clerics of the time resulted in a more liberal attitude towards the
Jews and a lessening of theological anti-Semitism, it is clear that both the
religious establishment as well as those who dissented from its teachings
maintained the classic negative Christian attitudes that went back to the
early church councils. As in the past, the legitimacy of Christianity was
strengthened by the degradation of the Jewish people.

In *The Weekly Miscellany* for April 12, 1735, a newspaper that
vigorously defended the doctrines and the practices of the Anglican
Church against its various critics, there is a front page discussion of why
Christ did not appear in "a more public manner to the multitude of
unbelieving Jews." Both the tone and the content of the answer, which
appears just prior to Easter, reflect the religious establishment's
unchanging prejudice against the Jewish people, the "hardened infidels"
of history.

As to the Jews, in particular, if a more
extraordinary method of conviction seems
requisite for the conversion of such inveterate
enemies, than for others who are better
disposed to believe the truth of Christ's
resurrection, this gave them no right to
demand it; neither was it consistent with the
settled purposes of God that they should have

---

[16]Asa Briggs, *A Social History of England* (Middlesex, England: Penguin Books,
1985), pp. 177-78.

> been convinced in such an extraordinary
> manner. Their obdurate temper, which arose
> from their lusts and passions, was in itself
> highly criminal, deserving rather the Divine
> vengeance than any particular marks of favour
> and goodness. Their slowness of heart to believe
> the miracles of our Saviour, and to embrace his
> doctrine proceeded from their inveterate malice.

Judging from these statements and so many others like them, Christianity was by no means defunct, and It continued to sustain the stereotypical image of the Jew that was to influence both religious and secular thought. Even those who rejected much of its dogmatism still believed in its superiority over Judaism.

In the myriads of religious tracts that were circulated in England at this time, medieval legends that deal with Jewish inferiority were accepted as fact. For example, one writer believes that, when Jesus was born, the temple in Rome dedicated to Pan fell to the ground while in Spain a great light appeared that turned night into day. [17] In addition, he reiterates the classic Christian belief that the destruction of Jerusalem and the slaughter of its inhabitants was a punishment for the Jewish involvement in the Crucifixion. He notes that after the city had been razed to the ground, Jews came to lament at the sight of the ruined temple " bearing in their habits and bodies the sad characters of divine vengeance of whom the soldiers exacted a fee for weeping; and they who formerly sold the blood of Jesus were now forced to buy their own tears."[18] In this spirit, the following statement made by Nathaniel Lardner (1684-1768), a non conformist divine, could have been uttered by a host of medieval clerics or by any number of his contemporaries as well.

> God cast them off from being his people, as they
> had been, and poured down upon them tokens of
> his displeasure: yet not destroying them utterly, and
> making use of them, even under afflictions, to support
> the truth of his son's mission and authority, whom
> they had crucified.[19]

George Colebrook (fl. 1791) went one step further than classic Christian theology to blacken the image of the Jewish people. In his *Six Letters on*

---

[17]*The Captivities of Jerusalem Lamented or a Plain Description of Jerusalem* (Manchester: 1780), p. 10.

[18]Ibid., 23.

[19]Nathaniel Lardner, *The Circumstances of the Jewish People An Argument for the Truth of the Christian Religion Three Discourses on Romans XI:11* (London: 1752), p. 70.

Intolerance, he blames the Jews for Christian anti-Semitism. He believes that " this persecuting spirit, which infected Christians, came evidently from the intolerance of the Jews" which he feels was derived from the biblical mandate "to punish idolatry with fire and sword"(pp. 497-98). Here was a clear case of the oppressor blaming the victim for being persecuted.

The Anglican sermons of the period lack the fire and the passion of those of prior centuries. The great majority of them are stiff, tedious works that reflect practical morality and a calm, rational approach to life.[20] According to Leslie Stephen, "Dull duller and dullest are a sufficient vocabulary to describe their merits."[21] Although the modern reader may very well agree with this evaluation, pulpit oratory was, nevertheless, an important part of the mass media of the times. Not only were these lengthy discourses heard by the Sunday worshipers, but with Parliament's abolishment of the Restrictive Printing Act, there was, starting at the beginning of the century, a substantial market for religious texts. They were now directed to a reading public and not simply to please a particular patron. Printed sermons became a significant part of popular literature, and since it was a common practice among the clergy to borrow from a colleague's work, the impact of the leading preachers on the faithful was multiplied on any number of pulpits throughout the country.

The anti-Jewish sentiments found in eighteenth century sermons are essentially an extension of both the theology and the popular attitudes of past centuries. For example, the acceptance of the Jews as being God's chosen people continued to be a problem for eighteenth century clerics just as it had been for their predecessors in prior centuries who believed in the doctrine of Christian superiority over Judaism. In a sermon delivered to the Society for the Propagation of the Gospel in Foreign Parts, the Lord Bishop of Sarum notes that God did not intend to limit revelation to any one people and that the Jews were to be condemned for refusing to share their gift with others. God's name, he believes, should be magnified by all nations. He criticizes those Jews who "did rise to higher degrees of fury" when the Apostles preached to the Gentiles and put them on an equal footing with the Chosen People without

---

[20]C.H. Sisson, ed. *The English Sermon 1650-1750* vol. II (Surrey, England: Cancanet Press, 1976), p. 14 and Rolf P. Lessenich, *Elements of Pulpit Oratory in Eighteenth Century England* (1660-1800) (Vienna: Bohlau-Verlaag, Koln, 1972), p. ix.
[21]Leslie Stephen, *History of English Thought in the Eighteenth Century* vol. II (New York: G.P. Putnam's Sons, 1927), p. 336.

demanding from them either circumcision or the observance of the Mosaic Code.[22]

Perhaps the most powerful theological condemnations of the Jewish people appear in the sermons delivered by members of The Society for the Propagation of Christian Knowledge. In these discourses that were first delivered from the pulpit and then printed and widely circulated, a popular theme is the punishment of the Jews throughout history for their role in the crucifixion of Jesus. As in the medieval past, it was a means of elevating Christianity by degrading the Jewish people. James Robertson (1714-1795) is but one of many clerics of the Society who preached that:

> This sinful nation rejected the Messiah and crucified the
> the Lord of Life; and not only fastened the guilt of that
> atrocious crime upon themselves, but entailed the same
> upon their posterity....all the people in the fullest sense
> of the expression, answered and said, "His blood be on
> us and our children.[23]

The fatherhood of God and the brotherhood of mankind, a common theme among those clerics interested in ameliorating some of the more serious problems of society, did not, in most instances, apply to the Jewish people. In his sermon, "The influence of Christianity on the Condition of the world," Thomas Coombe speaks of the Christian responsibility to deal compassionately with the inhabitants of Africa who are "equally entitled to all the privileges of humanity" (p. 10). Furthermore, "We owe it, as the best atonement in our power, to the God and father of mankind, whose image we have so long vilified and degraded, in the person of these our unhappy brethren" (p. 10). Coombe also views the Jewish people theologically, but in their case he comes to a different conclusion. He believes that they are really not flesh and blood creatures but proof of Christian belief. "The Jews under circumstances which must long since have exterminated any other people, remain a standing memorial that the invisible arm of Christ still rules his kingdom" (p. 12).

As in the past, any number of preachers used the classic negative Jewish stereotypes as a contrast to what they believed were the inherently superior qualities of Christianity. For example, in his comparison of the ancient Jews with the early Christians, Isaac Barrow(1630-1677), a seventeenth century divine whose influence

---

[22]Gilbert, Lord Bishop of Sarum, *A Sermon Preached at Mary-le-Bow February 18, 1704* (London: Printed for D. Brown, 1704), p. 2.

[23]James Robertson, *The Resemblance of Jesus to Moses Considered, and the Extraordinary and Continued Punishment of the Jews Shown to be a Standing Evidence of the Truth of Christianity.* (Edinburgh: Society for the Propagation of Christian Knowledge, 1765), p. 43-4.

continued for many years after his death, notes in one of his sermons that the Jews by their "seditious and turbulent practices and by their insolent contempt and implacable hatred for others" gained few converts. The Christians, on the other hand, by demonstrating " a mild patient and peaceable behaviour and perfect innocence and abstinence from doing injury" persuaded great numbers to accept their faith.[24] The popular and often quoted preacher, John Tillotson, (1630-1694) repeated the charge that the Jews of ancient Israel, in contrast to the early Christians, gave charity only to their own people and they were hostile to their neighbors. It was Jesus, Tillotson notes, who was responsible for restoring the true concept of love and charity by extending it to all people.[25] Tillotson was particularly hostile towards the Jews when he defended the truth of Christian tradition. In a series of sermons designed to buttress the faith of the Anglicans, he makes both the ancient and modern Jews adversaries of the worst sort. He believes that the Jews of Jesus' time did not understand the true meaning of messianism while " nothing but plain malice against Christ, and the Christian religion, makes the modern Jews to depart herein from the sense of their ancient masters."[26] Tillotson often refers to the "malice of the Jews" when they do not accept such concepts as Mary's Davidic lineage or Jesus' resurrection.[27] Jewish and Heathen writings are "the testimonies of enemies," and on several occasions he notes that it was the " unreasonable obstinacy " of the Jewish people that brought about the destruction of their temple.[28]

Whenever a more odious group could be found, the Jews would temporarily be relieved from bearing the brunt of the preacher's venom. Thus, in his sermon, "Jewish and Popish Zeal Describ'd and Compar'd," Simon Browne (1680-1789) repeats the age old theme that "Jews were instigated to persecute our Saviour to death and vex and murther his faithful disciples" (p. 4). Christianity, he believes, stands for love and goodwill to all humanity in contrast to the Jews' hateful ways. But, he notes, the "Romanists have exceeded them in their rage against all who stood in their way." (p. 40)

The animosities that erupted between the religious establishment and its Deist adversaries during the first half of the eighteenth century

---

[24]Isaac Barrow, " Of a Peaceable Temper and Carriage" in Sasoon *English Sermons* vol. II p. 73.
[25]John Tillotson, "Of Doing Good" in *Sermons* vol. 6, pp. 409-10 cited in Rolf P. Lessenich, *Elements of Pulpit Oratory in Eighteenth Century England: 1660-1800* (Vienna: Bohlau-Vertag, Koln, 1972), p. 230.
[26]John Tillotson, *Several Discourses of the Truth and the Excellancy of Christian Religion* (London: 1703), p. 16.
[27]Ibid., p. 80.
[28]Ibid., p. 110, p. 134.

was centered around the interpretation of the basic tenets of Christianity, and it was, at first glance, not a Jewish problem. Yet, Jews found themselves mentioned in the sermons and the religious literature that was circulated by both sides. Although they were scorned by those who attacked Christianity, they did not fare any better with the establishment. Anglican clerics considered Jews to be outsiders whom they lumped together with all those who threatened traditional religion. Thus, both sides used them for their own purposes, and neither group had very much sympathy for either ancient or modern Jewry. The greatest minds were arrayed on the side of the orthodox.[29] But all of their ability and learning had no effect upon their anti-Jewish sentiments that were a carry-over from previous centuries.

The conflict between the religious establishment and the Deists was reflected in the Boyle Lectures which contained the definitive arguments of the Anglican Church against its most strident enemies. These lectures, which have been credited with setting the content and the tone of eighteenth century natural religion, were very popular among the educated classes who were more familiar with their contents than with the scientific treatises of Newton.[30] Their purpose was to prove the truth of Christianity against such notorious infidels as "Atheists, Deists, Pagans, Jews and Mahometans."[31] They contained numerous tirades against the Jewish peoples as well as appeals to convert them to Christianity. The traditional role of the Jews as the adversaries of the true faith was stressed in these lectures by clerics who were anxious to please their superiors and to advance themselves in the Church's hierarchy.

The first Boyle lecturer, Richard Bentley (1662-1742), was more concerned with denouncing the growing secularism of the time than attacking either Deists or Jews. Only scattered and rather innocuous references to Jews can be found in his sermons. In one of his discourses, The *Folly of Atheism*, he equates the Sadducees with the Epicureans, and he notes that they "were not only rough and cruel to men of a different sect from their own but perfidious and inhuman one towards another"(p. 24). In another of his lectures, *Of Revalation and the Messias*,"

---

[29]Stephen, vol. II, p. 86.

[30]Margaret C. Jacob, *The Newtonians and the English Revolution 1689-1720.* (Ithaca, New York: Cornell University Press, 1976), p. 162-3.

[31]The full statement of purpose for these lectures that were endowed by Robert Boyle reads as follows: "To preach eight sermons in the year, for proving the Christian religion against notorious infidels, viz. Atheists, Deists, Pagans, Jews and Mahometans: not descending to any controversies that are among Christians themselves. Cited in Richard Bentley, *Sermons Preached at Boyle's Lecture.* (London: Francis Macpherson, 1838), p. XV.

he points out how the Deists use "Jewish objections" to Jesus' messianism even though they do not believe in them (p. 222).

The lecturers who follow Bentley are much more hostile to the Jewish people; they expand his references to Jewish cruelty and the arguments that he claims the Jews raised against Jesus' messianism. For example, Ofspring Blackall (1659-1716), in his sermon, *The Excellancy of Christian Revelation, as it Removes the Guilty Fears of Sinners, and their ignorance of God,"* points out that the Almighty appreciated the "weakness and Rudeness" of the Jewish people and he revealed to them only as much as they could bear. It was preparatory for a more complete revelation that would appear with the coming of Jesus(p. 18).

William Berriman (1688-1750), in *The Gradual Revelation of the Gospel: From the Time of Man's Apostacy,* condemned the Jews for their mistaken notion of the nature of the true messiah. He believed that their partiality, national prejudice, "carnal conceits", and "disrelish of all but sensual satisfactions" made them blind to the true meaning of the scriptural prophesies that made Jesus the Messiah (p. 48-49). He lumps modern Jews together with the infidels of his time, and he believes that their "heated prejudice" against Christian doctrine keeps them out of the mainstream of English life (p. 316). Like other clerics of his time, he believes that Jewish texts like the Targum, an Aramaic translation of Hebrew Scriptures, contains many latter-day fabrications. Therefore, Jews have their old prejudices confirmed by new forgeries (p. 348).

Leonard Twells (d.1742), another Boyle lecturer, refers to the Jews as " enemies to Christianity" who provide the modern day infidels with ammunition in their battle with the religious establishment. The Deists,he notes, argue on Jewish principles to undermine traditional Christian religion.[32] In addition, the Jews are evil in their own right. They view the Messiah as a "blessing to themselves only" a figure who will reduce all the families of the Earth to his obedience and to the religious and civil Jewish customs as well. He claims that the Jews are so narrow minded that they believe that the Messiah will even force Christians to become circumcised.[33] Twells also condemns them for being so blinded by prejudice and " judicial delusion" that they refuse to accept the prophesies of Isaiah as evidence of the truth of the Gospels.[34]

Throughout the Boyle Lectures and in a host of Anglican sermons, tracts and journals, there is a very real concern, bordering on militancy, for maintaining the moral climate of English society. The Jews appear as a stumbling block to achieving a truly Christian nation, but they are not

---

[32]Leonard Twells, *Twenty-Four Sermons* (London: 1743), p. 129.
[33]Ibid., 130-31.
[34]Ibid., Vol. II p. 6.

alone in their villainy. Of even greater concern are the Atheists and the Deists who are far more numerous and who pose a greater threat to law and order and a cherished way of life than the Jews. The bishops blame them for both the poor attendance at worship services as well as the general decline in morality. The combined forces of ridicule and reason, the clerics believed, could undermine the Protestant succession and ferment civil strife in the country.[35]

> When men can set no bounds to their
> impudence, we ought not to set common
> bounds to our zeal. Shall a villain dare
> openly to blaspheme my Lord and my
> Saviour and I not dare to call him an
> Infidel and an apostate for so doing?
> Away with such notions of moderation!
> They are the scandal of our times, and the
> reproach of our nation. If such miscreants
> don't care to be called atheists, they ought
> to take care not to deserve to be call'd so.
> The name is purely reproachful, but the thing
> is damnable.[36]

Though misguided, the Jews did have a sense of morality that was based on a belief in God. In the eyes of the Anglicans, they stood on much firmer ground than those who rejected any belief in a Supreme Being.

The preachers who display any sympathy for the Jewish people are invariably motivated by a desire to convert them. They view the sermon, in both its oral and written form, as an important tool to guide this wayward people to the true faith which, for so many centuries, they have stubbornly rejected. On the frontispiece of William Cooper"s sermon, The *Promised Seed*, the preacher notes that his motive for publishing his discourse is to use the profits to provide free copies of his text to the Jews. The sermon follows the usual pattern of the conversionist literature of the time. First, there is praise for the Jewish people's noble ancestry which is expressed in Cooper's self-deprecating statement: "You are the lineal descendants of God's ancient chosen people, we are the children of idolatrous and execrable gentiles" (p. 9). Furthermore, "The meanist Jew has in his respect more dignity than the greatest princes"(p. 13). Following this, he offers his proof of Jesus' messianism to his Jewish audience, and he offers the prayer that " the God of Abraham, the God of Isaac, and the God of Jacob, look down upon you with complacency and

---

[35]John Redwood *Reason, Ridicule and Religion: The Age of Enlightenment in England 1660-1750* (Cambridge, Massachusetts: Harvard University Press, 1976), pp. 16-18.
[36]*The Advocate* 9 (December 28, 1720): 2.

enlighten your dark understanding and may you witness with me, that Jesus of Nazareth is the true Messiah" (p. 36).

In addition to the hope of converting Jews through Christian love, concern about the growing power of the Deists made some Anglican clerics to draw closer to the Jews to buttress their theological arguments against those who had become their common enemies. This is particularly evident in Charles Leslie's work, *a Short and Easie Method With the Deists to Which is Added a Second Part to the Jews*.. Here, after the author attacks the Deists in the usual fashion, he then turns to the Jews and makes them partners in the struggle against the new idolaters in English society. Leslie claims that they who deny the validity of "instituted and reveal'd religion" are equal enemies to Jew and Christian alike for "if the revelation of Moses be true, that of Christ must be true also" (pp. 63-4). Though Leslie would like the Jews to convert to the Anglican faith, he acknowledges the debt that Christians owe to them.

> Christ preach'd to none but the Jews, before
> his death....He shewed himself to none other
> but to them. And from the Jews only have we
> Gentiles receiv'd the knowledge of his resurrection
> and of all the Gospel (p. 420).

When intellectual historians consider the spirit of the Age of Reason, they tend to emphasize the importance of the Deists, the "enemy camp" for most Anglicans, whose works were popular from the later part of the seventeenth century through the middle of the eighteenth. Though they were a definite minority who gained few converts from the masses, their writings did appeal to a growing reading public who gathered in the coffee houses to discuss the affairs of the day. Deistic works are not always of the highest caliber, but they reflect some of the changing religious attitudes of the time; how the Jews were viewed by many of the rationalist thinkers of this complex age.

The Deists, as a group, are difficult to define and to categorize. They represent virtually all shades of political opinion and some very diverse religious views as well. A small group who never established any formal party, they were, in many ways, more a state of mind than a school of philosophy. Only a few of the Deists knew each other, and rarely do they refer to kindred spirits in their writings. Although they have been credited with being the first significant group to challenge the fundamental beliefs of Christianity in England, Deists and traditional Christians were not always separated from each other by clearly marked boundary lines. As Hunt points out, "There were Deists whose Deism embraced Christianity and there were Christians whose Christianity impinged on Deism."[37] Deists vigorously rejected the notion that they were atheists. Their prime concern was to establish a universal religion that was based on nature and on reason. This natural religion was not transmitted by tradition, nor was it accepted on external authority. Since the Deists believed that reason was the sole criteria for determining truth, they had little use for revealed religion and for church hierarchies who sustained what they believed was the word of God. Their radical ideology made them the objects of suspicion by the overwhelming majority of the English people. The very word "Deist" was used to label anyone who was critical of divine revelation or who questioned the miracles of the Bible. It was a term that was used indiscriminately by the orthodox clerics in their battle against people or ideas that did not meet with their approval.

Although, in their quest for a rational, natural religion, the Deists rejected the demonology and the crude anthropomorphisms of the past, they could not shake off all of their old prejudices. They covered them over with a thin veneer of intellectualism which often wore thin in their disputes with the religious establishment. Though the Deists were not obsessed with the Jews, their anti-Jewish bias became quite apparent when they directed their attacks against their main target, the foundations of traditional Christianity. Since they were determined to detach Christianity from its Hebrew Scriptural roots that were based on divine revelation to a particular people, the Deists cast aspersions on Jewish law, traditions, and beliefs, All that was noble, rational, and moderate in the Bible was Christian, while that which did not comply with the spirit of the Age of Reason was considered to be Jewish. They believed that the errors that had besmirched traditional Christianity were almost entirely due to the Jews. Thus, by promoting this image of the Jew as the corrupter of the Christian religion, they were to provide "the first historic landmarks on the slippery path of modern anti-Semitism."[38] Though their anti-Jewish bias did not have any major effect upon their own generation in England, it did influence Voltaire and those who came after him. In essence, Deism served as a bridge for the transfer of ancient

---

[37]John B. Hunt, *Religious Thought in England, From the Reformation to the End of the Last Century; A Contribution to the History of Theology* Vol. 3 (1870-73;rpt. AMS Press, 1973), p. 159.
[38]Leon Poliakov, The *History of Anti-Semitism: From Voltaire to Wagner* Vol. 3, trans. Miriam Kochan (New York: Vangard Press, 1975), pp. 63-4. In addition, Poliakov believes that "their universalist-inspired thought- enriched by theories with scientific pretensions in the nineteenth century or by some other admixture- reached the twentieth century under the cloak of so called 'Aryan' internationalism as the racist dogma of Hitlerism." p. 69.

anti-Semitism to the Age of Enlightenment.[39] "The Church blamed the Jews for killing their Christ; the philosophers blamed the Jews for fathering him."[40]

Although some scholars assume that because the Deists were opposed to traditional Christianity, they were advocates of religious toleration. This is far from being true. A brief study of the writings of some of the key Deists of the period can demonstrate the sources and the depths of their anti-Jewish sentiments.

Lord Herbert of Cherbury (1563-1648) has been considered to be the father of English deism. However, as Hutcheson notes, "his children did not recognize his paternity."[41] Except for Charles Blount (1654-1693), he was ignored by those who followed him. Yet, many of his basic ideas, by accident or by design, are found in the works of the eighteenth century Deists. Lord Herbert, like those who followed, sought basic religious truths – fundamental principles of natural religion that could unify humanity. He stresses the importance of what he called Common Notions, innate ideas found in all people which could sweep away all of the falsehoods of traditional religion. In his most important work, De *Veritate,* he writes:

> ....I am not concerned with superstitions and sacred
> rites; it is not what a large number of men assert
> but what all men of normal mind believe that
> I find important. Scanning the vast array of
> absurd fictions I am content to discover a tiny
> Common Notion(p. 301).

Lord Herbert was severely critical of Hebrew Scriptures. Whatever he found to be good, like the Ten Commandments, for example, he attributes to Common Notions. That which was barbaric was the product of crafty priests who interpolated their superstitions and barbaric rites into the biblical text. He had few positive statements to make about the Jewish people. Here again, that which was good came from the neighboring cultures that had influenced them in biblical times. Thus, Abraham and Moses had been molded by Egyptian culture. On the other hand, Jewish revelations, which in reality were invented by their priests, encouraged the people to commit crimes against humanity. He believes that Jews were more despicable to the Gentiles than any other people;

---

[39]Samuel Ettinger, *Yehudim Ve-Yahdut Beinei Ha- Deistim Ha -Angliyim Be Meah Ha-18.* Zion 29 (1964) p. 205.

[40]Edgar Rosenberg, Tabloid *Jews and Fungoid Scribblers* (Hoboken, New Jersey: KTAV, 1973), p. 8.

[41]Herbert of Cherbury *De Religione Laici* ed, by Harrold Hutcheson(New Haven: Yale University Press, 1944), p. 55.

that the history of few nations could parallel their "mischiefs, murders, treacheries, falsehoods, rapes, incests, etc."[42]

Mathew Tindale (1656-1733) is the best representative of the English Deists. His fame rests on one major work, *Christianity as Old as the Creation: or the Gospel a Republication of the Religion of Nature*, which was published when he was seventy-four years old. The book has been called the "Deistic Bible" because it discusses so completely the views shared by most Deists of his time, and it expands the ideas of earlier thinkers as well. In this work, Tindale claims that no later revelation could possibly improve on the religion that was given to man at the time of Creation. In addition, God would not choose any one people to be the special recipient of his message. Through reason, God gives humanity the means of knowing what He requires of them. The purpose of scripture, Tindale believes, is to make sure that superstition does not become part of natural religion. Unfortunately, the Bible is filled with errors and distortions that make it a worthless document. Tindale has nothing positive to say about the Jews who claim to have received divine revelation and who brought this book to the world. He believes that much of what they claimed to do in God's name, like the conquest of Canaan, was motivated by self-interest (p. 273). In addition, the Jews are a superstitious people who place the observance of the Law over everything else. He notes, for example, that they think that self-defense on the Sabbath is unlawful even though it has resulted in slaughter at the hands of their enemies.[43] Tindale views the Jewish people as the most cruel nation on the face of the earth. He compares them to the Catholics who, he believes, have brought so much misery to the world.

> The Jews, as they were most superstitious, so
> were they most cruel; and as the Papists have
> beyond all other Christians, introduced into
> Religion, Things which are far from contributing
> to the Good of Mankind; so they have exercis'd
> a matchless Cruelty for the Support of them..(p. 274).

John Toland (1670 -1722) was one of the more philo-Semitic of the Deists. Along with stock criticisms of the Jews, his works reflect an appreciation of their economic usefulness, concern for their toleration in English society as well as their need to return to Zion. Toland was born a Catholic, but he subsequently became a Protestant, a Latitudinarian, a Socinian, a Deist, a Pantheist, and a Materialist. Toland's integrity and

---

[42]Edward, Lord Herbert of Cherbury, *A Dialogue Between a Tutor and His Pupil* (London: Printed for W. Bathoe, 1768), p. 240.
[43]Ibid. p. 47.

originality have been questioned by some scholars.[44] Yet, there are those students of the period like Heineman who believe that he anticipated trends of thought which would be developed over the course of centuries; that his "invective against tyranny and prejudice sounds as though it were spoken not yesterday, nor today, but tomorrow."[45]

The first of Toland's major works, Christianity *Not Mysterious*, is credited with marking the opening of the Deist-Orthodoxy controversy. Its purpose was to demonstrate that nothing in the Gospels can be considered contrary to reason and that no Christian doctrine can be properly called a mystery. In the preface to his book, he states that he uses reason "to confirm and elucidate revelation" and that by no means is it dangerous to religion (p. VII). Although Toland is primarily concerned about formulating a reasonable approach to Christianity, the traditional anti-Jewish sentiments of his predecessors appear throughout the book. Toland contrasts the "plain convincing instructions of Christ" with the "intricate effectual declamations of the scribes." He believes that it was the "Jewish Rabbies" and their "cabalistick observations" who were able to convince the people of the mysteries of the Bible (pp. XIX-XX). Toland believes that Christianity was intended to be a rational and intelligible religion. Jesus, however, was forced to perform miracles so that the "stiff necked" Jews could not deny his divinity (p. 47). He feels that any miracles contrary to reason are fictitious, and he scorns both those who believe them to be true as well as those who perpetuate them in their religious teachings. In his work, *Tetradymus*, a lengthy dissertation concerning the miracles that the Israelites experienced in the wilderness on the way to the Promised Land, he criticizes those like the seventeenth century sage, Menasseh Ben Israel, who accepted the literal meaning of the biblical text. "No other creature," he believes, " but an enthousiastical Christian Father, or his more credulous modern disciple, instructed by a fabulous Jewish Cabalist cou'd be capable of conceiving or propagating such absurdities, as are vended on this subject" (p. 32).

Although Toland echoes many of the ideas of the earlier Deists, he breaks new ground in his book, *Nazarenus, or Jewish, Gentile, and Mahometan Christianity*. He believes that as far as the Jews are concerned, Jesus never intended to abolish the law. Therefore, they could believe in him and still maintain their own customs and traditions (p. vi). Toland blames the intolerance of the Church for frightening the Jews away from

[44]For example, Endelman considers him to be nothing more than a hack writer who was in the employ of various politicians. see Todd Endelman, The *Jews of Georgian England 1714-1830: Tradition and Change in a Liberal Society* (Philadelphia: Jewish Publication Society, 1979), pp. 26-7.
[45]F.H. Heineman, "John Toland and the Age of Enlightenment," *Review of English Studies* 20(April, 1964):146.

Christianity (p. 56). Equally to blame, in his opinion, are the obstinate Jewish Priests who distorted the original law of Moses and caused the Jewish people to reject Jesus. Weiner feels that by blaming the religious leaders for rejecting Jesus, Toland tends to lessen the blame that the official Church teachings placed upon all the Jews of the time.[46] Toland's philo -Semitism is more evident in his work, *Appendix, Containing Two Problems Concerning the Jewish Nation and Religion.*, where he praises the Jews for remaining, through the centuries, a distinct people in race and religion. Furthermore, he states:

> ...if they ever happen to be resettled in
> Palestine upon their original foundation,
> which is not at all impossible, they will then,
> by reason of their excellent constitution be
> much more populous, rich and powerful than
> any other nation now in the world. I would have
> you consider whether it not be both the interest
> and duty of Christians to assist in regaining
> their country (p. 8).

Toland's liberalism is tainted, however, with some very definite conversionist tendencies. In this regard he continues an English tradition of using the carrot and not the stick to encourage the Jews to assimilate into Christian society.

If John Toland can be considered to be the Deist who was most tolerant of the Jews, Thomas Morgan (d.1740) was certainly the most rabid Jew hater of the group. He was not a particularly original thinker, and he adds little to the philosophical ideas of his predecessors. In his major three volume work, *The Moral Philosopher*, he continues the deistic tradition of detaching Christianity from its Hebraic roots. Morgan considers himself to be a "Christian Deist" in contrast to those "Christian Jews" who stress the Jewish influence upon Christianity. In an imaginary dialogue between representatives of these two groups, Morgan states his case in very crude language that gets progressively worse. He begins his attack against the Jewish people by noting that Paul and the prophets who came before him were obliged to treat them in a very "grave and solemn manner" because they were a "sullen, morose and severe people who lacked wit and a sense of humour" (I: 21). After accusing the rabbis of twisting the message of the Scriptures to suit their own needs through the use of Cabalistic techniques that are similar to those employed by the Papists, he lets loose with a barrage of condemnations that are unparalleled in deistic literature. The Jews, he claims, are an example to the world of "the natural effects and consequences of ignorance,

---

[46]Max Weiner, "John Toland and Judaism," *H.U.C.A.* 16 (1941):18.

superstition, presumption and Immorality"(I: 255).They are a stupid, stiff-necked people, a true generation of vipers who "could scarce be parallel'd by any other nation upon Earth for their gross ignorance, superstition, and moral wickedness which ran through their successive generations" (I: 257-9). Morgan continues his diatribes against the Jews by noting that they are a wretched, deluded people, a most untoward grossly ignorant, amazingly superstitious and desperately wicked generation of men – an army of bigots and blind enthusiasts" (I: 265, 269). In addition, the Jews are guilty of being Christ killers. He claims that when Jesus refused to join in their battle with Rome, those Jews who thought that he was their national redeemer turned against him and they sought to have him crucified (I:325). Paul understood the extent of their enthusiasm, persecution and superstition; he realized that Christianity, which represented true religion and liberty of conscience, could never share a common tradition with Judaism (I:359). Morgan, like other Deists, can not believe that the Jewish people were "chosen, separated, and set apart as God's peculiar people." He believes that this appeal to national vanity was the only way that the prophets could control such a "wild, fierce, ungovernable mob....a brutish generation, and a people of no understanding" (II: 56-57). According to Morgan, both the ancient and the modern Jews believe that the concept of choseness implies that all the nations who do not subject themselves to the laws of the Hebraic constitution are forever rejected and forsaken by the God of Israel. He asks if this was not "designed and calculated for universal empire and dominion, or to enslave all mankind to this nation?"(III:356)

Thomas Chubb (1679-1747), like Morgan claimed to be a Christian Deist. Unlike his predecessor, however, he was able to control some of his anti-Jewish sentiments, and his language is less abusive. Chubb was critical of both Hebrew and Christian Scriptures. In his work, Concerning *Divine Revelation*, he notes that both Judaism and Christianity are centered around God revealing his will to a specific people. In both cases God's clearly specified expectations of human conduct were distorted by religious leaders to meet the needs of their generation. The Jews, a credulous people who needed "signs, wonders and mighty deeds " to sustain them, were guilty of adding these elements to the Bible (pp. 24-25). Chubb warns his readers that they should be careful when they study this adulterated text. It is, after all, the product of many centuries of historical and theological evolution at the hands of fallible men (pp. 62-63). In addition to challenging the validity of the text of Hebrew Scriptures, Chubb is critical of the Jewish teachings concerning God, the Law, and the choseness of the ancient Israelites that are derived from biblical texts. He believes that the image of a wrathful and jealous Deity is not in keeping with the moral character of God who seeks true goodness from his creatures. Chubb also notes that Jewish law, with its emphasis on meaningless ritual and empty ceremonies is beneath the dignity of God. In addition, the concept of the chosen people is another doctrine that further distorts the meaning of God and the true purpose of religion. Chubb believes that this improper understanding of what was expected of the Jewish people encouraged them to commit murder in His name.[47]

For political reasons, some of the Deists kept their writings secret during their lifetime. Henry St. John Viscount Bolingbroke (1678-1751) was one of those who left instructions that his philosophical works were not to be published until after his death. When these writings were ultimately made public, the Deistic controversy was just about over and they had little effect upon the intellectual life of the times. Their immediate effect upon the Jews of England was equally negligible. However, whether private or public, his thoughts reflect some of the important underlying feelings of the Deists towards Judaism and the Jewish people.

In his writings, Bolingbroke repeats much of what was written by his more talented predecessors. Following in their footsteps, he criticizes traditional religion for its lack of concern for morality and for its excessive emphasis on ritual practices The Jewish people, he believes, is a classic example of a nation who is "superstitiously zealous" in ceremonial practices and who lacks any sense of charity and human kindness (V:548). Bolingbroke blames the Jews for distorting Christianity. He believes that the early Jewish converts to the new faith, who had been trained in both Kabbalah and Platonic philosophy, brought Eastern superstitions to what was originally a very plain system of natural religion. In addition to corrupting the teachings of Jesus, the Jewish people, in the course of their history, proved that they lacked any decent qualities. Bolingbroke believes that in reality, "ignorance and superstition, pride, injustice, and barbarity were the true characteristics of this people "who boasted that they were a nation of sages and philosophers.

Bolingbroke scoffs at the notion that God would bestow special favors on any nation; he feels that in the case of the Jewish people this belief has led to all kinds of excesses. Whereas the pagan philosophers did not limit their concept of benevolence to any particular society, the ancient Israelites considered themselves to be a chosen people. As a result of this mistaken theological belief, they viewed the other nations as inferior beings. This attitude, he believes, was reinforced in their laws,

---

[47]Thomas Chubb, "A Vindication of God's Moral Character," in *A Collection of Tracts on Various Subjects* (London: Printed for T. Cox, 1730), p. 277.

which "took them out of all moral obligations to the rest of mankind" as well as in the teachings of their priests and prophets (III: 290).

Through his writings, Bolingbroke intended to clear away myth and superstition. In reality he merely repeats and reemphasizes the stock anti-Jewish sentiments of both the traditional clerics and his fellow Deists.

Anthony Collins (1676-1729) was one of the best educated and most intellectually gifted of the Deists. Unlike Bolingbroke, he did not hesitate to express his opinions freely and openly, and he became a key spokesmen of the group. Collins was a close friend of both John Locke and John Toland; their ideas helped to shape his own role as a strong advocate of free thought and free inquiry. Ultimately, he became a major architect of anti-Christian scholarship. Although Collins' most vitriolic attacks are primarily directed against Christianity, he is markedly hostile towards both biblical and rabbinic Judaism. In order for him to discredit Christianity, it is necessary to cast doubt on the value of the prophecies found in Hebrew Scripture that are usually cited to validate Jesus' messianism. Therefore, Collins dismisses them as being either mystical or allegorical; they can not be taken literally. He believes that "to pretend that they prove what they are produc'd to prove is to give up the cause of Christianity to the Jews and other enemies thereof. "[48]

Collins praises free thinking as a means of overcoming the prejudices and superstitions that are such an integral part of organized religion. Yet, like many free thinkers of his time, he displays a strong hatred for the Jews that goes beyond the rational approach to life that he and the other Deists of his time prize so highly. For example, in his *Discourse of Free Thinking*, Collins pays tribute to Josephus, the most learned scholar that the Jews ever had, and one who was not inferior to the great Greek and Roman historians. Collins laments that a man of such talent did not have a better subject for his historical writings.

In a long footnote to this statement, he lists a host of quotations to highlight the negative qualities of the Jews. In his eyes they are a cross, odd, untoward people who are superstitious, illiterate, brutish, crafty, barbarous, and "incapable of understanding either the things of this world or the other"(p. 124- 5).

Thomas Woolston (1670-1733), the most eccentric of the Deists, as well as one of the few eighteenth century free thinkers who was fined and imprisoned for his writings, mounted a parallel assault to that of Collins on prophesy and miracles. In his *Six Discourses on the Miracles of our Saviour*, Woolston uses a mythical rabbi as his spokesman to

---

[48]Anthony Collins, *A Discourse of the Grounds* cited in O'Higgins *Anthony Collins the Man and His Works* (The Hague, Netherlands: Martinus Nijhoff, 1970), p. 48.

challenge the divinity of Jesus and the historicity of the miracles attributed to him in Christian Scripture. Woolston's fictitious rabbinic friend views the resurrection of Lazarus as nothing more than a deception perpetrated by Jesus to defraud the people. He argues that if it was a true miracle, then the Jews would not have persecuted Lazarus; they would have accepted the divinity of Jesus and his power to raise the dead. Obviously, nothing miraculous took place; they were justified in their actions against the two confederates (p. 44). Woolston believes that "this was one reason among others for that vehement and universal outcry and demand, at Jesus' tryal for his Crucifixion "(p. 52). Thus, he uses an imaginary Jewish figure to denounce Christianity's traditional beliefs in Jesus' supernaturalism and to link the Jewish people with the Crucifixion. Woolston is one of several thinkers who brings the Jew into the clash between the Deists and the religious establishment. The implications for the Jewish people of being caught in the middle of a major controversy will be touched upon later in the book.

Edward Gibbon (1737-1794), a classical historian, never counted himself among the Deists of his time. But, as a scoffer at all supernatural religion, he amplifies many of their ideas both in his attacks upon Christianity and in his anti-Jewish slurs. Commager considers him to be a major figure in the criticism of the Church during the Age of Reason.[49] Carswell believes that Gibbon's monumental work, The *Decline and Fall of the Roman Empire*, is "the supreme literary product of English civilization between the English and American Revolutions" that reflects "the virtues and faults of the age that formed its author."[50] Gibbon is enamored with the tolerant paganism of the ancient world which he contrasts with the zeal and "enthusiasm" of early Christianity that undermined the foundations of the Empire. In the spirit of the Deists and other enlightened thinkers of his day, he attacks the Church by ridiculing its Jewish roots.

In his writings, Gibbon paints a distorted picture of the Jewish people that combines the prejudices of Roman satirists, like Juvenal, with those of contemporary Deists. [51] The Jews, he believes, are one people who has refused to join in the common intercourse with the rest of mankind. Sullen and obstinate, they have maintained their peculiar rites and unsocial manners while managing to disguise their implacable

---

[49]Henry Steele Commager, *The Empire of Reason: How Europe Imagined and America Realized the Enlightenment* (rpt. Garden City, New York: Anchor Books, 1978), p. 49.

[50]John Carswell, *From Revolution to Revolution: England 1688-1776* (New York: Charles Scribner's Sons, 1973), p. 1.

[51]The following citations are from Chapters XV and XVI of *The Decline and Fall of the Roman Empire*.

hatred of the rest of humanity. Gibbon condemns the "stubborn incredulity" of their forefathers who believed that they alone were worthy to receive the Ten Commandments on Mount Sinai. He goes beyond the usual Deistic diatribes when he claims that those Jews who did convert to Christianity did not change their nefarious ways. Even those who accepted Jesus as their Messiah "obstinately adhered to ceremonies of their ancestors and wanted to impose them on the gentiles." In addition, the first fifteen bishops of Jerusalem were all circumcised Jews, and he leaves it to the readers' imagination to determine their Judaic influence upon the new faith.

Gibbon blames the victims for their suffering at the hands of their oppressors. Thus, it was the Jewish people's fanaticism that brought on the Hadrianic persecutions and which forced the Romans to turn Jerusalem into the pagan city of Aelia Capitolina. "We are tempted to applaud," he notes, "the severe retaliation....against a race of fanatics whose dire and credulous superstition seemed to render them implacable enemies not only of the Roman government but of humankind." He fails to find any traces of Roman intolerance during the entire turbulent period leading up to the revolt in the year 70.

Gibbon was challenged by contemporary thinkers for his narrow-minded approach to Christianity and to Judaism as well. He was criticized for relying too heavily on Juvenal, a Roman satirist, who was prejudiced against the Jewish people as well as for his own lack of knowledge of both Hebrew Scriptures and rabbinic writings.[52] In order to defend the roots of Christianity, Gibbon's critics challenged his condemnation of ancient Israel – his belief that the Jews borrowed some of their key rituals from the Egyptians. However, this did not affect his challengers scorn for contemporary Jewry. As one critic noted, "...yet does it follow that because the Jews are now a contemptible people, that therefore none of their ancestors were ever in favour and esteem among the Egyptians."[53] As in the case of the Deists, neither Gibbon nor his detractors added any philo-Semitic sentiments to the spirit of the times.

In eighteenth century France, those enlightened thinkers who examined the nature of the physical world were, for the most part, militant enemies of organized religion. In England, however, there was a holy alliance between science and religion that continued until the end of the century.[54] David Hartley (1705-1757), physician, philosopher, and

---

[52]Shelby T. McCloy, *Gibbon's Antagonism to Christianity* (London: Williams and Norgate Ltd., 1933), p. 57 and the *Gentleman's Magazine* 46(October, 1776), pp. 441-42.

[53]*Gentleman's Magazine* 46 (November, 1776), p. 495.

[54]Basil Wiley, *The Eighteenth Century Background: Studies on the Idea of Nature in the Thought of the Period* (London: Chatto & Windus, 1940), p. 136.

Christian apologist was an important member of this group who combined scientific objectivity with religious teachings. His major work, *Observations on Man*, is primarily devoted to ethics based upon the study of human psychology. However, it also contains some interesting insights into his very traditional Christian attitudes towards the Jewish people that are an integral part of his religious outlook. Harley accepts without question the account found in Christian Scriptures of how Jesus was "crucified under Pontius Pilate at the instigation of the chief men among the Jews," and he believes that the stories found in the Gospels are supported by secular historians (p. 118). All the great events in world history, from the growth of Islam through the dispersion of "Jews and Jesuits" are part of a divine plan that will hasten the coming of the "Kingdom of Christ"(p. 136). The Jewish people, a key factor in the Second Coming, are the keepers of the oracles of God: their suffering is a necessary precondition of their final restoration in their ancient homeland. Hartley believes that "without the shedding of blood there is no remission of sins"(p. 181). Thus, those who afflict the Jews are "scourges in the hand of God" who prepare them for their unique destiny (p. 182). In a logical and systematic way, Hartley explains why, in all probability, they will soon be restored "after they have suffered the due chastisement"(p. 374). Hartley has no sympathy for the Jewish people. They are simply the means of fulfilling scriptural prophesies that establish the legitimacy of Christianity. The Restoration of the Jews, which is connected to the Second Coming, will open the eyes of the world to the true faith (p. 377).

Joseph Priestly (1733-1804), chemist, metaphysician, political scientist, humanist, teacher, and author of 150 books and pamphlets, was an enthusiastic admirer of David Harley. Priestly stands as one of the great intellectual forces of the Age of Reason, and he has been called the English Benjamin Franklin and the Leonardo da Vinci of dissent. Though Priestly's imagination touched on a number of practical areas, and he is credited with discovering oxygen, soda water, carbon monoxide, and hydrochloric acid, he thought of himself to be primarily a theologian.[55] In his writings, he sees no incompatibility between religion and science; his mind can grasp both the principles of scientific experimentation and the doctrine of bodily resurrection. The theory and practice of religion is always part of his thinking, and he believes that true Christianity, removed of its superstitions, can be an instrument of human

---

[55]Commager *Empire of Reason.* pp. 31-33. See also James J. Hoecker *Joseph Priestly and the Idea of Progress* (New York and London: Garland Publishing Inc., 1977), p. 32 and Watts *The Dissenters* p. 472.

perfectibility.[56] Although many of Priestly's criticisms of the Anglicans and the Catholics are similar to those of the Deists, he is not one of them. First and foremost, he believes in revealed religion's "superiority in sentiment and practice " over paganism[57.] He feels that both miracles and biblical prophesy can exist side by side with the rational discovery of the laws that govern the universe. Prophesy plays such an important role in his life, that he is convinced of the imminency of the Second Coming of Christ and the Restoration of the Jews. Through his interpretations of the Book of Daniel, he sees the French Revolution as the beginning of "those calamitous times when divine judgments will fall upon all the nations who have oppressed the Jews, particularly those in Western Europe."[58]

As a Dissenter, Priestly appreciates the need not only for religious freedom for all people, but for human dignity as well. In *A Sermon on the Subject of the Slave Trade,* he notes:

> As men, and as Christians...we should interest
> ourselves not only for our relations and particular
> friends, not only for our countrymen; not only for
> Europeans, but for the distressed inhabitants of Asia,
> Africa, or America; and not only for Christians, but for
> Jews, Mahometans, and Infidels. And as we ought, to
> feel for our fellow men, we ought, to the utmost extent
> of our influence, to exert ourselves to relieve their distress (pp. 1-2).

Priestly criticizes those who "plead strongly for the rights of conscience, or of private judgment and of free inquiry: but when they have gotten room enough for themselves, they are quite easy and in no pain for others." [59] In the Birmingham Riots of July 1791, he personally suffered at the hands of the mob. The meeting house where he preached was set ablaze, and his library and laboratory were ransacked by those proclaiming loyalty to "Church and King." Ultimately, because of his fear that a trumped up charge of treason might be brought against him for his support of the French Revolution, Priestly followed his three sons who had already sailed to America.

Priestly believes that in religious matters every individual should be " at liberty to think and choose for himself and to support that which he

---

[56]Hoecker, p. 123.

[57]Joseph Priestly, *A Comparison of the Institutions of Moses With those of the Hindoos* (Northumberland: 1799), p. vii.

[58]Joseph Priestly, *The Present State of Europe compared with Ancient Prophecies* (London: Printed for J. Johnson), p. 2, p. 17.

[59]Joseph Priestly, *Essay on the First Principle of Government* in *Priestly's Writings* ed. by John A. Passmore (New York: Collier books, 1965), p. 238.

prefers."[60]Yet, he sees no contradiction between his noble sentiments concerning human rights and his very strong desire to convert Jews to Unitarianism. In his essay, *An Address to the Jews*, he begins by declaring his "respect and veneration" for the Jewish people as well as for the faith of Israel which he believes is superior to all other ancient religions and which contains the purist worship of God and the purist morality. He praises the Jewish people for their ability to accept trials and tribulations and to still maintain a faith which is "as firm at this day as it was two thousand years ago"[61](p. 394). Soon they will experience the dawn of a glorious day when they will be restored to their ancient homeland. Hopefully, before this takes place, they will be convinced of the sin of their ancestors who were guilty of the Crucifixion. Jesus, Priestly believes, was the greatest prophet ever sent to the Jewish people, and he hopes that at least a few candid individuals "will see the light and urge the rest of the people to appreciate his teachings (pp. 424-25). He concludes his essay with the statement:

> Your restoration cannot fail to convince the world
> of the truth of your religion; and in those circumstances
> your conversion to Christianity cannot fail to draw after
> it that of the whole world (p. 428).

Priestly's use of humanitarianism as a means of converting the Jewish people is quite evident in his *Letters to the Jews*, a book which he printed with the hope that it would be translated into Hebrew and distributed throughout the world as a catalyst for Christian-Jewish dialogue. His work begins with words of praise for Jewish perseverance in the face of persecution and oppression. Considering all that the Jewish people have experienced, he is not surprised that they dislike Christians and Christianity(p. 1). Priestly admits that both Jesus and his disciples were Jewish and that they "conformed to all the rites" of Judaism (p. 5). They are truly the "elder branch of the family" and the "salt of the earth "(p. 6, p. 8).However, after he uses these laudatory phrases, Priestly echoes the classic Christian belief that the Jewish people are "under the cloud of Divine displeasure" because of their "obstinacy and incredulity" in both ancient and modern times (p. 12, p. 28). In the past they were responsible for putting Jesus to death and for persecuting his followers; they have continued to maintain this attitude towards Christians through the centuries (p. 15). Priestly understands the importance that the Jewish

---

[60]Joseph Priestly, *A Letter to the Right Honorable William Pitt on the Subject of Toleration and Church Establishments*. London: 1787 p. 24 cited in Scult, p. 68.

[61]This citation, as well as the two that follow, are from the essay that is found in the conclusion of Priestly's work, *A Comparison of the Institutions of Moses With those of the Hindoos and other Ancient Nations*.

people place upon maintaining their identity, and he suggests that they establish a separate church where they can keep the Sabbath and some of their unique rituals. He claims:

> There is no occasion for you Jews to connect
> yourselves with any class of Christians. On the
> contrary, since you are still to be distinguished
> as Jews, no less than as Christians, it will be more
> convenient for you to form a separate church, and to
> keep your Sabbath as you now do (pp. 42-3).

Furthermore, he reminds his Jewish readers that many Christians reject the Trinity. Therefore, they have no need to accept the divinity of Jesus (p. 42). Priestly urges them to overcome their prejudices against Christianity and to accept a form of Unitarianism that is steeped in Jewish culture and tradition. He hopes that they will see for themselves just how his brand of religion and their beliefs are so very compatible with each other (p. 53). In the conclusion of his work, he urges the Jewish people to compare the historical evidence of the two religions. The Jews must realize that, in reality, they and the Christians are of one faith and that they must "stand or fall together" (p. 64).

One of the most complex indicators of the temper of the times can be found in the attitudes of the "reasonable" luminaries of eighteenth century England towards the toleration of minority groups in their midst. The intellectual, political, and religious issues that were brought to the surface over this issue, represent both the best and the worst sentiments of the Age of Reason. In many instances, the Jews were viewed as part of the larger issue of accepting non-Anglicans and foreigners into the mainstream of English life. On other occasions, they were singled out for special consideration. Party politics often clouded issues and distorted the true sentiments of many key figures. In addition, starting with John Locke (1632-1704) who, more than any other Englishman of his time, set the tone for toleration, age-old prejudices were often mingled with the more enlightened sentiments of the time.

In his Third *Letter on Toleration*, Locke notes that the state should not attempt to propagate religious creeds by force, and those who dissent from these doctrines are harmless as long as they are not oppressed. He believes that if such people would be put on an equal basis with the rest of society, it would be to the benefit of all citizens. The toleration of individuals who differ from the tenets of the Anglican Church, he believes, is in accordance with the teachings of the Gospels, and it is the sign of the true church. "Jews, mahometans and pagans" should not be subjected to physical harm because of their beliefs; Locke advocates toleration as long as the welfare of the state is not endangered. He does not believe that these three groups would "infect" the English

Protestants, and there is no valid reason for them to "be shut out of the commonwealth "(VI: 231). The Catholics, whom he could not trust, were another matter.

Behind Locke's enlightened attitude towards the Jews, there is a sense of economic pragmatism that reflects the mercantilistic spirit of the time. His toleration of the Jewish people is not based on a repudiation of past theological prejudices. In fact, in some of his later works such as *The Reasonableness of Christianity as Delivered in Scripture*, he expresses classical Christian anti-Semitic sentiments that are based upon his understanding of Christian Scripture. He does not question, for example, the Gospels' account of the Jewish role in the Crucifixion. He claims that after Jesus raised Lazarus the "Chief priests and the Pharisees counseled together to put Jesus to death." The Jewish leaders set traps to get evidence against him so that they could turn him over to the Roman authorities. Locke believes that, had they the power, they themselves would have put Jesus to death (VII:38). In his work, *A Second Vindication of the Reasonableness of Christianity*, he expands upon this theme of the guilt and cruelty of the Jewish leaders at the time of Jesus. Locke feels that the idolatrous heathen priests of the time were far better than those who tended the Temple and who had designs upon Jesus' life (VII: 423).Thus, only by accepting Christianity could the Jewish people become, once again, the people of God. As Barzilay notes, "Locke's apparent liberalism was strongly tainted with overt conversionist tendencies."[62]

When the entire scope of Locke's writings is considered, particularly his extensive work in Christian Scriptural paraphrases and commentaries, he is more a transmitter of old prejudices against the Jews than an innovative thinker who is anxious to right old wrongs. For Locke, the main value of the Hebrew Bible is to serve as proof of the validity of Christianity. In the final analysis, toleration of the Jews is simply a political necessity – a concession that the state makes not to interfere with Jewish ritual practices. He, like so many of those who followed him, is weighed down by past prejudices against racial and religious minorities. According to Popkin, Locke and his disciples found that those individuals with either wrong or inferior mental powers " just happened to have wrong skin color or religious beliefs."[63]

---

[62]Isaac Eisenstein Barzilay, "John Toland's Borrowing From Simon Luzzato." Jewish *Social Studies* 31(April, 1969): 75.

[63]Richard H. Popkin, "The Philosophical Basis of Eighteenth-Century Racism," in *Studies in Eighteenth-Century Culture: Racism in the Eighteenth Century*, ed. Harold E. Pagliano (Cleveland: Case Western Reserve University Press, 1973), p. 254.

For both the Jews and other non-Anglicans, religious freedom is by no means an inalienable right.

In 1689, the same year when Locke's *Epistola de Tolerantia* w a s translated into English, a toleration act was passed that expressed the pragmatic spirit of the time. It ended all attempts to coerce the English people into religious uniformity, and it allowed them to be citizens of the country without being members of the Anglican Church. Though most Protestant Dissenters were now granted the rights that they had sought for many years, Roman Catholics and anti-Trinitarians were excluded from these benefits. In the spirit of John Locke, toleration within the boundaries of national security was acceptable, and those who preached the religious fanaticism of previous centuries were suspect. These sentiments are echoed by Thomas Barlow (1607-1691) in his work, *The Case of Toleration in Matters of Religion.* He believes that toleration is "most consonant to the principles of right reason and the perpetual procedure of all nations." Rather than risk future sectarian strife, he feels that it is more prudent to pardon than punish dissenters (pp. 15-16).

While the Anglicans wrestled with the problem of the need for a national church to unify the country and the right for individuals to worship in accordance with the dictates of personal conscience, the Dissenters pushed for reforms that would remove the discriminations against them. However, with the exception of the Baptists, they were champions of civil and religious toleration only for themselves: they were not interested in granting it to other groups, especially the Catholics. In addition, although they believed that all people were equal in the sight of God, this did not apply to the poor who, they felt, were not qualified to participate in political life.[64] The dissenters' self-centeredness did not directly help the Jewish cause. But their very presence made the Jews only one of several minorities who were the objects of religious hostility.

The Jewish people were carried along with the tide of "others" who struggled for an equal place in English society. Economic necessity proved to be an important factor to help many achieve at least part of their goal. It is Adam Smith (1723-1790), the first prophet of free trade, who believes that the natural effort of every person is to improve his own lot ; that the fewer restrictions that are placed on an individual the better it will be for society as a whole. People should be allowed to follow their natural instincts as long as they do not infringe upon their neighbor's well being. Governments should encourage a number of small sects to function so that "philosophical good temper and

---

[64]Carl B. Cohen, *The English Jacobins: Reformers in Late Eighteenth Century England* (New York: Charles Scribner's Sons, 1968), p. 13.

moderation with respect to every religious creed" would fill the country.[65] For Adam Smith and his disciples, any form of persecution or discrimination would hinder the production and the distribution of goods, and it would be detrimental to the best interests of society.

Adam Smith's abstract ideas were concretized into specific recommendations in several of the pamphlets that were circulated when Parliament was considering the passage of legislation for the naturalization of foreign Protestants and "others." Whether or not Jews were the main focus of these works, their future was tied to the fortunes of various groups on the Continent who were anxious to enter into England 's commercial world. In a pamphlet, *The Considerations Concerning the Expediency of a General Naturalization of Foreign Protestants and Others* (1747), the anonymous author argues primarily on economic grounds for allowing foreigners to settle in the country. He claims that the "increase of people is the means of advancing the wealth and strength of a nation" (p. 5). Citing Josiah Child's work, *Discourse on Trade.* he notes that the naturalization of foreigners would advance trade and increase the value of land in the kingdom (p. 6). In addition, he uses Locke's *Essay on Civil Government* to support his argument that increasing the general population will increase the standard of living of the country (p. 9).The author believes that since England's population has been diminished through military casualties and intemperate living, it is the appropriate time for a general naturalization of not only foreign Protestants, but Jews as well. Although this is opposed by "persons of narrow principle," he points out that Jewish financiers who reside outside of the country hold two million pounds of government debt securities. Allowing them to live in England would keep both the principle and the interest at home. Furthermore, since Jews have no country of their own, they have no place to retire to or to show favoritism in trade. Since the Jewish people have the reputation of taking care of their own poor, they would not be a burden on their new neighbors. Therefore, whatever they would bring to England would be a net gain (P. 11). This was in keeping with the sentiments expressed in earlier pamphlets where it was suggested that poor foreigners who would become a burden to native Englishmen should not be encouraged to enter the country. Only the "rich and wealthy", who would become truly useful subjects, were welcome (p. 13).

The commercial spirit of the times and its implications for greater toleration permeated diverse strata of English thought which included both the press and the pulpit. In an article," Good effects of the

---

[65]Stephen, p. 324.

Toleration of Religion," that appears in *Common Sense* and The *Gentleman's Magazine,* the author points out how Louis XIV lost both skilled workers and considerable treasure when he forced the Huguenots to leave his country while England, Holland, Germany, and Switzerland benefited from these refugees. England too, he notes, lost great numbers of industrious people during the persecution of the Dissenters at the time of Charles II. It is "impolitick" to force people to give up their beliefs and to punish them for their convictions. [66]

Josiah Tucker (1713-1799) was one of the rare clerics who combined a religious sensitivity with a shrewd business sense. His critics called him the "Commercial Clergyman", and in many ways he lived up to his reputation. Though not an advocate of laissez-faire capitalism, Tucker believes that Providence had made different nations to supply each others wants; to advocate free trade was to practice pure Christianity.[67] He condemns the creation of monopolies as an abuse of self-love which ultimately destroys those who found them; it is also harmful to the public good.[68]

Tucker's interest in immigration led him to advocate a more liberal policy of naturalization. In his two part pamphlet, Reflections *on the Expediency of a Law for the Naturalization of Foreign Protestants,* which was printed in 1751-2, he criticizes those narrow commercial and sectarian interests which encourage national prejudice against foreigners to the detriment of the country. He contrasts this xenophobia to the more liberal policies of Holland and Prussia.[69] Tucker believes that the fears concerning the consequences of increased immigration are unfounded; newcomers would increase employment and improve the quality and the quantity of land under cultivation.[70]In addition, foreign Protestant merchants and mechanics would prove useful to the state while those wealthy foreigners who hold government bonds should be encouraged to live in the country so that interest payments could be spent or reinvested in England.[71] Reverting back to his clerical role, Tucker reminds his readers of the earthly rewards for fulfilling their religious obligation to receive persecuted and distressed Protestants from lands of Catholic oppression. He notes:

---

[66]*Common Sense* 346 (October 1, 1743) reprinted in *Gentleman's Magazine* 13 (October 1743): 532-33.

[67]Josiah Tucker, *Two Sermons* cited in Leslie Stephen p. 303.

[68]Josiah Tucker, The *Elements of Commerce and Theory of Taxes* reprinted in Robert Livingston Schuyler, *Josiah Tucker: A Selection From His Economic and Political Writings* (New York: Columbia University Press, 1931), p. 58.

[69]Schuyler, p. 19.

[70]Ibid.

[71]Tucker, *The Elements of Commerce,* p. 81.

> But as it is our duty, so it is our interest to
> naturalize the virtuous and industrious of every
> nation, and to make them one people with ourselves.
> For numbers of inhabitants are the strength,
> riches, and security, nay the beauty of a country: -
> whereas the depopulation of a territory is not only
> its ruin, but its deformity.[72]

The commercial spirit and its effect upon the toleration of ethnic and religious minorities, especially the Jews, is noted by a foreign visitor, Cesar De Saussure (1705 -1783). In comparison to what he had observed on the Continent, he was impressed with the status of the Anglo-Jewish community. He writes:

> Commerce is considered to be England's
> strength, and care has been taken not to drive
> away anyone who contributes to build it up.
> Jews therefore are protected by laws, and are
> even granted certain privileges. They are not
> forced to bear a distinctive mark, as in the case in
> many countries....[73]

Commerce was indeed England's strength, and the Jewish people benefited from a society that prized it so highly and which was willing, on many occasions, to overlook their "otherness." But of equal, if not greater importance, was the diversity of religious and ethnic groups who, as previously mentioned, deflected the kinds of prejudice that historically the Jewish people had so often experienced. Though often glossed over by the Anglo-Jewish historians, they provided a host of new stereotypes for the multitudes. A critical understanding of the nature of these groups, the baggage that they carried with them as well as how they were viewed by the Establishment and by each other, can shed light on anti- Semitism in the context of the Protean prejudices of the time. In addition, English nationalism during this period was defined in terms of the conflict with "others" beyond the country's borders. As Linda Colley notes:

> They defined themselves as Protestants struggling
> for survival against the world's foremost Catholic
> power. They defined themselves against the French
> as they imagined them to be, superstitious, militarist,
> decadent and unfree. And, increasingly as the wars
> went on, they defined themselves in contrast to the
> colonial peoples who were manifestly alien in terms

---

[72]Ibid., p. 83.
[73]Muyden, Madame Van, ed. and trans. *A foreign View of England in the Reigns of George I. & George II.: The Letters of Monsieur Cesar De Saussure to his Family* (London: John Murray, 1902), p. 328.

of culture, religion and colour.[74]

The Jews, the classic enemy of Christianity who for centuries served as a foil to demonstrate the strength of the true faith, were no longer alone in their villainy.

---

[74]Linda Colley, *Britons: Forging the Nation 1707-1837* (New Haven: Yale University Press, 1992), p. 5.

2

Religious "Others"

The Catholics

Popery is such a composition of corruption,
superstition, bigotry, and ignorance, that
the very appearance of her, at a distance
both frightens and shocks us, especially
as she comes presenting to us the yoke of
spiritual tyranny in one hand and persecution
and fire in the other.[1]

....and they can also, whenever the good of the
Church requires it, have a dispensation for the
denial of every religious principle and the breach
of every moral duty: They can dethrone princes,
absolve subjects from their allegiance, and consecrate
murders, massacres and assassinations.[2]

....another soldier who was enlisted in Ireland,
and at the same time profess'd himself a Catholick
was whipp'd two days together with a cat of nine-
tails, for perserving in his religion, and refusing to
go to church, and with that severity, that he begg'd
to be shot or hang'd.[3]

Catholics were, by far, the most despised and feared minority group
in England. Although it is difficult to determine with any certainty their
exact numbers, there was a community of about 60,000 in the country at
the turn of the century which grew to approximately 100,000 by the year

---

[1]Benjamin Nicholls, *A Sermon Preached on the Occasion of the Present Rebellion at St. Anne's Church Manchester, October 13, 1745* (London: Henry Whitridge, 1745), p. 17.
[2]*London Magazine* 1 (December, 1732): p. 474.
[3]*Mist's Weekly Journal* (June 22, 1728).

1800.[4] If, through the years, they had been guilty of portraying the Jew as the nefarious "other" who proved the superiority of Christianity by his own sinister behavior, they, in turn, were viewed in this same way by the Protestant majority. During this period of reason and moderation, they were subjected to legal discrimination and, at times, pogrom-like violence that eclipsed anything that the Jewish community of England experienced.

Anti-Catholic sentiment like anti-Semitism was part of the fabric of the times, but its roots ran much deeper and occupied a more significant place in English life than many English historians are willing to admit.[5] Preachers exploited these deeply ingrained fears of the Papists to support their own doctrinal points of view as well as to unite Protestants in a common cause. Clerics often criticized the use of Latin in the Catholic worship service which they claimed concealed superstition and idolatry. The purchasing of indulgences and pardons was "a holy bribe which....procures a ready entrance into the strait gate of heaven,"[6] while the deathbed confession and absolution were dangers to Christian morality. They viewed transubstantiation as something utterly inconsistent with reason and notions of natural philosophy. It was, along with the veneration of relics and "image worship," more gross than paganism. In addition, they criticized the unlearned priests who did not allow the common people to read Scriptures and the infallible Pope and his followers who were the successors to the hated Pharisees.

> The same Popish grandeur and ecclesiastical
> tyranny and usurpation; that the same avarice

---

[4]Gordon Rupp, *Religion in England* (Oxford: Clarendon Press, 1986), p. 190. and Sheridan Gilley, "Roman Catholicism" in D.G. Paz, ed. *Nineteenth Century English Tradition Retrospect and Prospect* (Westport, Connecticut: Greenwald Press, 1995),p. 33. Gilley points out that in light of the increase in the general population, by 1800 England was actually becoming more Protestant not less so.

[5]An exception to the standard approach of most historians of the period that anti-Catholic passions had cooled during the eighteenth century can be found in Colin Haydon, *Anti-Catholicism in Eighteenth-Century England, 1714-80* (Manchester: Manchester University Press, 1993).He believes that this period "constituted a bridge, not a hiatus, between the better-researched ' No Popery ' troubles of the Stuart and Victorian eras (p. 2). See also David Hempton, *Religion and Political Culture in Britain and Ireland* where the author, citing the work of Colin Haydon, claims that not only were there more widespread anti-Catholic disturbances in 1745 and 1780 than was previously noted, but this virulent hatred "remained a strong element in the traditional beliefs and moral economy of the English lower orders throughout the period"(p. 145).

[6]Henry Stephens, *A True Representation of Popery as it Appears in Foreign Parts: Designed as a Preservative Against its Contagion; Particularly Recommended to British Protestants During their Residence in Popish Countries* (London: Printed for James and John Knapton, 1728),p. 24.

> and pride, superstition, and hypocrisy; the
> same ambitious, oppressive, persecuting
> and cruel spirit, in Scripture charg'd so heavily
> on the Pharisees and elegantly stil'd their leaven;
> have in the full extent and aggravation of guilt....
> been transmitted to these their true successors....
> or rather their not only genuine but improv'd off-spring.[7]

The condemnation of the dreaded Inquisition, with its use of torture to seek out heretics and to "force men's conscience", rounded out the litany of complaints against the Catholic Church that reverberated from pulpits all over England.

The press added its own touch of sensationalism to the preachers' diatribes against the Papists. Stories of the sexual misconduct of priests and nuns, the subject of numerous articles, were always of interest to the reading public. For example, *The British Journal* of November 24,1722 carries a story of a priest who "is accused of some criminal gallantries with the fair sex, which went smoothly on for some time under the name of confession." The reporter notes the priest's hypocrisy and how "the good man was much commended for his pious pains till the visible fruits of his amours confuted that opinion." In addition, it is noted that "About the same time, a certain young lady receiv'd two stabs by a stiletto from her lover, who was grown jealous by her familiar conversations with the said Ecclesiastick." In the October 19,1723 issue of *The British Journal* there is a story of both illicit sex and Catholic hypocrisy. An amorous cavalier, disguised as a deaf and dumb gardener, was employed in a convent where he enjoyed the sexual favors of the abbess and the younger nuns. "Finding more work than he was able to perform," the cavalier asked to be discharged from his position. "To cover the intrigue, it was recorded among the miracles of the convent, that the poor deaf and dumb was there restor'd to his hearing and speaking." In the February 2, 1723 issue of *The British Journal* the alleged immorality of the Catholic clergy is explained to the reading public in the following way:

> In Popish countries their Ecclesiastics living
> in idleness and riot, must be more lascivious
> than if otherwise employ'd; and by the means
> of confessions, and other secret communications
> with women have better and frequenter opportunities
> to debauch them themselves and to carry on
> intrigues for others.

The amorous priest and nun competed with the lecherous Jew for the attention of those readers looking for titillating tales.

---

[7]Ibid., p. 63.

The wide gulf between Protestantism and Catholicism that had been nurtured by centuries of hatred and fear was now also reinforced by the presence in England of a flood of refugees, victims of Catholic persecution in France, Bavaria, the Savoy and the Palatinate, who sought refuge in England or who were using the country as a way station on their journey to the North American colonies. The physical state of many of these miserable refugees, when they arrived in England, not only created anxiety about Protestantism on the Continent, but it was graphic proof to the British people of what they would experience at home if the Papists should ever seize power. The stories of persecution and degradation spread by these newcomers, strengthened the already strong selective remembrances of past events when Protestants were at the mercy of the Catholics.[8]

In the eyes of the English people, the Papists were responsible for the plot to blow up James the First's Parliament, the St. Bartholomew's Day Massacre of 1572, the Irish disturbances of 1641, and the Great Fire of London in 1666. Just as Easter was a traditional time for preachers to remind the faithful of the Jewish involvement in the Crucifixion, the anniversary of these events provided opportunities for anti-Catholic diatribes. Perhaps the most impressive service of remembrance took place each year on November fifth. According to *The Book of Common Prayer*, it marked "the happy deliverance of King James I, and the three estates of England, from the most traitorous and bloody intended massacre by Gunpowder" and also the deliverance of the nation at the time of William. In addition to impressive prayers that denounced the Papists' schemes and biblical readings that expressed thanksgiving to God for His power to save the faithful from their enemies, sermons were given at these services that reinforced past hatreds.

Richard Bentley (1662-1742), in *A Sermon on Popery Preached Before the University of Cambridge November 5th 1715* that was delivered at a convocation to mark the anniversary of the "intended massacre" at the time of James I, warns his listeners of the dangers of Popery in the strongest possible terms. After his opening remarks in which he points out that even in the city of Sodom there was one pious family and that "Not every single person within the limits of the Reformation is as good as his profession requires: nor every Papist as bad as the Popish system permits," he proceeds to spew his venom on the hated Catholics (p. 6). Bentley begins with a condemnation of the sale of relics and the use of "prayers and Masses for the dead to ease and shorten the pains of purgatory "to raise money for the Church (pp. 13-16). He continues with an attack upon the Mass where consecrated bread and wine is "easily

---

[8]Rupp, p. 76.

rais'd by superstition and ignorance to the highest excess, to notions improbable and impossible" (p. 21).This is followed by a criticism of the pomp of the Church, which Bentley believes is even greater than the practices of ancient Paganism, and a reminder of the cruelty of the Inquisition (pp. 21-23). Bentley saves his severest condemnation of Catholicism for the end of his sermon where he plays upon his listeners" real and imaginary fears of the power of foreign Popery.

> But if we are to watch against the silent
> tide of Popery in the small rivulets at home;
> much more against its inundation and deluge
> from abroad: which always mediates and now
> threatens to overwhelm us if foreign Popery
> once returns, and regain all the provinces that
> it lost at the Reformation: O the terrible
> storm of persecution at it's first regress!
> O the dark prospect of slavery and Ignorance
> for the Ages behind (p. 26).

Francis Haslewood (1661?-1722), in *A Sermon Preached Before the Right Honourable the Lord-Mayor, the Alderman and the Citizens of London, in the Cathedral Church of St. Paul on Nov. 5th 1720* to mark the anniversary of the Gun Powder Plot, warns of the dangers of any reconciliation with the Catholics. It was, he believes, the softening of animosity towards this group that increased its strength in the country." Our safety from Popery," he states, will always run parallel with our dread and abhorrence of it "(p. 21). In good demagogic tradition, he uses the hatred of the despised Catholics to foster greater unity among Protestants. He notes:

> As therefore friends naturally unite the closer,
> when they perceive the treacheries of an enemy;
> let this Popish snare prepare us with the greater
> alacrity to receive the light of our eyes(p. 27).

Benjamin Bennet (1674-1726) marked the one hundred and eighth anniversary of the Gunpowder Plot and the thirty-fifth anniversary of the Glorious Revolution with an equally stinging condemnation of Catholicism. The fact that his sermon, *The Persecution and Cruelty of the Church of Rome,* originally delivered in 1713, was reprinted as late as 1746 shows the popularity of his anti-Papist prejudices. Bennet believes that since the time of the Reformation, Rome has been waiting for the opportunity to regain power by any means possible. "Which of our kings," he asks, "have they not attempted to murder and slay"(p. 3). He views the coming of William of Orange as divine deliverance, an event that "should be to us like days of Purim among the Jews"(p. 5). The sermon contains the usual tirades against the Pope's infallibility as well as the "arbitrary injustice and inhumane cruelty "of the Inquisition(p. 16). Bennet dwells at length on the Saint Bartholomew Massacre of 1572 when, he claims, the Catholics took "pleasure and glory" in the barbaric massacre of some 200,000 innocent people(p. 23). He believes that through the years they have "actually enslaved the greatest part of the world and wait to enslave the rest (p. 30). Thus, it is incumbent upon all good Englishmen to remember what the Glorious Revolution represents.

> That it was a deliverance from Popish tyranny and
> cruelty 'tis plain the design was to have converted this
> nation by French Dragoons, Irish cut-throats and
> spiritual inquisitors. The only choice you must have had
> would have been Popery or death (p. 31).

In addition to prayer services and powerful sermons condemning Catholicism, it was also customary on these days of remembrance to burn the Pope and the Pretender, dupes of the Devil, in effigy. Prior to the actual ceremony, a parade of mock cardinals, priests and nuns would slowly wind through the city streets proclaiming the sins of the Papists. Like the church plays of the Middle Ages that condemned the Jews for crucifying Jesus, dramas reflecting Catholic plots to seize power in England were performed in a carnival-like atmosphere along with displays of fireworks for huge audiences from all social classes. But their impact upon the people was no laughing matter. These prayer services, sermons, Pope burnings, and spectacles, perpetuated old hatreds and encouraged new ones to be created. They reflect the very real fear of the power of the Catholic nations who had gained ground in the seventeenth century European rivalry between Protestantism and Catholicism and who now threatened the security of England. They also reveal a deep distrust of an alleged subversive minority group who, like the Jews, obstinately refused to disappear. Catholicism's durability was an embarrassment to those who believed in the superiority of the Protestant faith. These "celebrations," therefore, justified the treatment of Catholics as second class citizens.

In a number of articles that were designed to alert the Protestants of England to this threat to their cherished way of life, the press reinforced the theme of Papist subversion and the need to control the spread of their vile, blasphemous religion. Danger to the Protestant cause lurked everywhere. For example, in the *London Magazine* for January, 1735, readers were warned that there is "Scarcely a petty coffee house in any quarter of the town, where there is not a Popish lecture read on Sunday evenings to a set of apprentices, and such sorts of persons drawn together to be instructed in the great mysteries of Popery"(p. 2). The Catholics, especially the Jesuits, were believed to be so rich and powerful that they could use ministers of state as instruments for the destruction of liberty; soon they would be able to corrupt and rule all of Europe,[9] They were accused of not only teaching their poison, but also encouraging the general growth of irreligion which would destroy the foundations of society. Jesuits were blamed for seeking to undermine classical scholarship so that their own "Fopperies, Superstitions, and Corruptions" could influence the people. In this spirit, they were also guilty of spreading licentiousness and the "vice of luxury" in the country so that "idleness and ignorance" would follow."[10] In addition, in contemporary periodicals the fear was often expressed of some impending danger that would soon be touched off by the Papists and their traitorous allies within the country. For one writer in the *London Magazine* of November, 1733, the presence of what was alleged to be many thousands of Irish and French Catholics and their priests in both the city of London and its environs, was proof that the day of this uprising was near (p. 569). One observer of the contemporary scene, writing in the *London Magazine* for April, 1735, notes:

> The number of Priests about this city,
> is said to be no less than 10,000 and
> the number of the Papists in the Kingdom
> to amount to 600,000. And are not these
> circumstances sufficient to excite us to a
> a sense of our Danger? 'Tis in the nature of
> things impossible, that Popery can prevail,
> but slavery must encrease in proportion with it (p. 177).

From the latter part of the seventeenth century until 1829, to counter this threat, there were two clear trends in anti-Catholic legislation which resemble the medieval and pre-modern treatment of the Jews. The first was to debar them from profitable employment; the second was to limit their political power. Catholics were discriminated against when they sought access to education. They could not enter the professions nor could they own arms and ammunition or a horse that was worth more than five pounds. They were not allowed to vote; they were excluded from state offices and Parliament, and they were subjected to special taxation. At the turn of the eighteenth century it was generally believed that Catholics, as a whole, were very wealthy, and the government was often pressured to extort money from them to wipe out the national debt that had grown during the wars of William and Anne. Stories were continually circulated of vast treasures that they had accumulated to

---

[9]*Gentleman's Magazine*, 1 (September, 1732): 290. See also *London Magazine*, 5 (November, 1736): 629.
[10]*Gentleman's Magazine*, 4 (May, 1734): 240. and *Gentleman's Magazine* 3 (May, 1733): 231.

support seminaries in foreign countries and of their substantial investments in stocks and bonds.[11] *The British Journal* of December 1, 1722 notes that a bill in Parliament to raise £100,000 through a special tax on the "Estates of Roman Catholics and Popish Recusants" is necessary "in order to defray the extraordinary expenses occasion'd by the plots and conspiracies that have lately proceeded from that quarter." Throughout the century, Catholics could not inherit land. Until 1791, when freedom of worship was officially granted to them, any priest who conducted a Mass was subject to life imprisonment. Although these statutes were rarely enforced, they branded English Catholics as traitors to the Crown, and they created potential targets for social ostracism, business boycotts, and ultimately, mob violence.[12] The fact that there were those who advocated that Catholics wear something equivalent to the infamous "Jew Badge" to separate them from their neighbors or that they be deported from the country, is further testimony to their precarious place in English society.

Unlike the Jews, Gypsies, and Blacks, Catholics represented a cross section of the populace that was very English in dress, social customs, and speech. As Gordon Rupp notes:

> Every Parish church, every English Cathedral bore
> on its walls the records of incumbents and dignitaries,
> a large part of whom belonged within a Catholic
> pedigree. And while perhaps the "Englishness"
> of the English Catholics has been a little exaggerated
> by some historians, yet the old Catholic families
> among the nobility and landed gentry were so
> obviously rooted in England that their Protestant peers
> and neighbours could indeed manage to live
> peaceably together since they were joined with them
> by deep spiritual and material ties.[13]

It was the practice of their religion that separated them from their neighbors and which also created a problem of dual loyalty. Starting in the sixteenth century with the establishment of a national church, their allegiance was divided between their native country and their faith. Like the Jewish people, they were branded as outsiders. But even more than the Jews, they were considered to be a direct threat to the establishment.[14] Throughout this period, Catholics, in a very limited

---

[11]M.D.R. Leys, *Catholics in England 1559-1829: A Social History* (New York: Sheed and Ward, 1961), p115.
[12]Colley, p. 19.
[13]Rupp, p. 181.
[14]Mary Dorathy Rose, *Catholics in England 1559-1829: A Social History* (New York: Sheed and Ward, 1961), p. 1.

way, tried to convince the public of their loyalty to the Crown. In one pamphlet, *A letter from a Catholic Gentleman to his Protestant Friend,* written in 1745, the author stated that he was neither a Frenchmen nor a Spaniard, but a true, sincere, Englishman who desired the peace and the union of England's three kingdoms. He admitted that he was in communion with the See of Rome, but if the Pope himself would invade England, he would kneel down and kiss his toe and then rise up and shoot him in the head (p. 8)! It is doubtful if during this point in time that very many took his argument seriously and actually believed that Catholics could be both good neighbors and good subjects.

For many "enlightened" Protestant clerics such a nefarious group could not endure either at home or abroad. William Lloyd, Bishop of St. Asaph and later of Worcester (1627-1717), announced in 1688 that Popery in England could not last another year. In 1691, based on his interpretation of texts in Daniel and John, he predicted that France would be destroyed. In 1712, he assured Queen Anne that in four years the Church of Rome and the Papal city would come to an end.[15] In spite of such dire predictions, with the exception of periods of national crisis, especially when the enemy was a Catholic state, a practical toleration existed for English Catholics. Fortunately for them, the upheavals created by the Jacobite rebellions of 1715 and 1745, where considerable violence was directed against the Catholic community, were followed by periods of relative calm. After the final defeat of the Jacobites in 1746, the Stuarts were no longer a serious threat to the Crown, and anti-Catholic legislation was, to a considerable degree, relaxed. From this point on, Catholics were more likely to suffer attacks at the hands of the mob than from official persecution. However, in spite of a laissez faire government that did not want to get too deeply involved in the private lives of its citizens, prejudice against them still remained very strong in the English Protestant psyche. By avoiding political entanglements and by confining their worship to the chapels of foreign embassies, private homes, and a few churches, the Catholics, like the Jews of the country, tried to maintain a low profile. As a minority group, they also created a similar tight knit community that supported its own schools and collected and distributed charity to its poor. There was, of course, a price to paid for this separateness. Colin Haydon points out that the pattern of Catholic settlement in England which consisted to a large degree of self-contained communities, metropolitan ghettos and rural enclaves comprising Catholic manor houses surrounded by the homes of Catholic tenants,

---

[15]Margaret C. Jacob, *The Newtonians and the English Revolution 1689-1720* (Ithaca, New York: Cornell University Press, 1976), p. 125.

gave the Protestants good reason to believe that they were a law unto themselves.[16]

In spite of their need for communal autonomy, in many areas throughout England, individual Catholics found a respected place for themselves in society. Thus, the stereotype of the subversive Papist could not easily be projected upon loyal friends and good neighbors. This prompted some of the more vicious anti-Catholic hate-mongers to admit that not all of the Papists actually believed in the tenets of their faith, and that there were some good people among them. As one cleric notes:

> It is almost needless to say, that I do
> not charge all Papists with the above
> principles. I myself know several worthy
> Roman Catholics, who detest and abhor
> them. But I shall be easy understood, when
> I say that they are principles of the Popish
> Church, though not of every Papist.[17]

In addition, other demagogues directed their caustic remarks to faceless and nameless Catholics who did not take on recognizable human characteristics or who lived in distant communities or in foreign countries.

Although the Anglicans had been vociferous in their anti-Catholic stand, it was, in reality, the Dissenters and the Methodists who were much more hostile than the established church in openly attacking Papists. They were the ones who promoted "No Popery "publications and who organized societies to keep them out of the mainstream of English life. Some of the Dissenters' attitudes were based on doctrinal differences: they strongly disliked the Catholic emphasis on ritual and tradition which ran counter to their rationalism. But both they and the Methodists also feared that priests would compete with their own ministers for the voluntary contributions brought by new members. In addition, the Methodists were sometimes accused of being "Papists in disguise" or "Popishly inclined." To prove that they were good Protestants, they went to great lengths to stir up the masses against the Catholics.[18]

Actual physical abuse usually occurred during times of war when England was fighting a Catholic power. Then, in addition to the destruction of property, Catholics were often dragged to nearby ponds where they were forced under water until they nearly drowned. This

---

[16]Haydon, p. 77.
[17]D. Grant, Two *Dissertations on Popish Persecution and Breach of Faith* (London: J. Murray, 1771),p. 6.
[18]Haydon, p. 64.

was the very same treatment that was traditionally reserved for reputed witches. It was now inflicted upon the new scapegoats, the new targets of the fears and frustrations of the time.[19] Whenever the international situation worsened, it was easy for public figures to gain popularity by damning Catholics as conspirators who belonged to a foreign and traitorous religion which threatened to bring "the rack and the Inquisition to England."[20] In the words of John Free (1711?-1791), a preacher who had an especially strong dislike of Papists and other enthusiasts:

> It may not be unreasonable here to ask
> the Papists, what sort of a religion they are
> propagating in the dungeons of the Inquisition?
> What sort of religion they were for establishing
> in these kingdoms, by their horrid plots and
> treachery and dark designs of death?[21]

During the tumultuous time of the Fall of 1745, another cleric, Benjamin Nicholls(1717?-1765), warned his congregation that if the rebellion succeeded,

> We should lose our religion, we should
> lose our liberty, the boasted perogative
> of the British people; the one, pure
> Protestant Christianity, we must exchange
> for bigotted ignorance, and anti-Christian
> Popery; the other, freedom and happiness,
> we must part with for Egyptian bondage and servitude.[22]

Colin Haydon believes that the survival as well as the continuing wide appeal of anti-Catholicism throughout the century was due to its important function of social bonding. He believes that it provided "a negative definition of what was good and acceptable, by showing its wicked, deviant antithesis." It could, therefore, bind a nation together during periods of ideological or political tension. For whenever Popery was viewed as a threat to the fabric of society, it was the common duty of all good Protestants to combat such an enemy.[23]

The most virulent outbreak of popular anti-Catholic fanaticism occurred in 1778 when the military campaigns in the American colonies were going poorly. In order to increase the strength of the British Army,

---

[19]Colley, pp. 22-3.
[20]Christopher Hibbert, *King Mob: The Story of Lord George Gordon and the London Riots of 1780* (Cleveland: The World Publishing Co., 1958) pp. 19-20.
[21]John Free, *A Sermon Preached at St. Mary's in Oxford Before the University on the 5th of November 1745* (London: Printed by D. Browne, 1745), p. 11.
[22]Nicholls, p. 17.
[23]Haydon, p. 253.

attempts were made to persuade the Scottish Catholics to enlist by offering them greater political freedom. The Catholic Relief Bill, which granted only limited benefits, was passed unopposed by Parliament. But before it was put into law, riots broke out in Edinburgh and Glasgow where Catholic schools and houses of worship were attacked. In London, Lord George Gordon, president of the newly formed Protestant Association made up of Methodists, Dissenters, Anglicans, and those who believed that the Catholics were a threat to religious freedom and to individual liberties, attempted to repeal this legislation through mass demonstrations and a petition to Parliament. Handbills were circulated urging the people to unite in the name of the tens of thousands of Protestant martyrs who had been massacred in France. Any toleration of Popery, they stated, would provoke God's vengeance upon the nation and destroy its army and navy.[24]

On June 2, 1780, after almost two full years of carefully organized and planned agitation, tempers reached a boiling point, and a chain of events was set off which unleashed the power of the mob. Gordon attracted all kinds of people to his cause who had but to put a blue cockade in their hats to be considered part of his supporters. For five days, until the military finally restored order, reason and moderation, the hallmarks of the period, were put aside as Catholic chapels and property were viciously ransacked by the unruly mob. In a rare pamphlet that displayed sympathy for the victims, the writer who witnessed the wanton destruction and killings in Edinburgh notes that, "The fear of Popery displayed by an artful hand is a bugbear which never fails to terrify the minds of the people of this country."[25] He claims that in this violent setting a Roman Catholic could not appear in the streets without being pointed at and attacked with such words as: "There is a Papist, a black Papist, knock him down, shoot him."[26] He blames this violence on the innumerable advertisements that had been placed in the newspapers prior to the riots that portrayed Catholics as "monsters of nature" as well as the pamphlets that labeled them as "enemies to every species of liberty and unworthy to live among men." In addition, he claims that Catholics were execrated from the pulpit and that Protestants were told that to extirpate them from the face of the earth "was a work of merit, and doing God a service."[27] Even if only a portion of what he writes

---

[24]Hibbert, p. 40.

[25]*A Memorial to the Public in Behalf of the Roman Catholics of Edinburgh and Glasgow Containing an Account of the Late Riot Against Them on the Second and Following Days of February, 1779* (London: J. Coghlan, 1779),p. 10.

[26]Ibid., p. 16.

[27]Ibid., pp. 41-42.

actually happened, it is another grim testimony to the dark side of the Age of Reason.

The Jews of London were so terrified by the ferocity of the mob that they followed the general example of writing on their shutters, "This house is a true Protestant."[28] Unlike other times in Jewish history when periods of turmoil were used as an excuse to also attack the Jews, they were left unharmed. Wanton violence against the papists and the destruction of their property and some public buildings was sufficient to satisfy the wrath of the mob.

Eugene Black believes that there were several significant factors which contributed to the devastating power of the rioters. They included the misguided religious zeal of those who looted and burned, the ineffectual police system of the time, and the inability of the magistrates to stand up against the Protestant Association. Of even greater significance, he notes, "Popery was a living symbol" that could stir the masses to wanton destruction.[29] According to Butterfield, the Catholic Relief Bill which triggered off the riots "proved to be a pitfall, offending not only rational prejudice, but deep dark passions strange as Nazi hatreds and as baffling as anti-Semitism."[30] As a result of this mob action, Catholics were pushed even further out of the mainstream of English life. Yet, in 1791 there was no popular outcry when Parliament passed the second catholic Relief act which gave them the right to worship freely and openly. It was not due to any new found respect for this minority group or because of a rising feeling of good will in English Society. Prejudices against the Papists were still in the hearts of the great majority of the masses. Only now, during the period of the French Revolution, the protean nature of prejudice was at work. In the words of E.P. Thompson, there was "a drastic redirection of hatred; the Pope was displaced from the seat of commination and in his place was elevated Tom Paine."[31]

The hatred of Catholics which continuously smoldered throughout this period not only drew attention away from the Jewish community, but it evoked a certain amount of compassion for Jews in foreign countries who were persecuted by them. In the pages of the *Gentleman's*

---

[28]Thomas Holcroft, *A Plain and Succinct Narrative of the Gordon Riots* (London: 1780), p. 30. A reprint of this pamphlet, with an introduction by Garland Garvey Smith, was printed by the Emory University Library in 1944.

[29]Eugene Charlton Black, *The Association: British Extraparliamentary Organization 1769-1793* (Cambridge, Massachusetts: Harvard University Press, 1963), p. 166.

[30]Gerald Newman, *The Rise of English Nationalism: A Cultural History* (New York: St. Martin's Press, 1987), p. 209.

[31]E.P. Thompson, The *Making of the English Working Class* (New York: Vintige Books, Random House, 1966), p. 391.

Magazine for November, 1788, there is an account of the murder of a Jew that took place in one of the German states. The author believes that it "proves the sentiments of the lower classes of people professing the Catholic faith, with respect to the natural rights of the Jews." These attitudes, he claims, are a result of the teachings of the illiterate and bigoted priests. One of the assassins is quoted as telling the tribunal that he had implored the aid of the Virgin Mary to carry out this deed and that the court should pay no further attention to it since the victim was "only a Jew." With righteous indignation the author concludes his account of the incident with the words, "O Popery what hast thou to answer for"(pp. 3-4). The story, an obvious anti-Catholic diatribe, made the Jews the innocent victim of the Papists, and it generated sympathy for them at the expense of a hated enemy. This same theme appears in other accounts of forced conversion or the expulsion of Jews from Catholic countries.

Christopher Hill believes that the relative absence of anti-Semitism during the seventeenth century was due to the rejection by Protestant theologians of the medieval Catholic belief that the Antichrist had not yet come and that he would be a Jew. The great majority of these clerics now identified the Pope with this evil eschatological figure – the pseudo-messiah who would be revealed in the end of days as the great enemy of Jesus. Despite occasional references to "Antichrist and his synagogue," the Pontiff was now the focus of their attention. In fact, many of these theologians believed that the conversion of the Jews was a prelude to the Antichrist's fall and to the coming of the millennium.[32] Although during the eighteenth century the Pope was not identified with the Antichrist as often as he had been in previous times, anti-Popery was far from waning. For many English people he continued to be the satanic ruler of the perfidious city of Rome – an ecclesiastical bogey man who could be blamed for the national disasters that struck the country. In popular imagination, the Pope's ultimate goal was to use the traditional enemies of England to reassert his power over the people and to bring the rack and the Inquisition to the land.[33]

Stories of Papist cruelty, treachery, and sedition were passed down through the generations, and they continued to flourish during the Age of Reason. One of the most popular works to describe the barbarism of the Catholic church was John Foxe's *Book of Martyrs, containing an account of the sufferings and death of the Protestants in the reign of Queen Mary.* This sixteenth century classic was now revived and vigorously promoted to

---

[32]Christopher Hill, *Anti-Christ in Seventeenth-Century England* (London: Oxford University Press, 1971), p. 175.
[33]Hibbert, *King Mob*, p. 38-9.

perpetuate old Papist stereotypes that were designed to unite Protestants against their traditional enemy. In order to reach as wide an audience as possible, a new edition of thirty-one installments was printed so that people of limited means, who could not purchase it all at once, could spread out their payments. As the century progressed, its popularity grew and repackaged editions of some eighty installments were made available to the masses.[34] Foxe's heroic Protestant martyrs who appeared in the text, as well as in some highly imaginative illustrations, were proof of the sinister nature of Catholicism. *The Pilgrims Progress* was another work with anti-Catholic stereotypes that continued to be reprinted throughout the eighteenth century. Papists were the ones who prevented the hero and heroine from reaching the Heavenly city. John Bunyan made his anti-Catholic feelings quite clear when he named the two sinister, tyrannical giants who guarded the cave in the valley of the shadow of death, Pope and Pagan.[35] But these kinds of sentiments were not limited to the printed page. In one instance, relating to the alleged Popish plot to destroy the city of London, they were literally engraved in stone. Following the Fire of 1666, Christopher Wren was commissioned by an act of Parliament to design a monument "the better to preserve the memory of this direful visitation." Years later, in June of 1681, after tales had been circulated that eighty Jesuits had been the cause of the conflagration, the words "begun and carried on by the treachery and malice of Popish faction" was engraved on the base of the pedestal. They were obliterated after the accession of James II, but incised once again when William and Mary were called to the Throne. The words were not removed until 1830.[36]

Throughout the century, a stream of books and pamphlets appeared that cautioned the public of the dangers that the Catholics, especially the Jesuits, posed to the religious and the political establishment. There were constant warnings that good Protestants should be on guard against the "crafts and assaults" of priests who are busier than ever with their nefarious schemes to proselytize the Protestants.[37] Catholics were often compared to the Pharisees of Christian Scripture who were willing to compass sea and land to make one convert. These modern-day missionaries were even more odious since their intention was not for

---

[34]Colley, p. 26.
[35]Ibid., p. 28.
[36]Walter George Bell, *The Great Fire of London in 1666* (London: John Lame Co., 1920), pp. 208-9.
[37]John White, *The Protestant Englishmen Guarded Against the Arts and the Arguments of Romish Priests and Emissaries* (London: 1753), Preface.

true religious purposes, but to recruit additional supporters for the Pope.[38]

Just as the previously mentioned sermons were delivered to mark special days of Catholic treachery, pamphlets served the same purpose. Writers dusted off old accounts of such events as the Gun Powder Plot and added new flourishes to them for popular consumption. The need for the English people to remember the evils of the Papists was related to the traditional Jewish approach to observing the Passover. One writer notes that, "When God delivered his people out of Egypt He instituted the Passover as a memorial that they and their children might forever remember it.[39] The deliverance of Protestants from the clutches of the Papists was equally worth remembering. The title of one contemporary pamphlet, *Reasons Humbly Offer'd For a Law to Enact the Castration or Gelding of Popish Ecclesiastics as the Best Way to Prevent the Growth of Popery in England*, sums up how seriously some Protestants viewed the corrupting power of the Catholic Church. The author scorns the immorality of the priests and how they cause a "deluge of uncleanliness to be poured upon England "(p. 7). He justifies his suggestion of using harsh measures to curb their influence with the words:

> It would be a punishment very proper for them,....
> since its evident that by their own personal
> villainy, and their loose doctrine of pardons etc.
> which incourages people in licentiousness,
> they make more proselytes than by any other method (p. 11).

Another source of anti-Catholic sentiment was the astrological almanacs. Although they were not as popular as they had been in past centuries, they were still widely circulated and read. Along with instruction and amusement, they ridiculed Catholic practices and beliefs. They, too, reminded their readers of such evils as the Inquisition, the persecution of the Huguenots, and the Gunpowder Plot as well as the hopes for the future downfall of the Papacy and Catholic France.[40]

Closely related to the Catholics in the eyes of Whig propagandists were the Jacobites, those who sought to restore the Stuarts to the throne and who backed the exiled James II. In a spurious work entitled, *A Genuine Intercepted Letter From Father Patrick Graham Almoner and Confessor to the Pretender's Son in Scotland to Father Benedick Yorke, Titular*

---

[38]Benjamin Bennet, *Several Discourses Against Popery* (London: 1714), p. 343.

[39]*The Gunpowder-Treason With a Discourse of the Manner of Its Discovery* (London: 1679), p. 7. This pamphlet is a reprint of an earlier work that contains a preface by Thomas Lord Bishop of Lincoln who added his own anti-Catholic diatribes.

[40]Bernard Capp, *English Almanacs 1500-1800: Astrology and the Popular Press* (Ithaca, New York: Cornell University Press, 1979), p. 251.

Bishop of St. David's at Bath, that was allegedly written after the Prince of Wales landed in Scotland, the mythical cleric spins a fanciful tale of Papist conquest. The Prince is pictured as a devout Catholic who, in his conversations, "can never omit declaring his detestation of heresy"(p. 4). The writer of the letter doubts that if he would be victorious he could ever bring himself to sign a declaration that "had in it even a promise of toleration" (p. 4). In order to send shivers up the spines of his Protestant readers and to galvanize their support for the administration, the author attributes the following words to Father Patrick:

> O my Lord what a glorious scene opens to my view,
> shall the Cross once more be erected in Britain?
> Shall our altars be again exalted? Shall our churches
> be restored to us? Shall our abbey-lands divert to
> their right owners? Shall the clergy have their due
> honours and weight? Shall we rush like a torrent upon
> the laity, and make'em know they are our people and
> the sheep of our pasture (p. 4)?

Under the new Catholic government the national debt would be canceled along with grants, peerages, and honors made after 1688 (p. 7).The letter concludes with the words, "Exert yourself then, inflame your friends with a zeal to destroy the enemies of our Church and King and to extirpate hereticks and traitors" (p. 8). This potentially dangerous anti-government group was made up not only of Catholics, but also of Scottish Episcopalians and English non-jurors. They were some of the best minds of the age who, as outsiders, supported this popular opposition faction. The French, engaged in a worldwide economic contest with England, supplied military and financial aid to the pretender to the throne, and they also encouraged a powerful Tory fifth column. The fact that France was a Catholic country, added an additional sinister note to its already black image. As one preacher noted in 1756, on the eve of an expected invasion from across the channel:

> It is a Popish power, and therefore to a
> Protestant country, a natural, and the
> bitterest enemy: an enemy from principles,
> such as they are: for Popery teaches her
> votarys to dispense with truth, when concerned
> with a Protestant enemy; nay suggests and
> sanctifies barbarities, at which nature, left to
> herself, would honestly shudder.[41]

---

[41]J. Grigg, *A Sermon Preached at St. Albans and at Box-Lane, Chiefly with a view to the Apprehended Invasion* (London: Printed for J. Buckland, 1756), p. 13.

Though plagued by bad luck, poor coordination and the inability to mount a successful military campaign, for over seventy years the Jacobites were a thorn in the side of the government and a threat to its security. The fear of the Jacobites encouraged the authorities to set up an elaborate intelligence system in order to keep them under surveillance.[42] The Jacobites' association with the Papists reinforced, in popular imagination, the "other" image of the native Catholics, and it kept negative stereotypes alive for many years to come.

One theme that runs through several of the anti-Catholic sermons and pamphlets, is the need of the English not to deny to other Christians the religious liberties that the Catholics refuse to grant to Protestants. In essence, to remove the bigotry in themselves that they see in the Papists.[43] A study of the negative attitudes of the Anglican Church to the "other" Protestants as well as the rivalries between the different groups of religious outsiders shows that this was a continuing problem during the Age of Reason that indirectly benefited the Jewish community.

The Dissenters

As the long, swelling waves succeed a hurricane,
so the tempest of the Puritan Revolution was followed
by continuous disturbances.[44]

Even in its shared Protestantism eighteenth- and
nineteenth-century Britain was deeply divided in
matters of religion: divisions between the orthodox
and the heterodox, between Episcopalians and
Presbyterians, between Churchmen and Dissenters,
between evangelicals and High Churchmen, between
clergymen and anticlericals and between adherents
of the political status quo and those who wanted to change it.[45]

Just as the real and the imagined deeds of the Jews and the Catholics of prior centuries were ingrained in the memory of many of the English people, so too were those of the Dissenters. Each year, on January 30, at special Anglican services, they were remembered and condemned by both the illiterate and the learned members of society for their part in the

---

[42]Paul S. Fritz, "The Anti-Jacobite Intelligence System of the English Ministers, 1715-1745." *The Historical Journal* 16 (No. 2, 1973): 265. Fritz Believes that the Jacobitess were a much more serious threat than earlier English historians were willing to believe.

[43]See, for example, *A Letter to a Friend in Lancashire Occasioned by a Report Concerning Injunctions and Prohibitions by Authority, Relating to Some Points of Religion, Now in Debate* (London: Printed for John Baker, 1714), p. 19, and Henry Mathew, p. 34.

[44]Rupp, p. 4.

[45]Hempton, *Religion and Political Culture in Britain and Ireland*, p. 174.

execution of Charles I. On such solemn occasions, marked by appropriate readings in Christian Scriptures and masterful Anglican preaching, their involvement in the regicide was often compared to the Jewish role in the Crucifixion. Though a comparison was made between the two groups by Anglican clerics and writers, the Dissenters were actually hated and feared more than the Jews. It was noted that in regard to these two events, "lasting monuments and memorials of the blackest scenes of villainy," that:

> What the Jews do this way, we hear very
> little of, they have at least the modesty to be
> silent to us, and if they do belch forth their
> malice in any blasphemies and slanders
> against the Lord of life and glory, they keep
> them private in their families; but what the
> inheritors of the principles of those who
> murder'd the royal martyr have to say, we hear
> from every apprentice boy; a sort of merit is plac'd
> in justifying the deed, and the only concern
> seemingly express'd about it, is, that they had not
> themselves a hand in it.[46]

As a result of the Dissenters' openly disrespectful attitudes, their religious and political activities were continually scrutinized and interpreted in the light of this infamous event.[47]

The Dissenters' economic strength and the skill, the determination, and the zeal of their spokesmen also made them appear to be a more serious threat to the established church than the Catholics and also the Jews and other non-Christians.[48] As Henry Stebbing (1687-1763) notes in *An Essay Concerning Civil Government:*

> For What is an establishment to guard against?
> Not Jews not Mahometans, but the various
> incompatible, I had almost said absurd sects of
> Christians, every one of them scriptural according
> to his own account and every one of which would
> be of the established religion if no subscription were
> required but the words of the scriptures.[49]

[46]*The Advocate* 12 (January 25, 1721): 1.
[47]Anthony Lincoln, *Some Political and Social Ideas of English dissent 1763-1800* (Cambridge: Cambridge University Press, 1938), pp. 4-5.
[48]John Carswell, *From Revolution to Revolution: England 1688-1776* (New York: Charles Scribner's Sons, 1973), p. 43.
[49]Henry Stebbing, *An Essay Concerning Civil Government*, pp. 20-1. Cited in Richard Burgess Barlow, *Citizenship and Conscience A Study of the Theory and Practice of Religious Toleration in England During the Eighteenth Century* (Philadelphia: University of Pennsylvania Press, 1962), p. 47.

The Dissenters were aliens among their own people. Like the Catholics who were often accused of being in the employ of France or Spain, it was believed that their loyalties were first and foremost to Geneva or to the Germanies. The Dissenters, a truly diverse group, were religiously, politically, and socially isolated from their peers, and in many ways, suffered more discrimination than the Jews. Although they did not attend the Church of England, they were still obligated to pay tithes and church rates. At times, because the Anglicans did not consider them to be properly baptized, they were denied burial in parish graveyards. Dissenters were excluded from Oxford and Cambridge, and since the Royal College of Physicians only accepted as fellows the graduates of these two schools, they were also denied the right to practice medicine. Their own schools, which were built to counter academic discrimination, were often attacked by the Anglicans on the grounds that their teachers had not obtained proper licenses from the local bishops. Sometimes, magistrates refused to register their meeting houses or to protect them from mob violence.

Just as Jews, who converted to Christianity, were mentioned in the press to enhance the position of the Christian faith, those dissenting ministers who decided to follow the tenets of the Anglican Church received similar treatment in order to bolster the image of the official religion. Thus, *The British Journal* of September 12, 1724 notes:

> Mr. Samuel Bernard, formerly minister of a dissenting
> congregation at Farehan, has lately conformed to
> the discipline of the Church. He has the reputation
> of being a great scholar, one of a clear head, and
> unbyass'd searching after truth: and as this change
> was not made on a sudden, but after long consideration,
> and upon thought well digested, it is probable, he will
> offer his reasons to the publick, and in them something new.

Historically, some of the causes of anti-Semitism have been the very visible Jewish involvement in business and the practice of Jews sticking together for mutual support. During the eighteenth century, it was the Dissenters who took advantage of family ties to raise capital for new enterprises. In the first part of the century, they were basically from the middle class, and they lived in the urban areas of England. Success brought several of them wealth, upward social mobility, and also a considerable amount of attention.[50]

Dissenters, like the Jews, were viewed as a special source of revenue. For example, the City of London, anxious to raise funds in 1742 for the

---

[50]Richard Brown, *Society and Economy in Modern Britain 1700-1850* (London: Rutledge, 1991), pp. 212-13.

new Mansion house, passed a by-law which stated that anyone declining to accept the nomination for sheriff would be subject to a fine of £400. In addition, those who refused to serve after their election would be liable for £600. Since, as a matter of conscience, Dissenters could not take Communion in an Anglican Church, a necessary prerequisite for the position, they became the source of a substantial amount of revenue. The practice continued for some twenty-five years, and it was not abolished until 1767.[51]

Another thorn in the side of the Dissenters was the charge that they were disloyal to the Crown. In 1715 and in again in 1745, they offered their services for "King and country" – willingly enlisting in the armed forces to fight the rebels. Their only reward for this act of patriotism, was an Act of Indemnity, a pardon for those who had violated the law by serving in the ranks during times of national emergency.[52]

The Test and Corporation Acts imposed upon the Dissenters their most serious disabilities. If they did not participate in the Communion Service according to the rites of the Church of England, they were officially barred from a substantial number of civil, military, and municipal offices. The Anglicans viewed the Test Act as a necessary instrument for the safety of both the Church and the State. They did not believe that it was unjust to deny political power to those who did not conform to the doctrines of the Church of England since they firmly believed that the majority faith, the established religion of the country, should be protected against those who would challenge it. They also feared that if the Dissenters would receive full toleration, the Jews, Deists, and Mohammedans would be next in line.[53] Some Anglicans believed that the Dissenters would join with the Jews in an alliance against the Church of England. This threat of a Jewish conspiracy was not taken very seriously; it was the Dissenters who were in the public eye. For several decades, their attempts to receive greater political freedom were the focus of the establishment's attention.

As long as the Dissenters, like the Jews, knew their place and were willing to accept an inferior legal status, they could count on the sympathy and even the active support of a number of liberal Whigs and Anglican clergy. However, in the 1770's and 1780's when they became more vocal in their demands for equality, their friends were neither willing nor able to overcome the hostility that was directed against them. Vigorous opposition to them was articulated at the time of Wilkes, and it

---

[51]Basil Williams, *The Whig Supremacy* 1714-1760 (Oxford: Clarendon Press, 1962), p. 71.
[52]Ibid., p. 72.
[53]Joshua Toulmin, *Two Letters*. Cited in Anthony Lincoln, p. 224.

continued to grow during the period of the American Revolution when Dissenters were accused of not only interfering with the conduct of the war, but of actually provoking it. Failure to secure the repeal of the Test Acts in 1787 heightened animosities which became full-blown during the time of the French Revolution. The Dissenters' admiration for the radicals across the Channel further alienated them from the establishment ; it brought on both governmental repression and the wrath of the mob. According to G.M. Ditchfield, for a brief time during the French Revolution, radical dissenters were regarded by the authorities as being much more dangerous than the Catholics.[54]

It was the Unitarians who were in the forefront of the campaign to abolish the Test and Corporation Acts. By May of 1789, they almost succeeded when their efforts for repeal were voted down by the House of Commons by a vote of only 124 to 104. The outbreak of the French Revolution encouraged them to demand a nation-wide union of Dissenters. However, their hope for a united front among the non-Anglicans was short lived. For many Baptists and Independents, the Unitarians were overstepping their bounds; they decided to part company with them.

In Birmingham, suspicion of Unitarian subversion produced bitter Anglican tirades which incited mobs to destroy their homes and meeting houses. In July of 1791, the city was subjected to three days of unrestrained riots and looting. Well-organized bands, under safe conduct of the magistrates, burned Joseph Priestly's house to the ground destroying his library and his laboratory. The Loyalist mobs who rampaged through the streets of Burmingham shouted, "Church and King" and "No Philosophes" as they burned and looted. In their minds the victims of their violence were part of an international conspiracy to undermine the authority of the Crown.

The next year, the scene was repeated in Manchester where again, in the name of "Church and King," mobs, incited by the Anglican clergy and protected by the magistrates, attacked Unitarian meeting houses. Liverpool, Yarmouth, Warwick and other townships also felt the wrath of angry mobs; many champions of the Unitarian cause emigrated to America or pledged their allegiance to the Establishment. Loyalist associations were formed, and the Anglicans unleashed vicious attacks upon all dissenting groups, Sunday schools and itinerant preachers.

Edmund Burke (1729-1797), probably the first person of importance in England to openly denounce the dangers of the revolution in France, believed that, by definition, the Unitarians were not really Christians.

---

[54]G.M. Ditchfield, "The Priestly Riots in Historical Perspective," *Transactions of the Unitarian Historical Society*, 20 (April, 1991): 8.

They were, in reality, a political faction who would not hesitate to destroy the Anglican Church, wreak the British Constitution, and dismember the Christian Commonwealth. He vehemently rejected the idea that religious freedom was an absolute right; he did not believe that refusing such a militant, infidel, minority unrestricted freedom to practice their faith was unjust.[55]

In 1792, the hostility directed against the Dissenters was, in turn, overshadowed by attacks against radicals and reformers in general. The government's and the property owners' very real fear of revolution at home, inspired by the violence across the Channel, led to the suppression of their allegedly politically subversive activities.[56] Under the threat of foreign invasion and internal dissent, Habeas Corpus was suspended in 1794; brute force was used to quell food riots and naval mutinies. Though there were now new targets of prejudice and repression which took some pressure off the Dissenters, these religious groups remained second-class citizens until the Test and Corporation Acts were repealed in 1828.

The history of the Dissenters during the eighteenth century highlights not only the repression of non-Anglicans, but also the extent of the sectarian rivalries and conflicts that were so prevalent within English society. The clash between them and the Methodists is a case in point. John Wesley (1703-1791) disapproved of Dissenters because of their separation from the Anglican Church. On the other hand, the Calvinists and the Presbyterians condemned the Methodists for their irrational, enthusiastic behavior and their undisciplined modes of prayer. They denounced their leaders as false prophets. By and large, Dissenters encouraged free inquiry and controversy to find the truth while Wesley and his followers placed strong emphasis on conformity and a rigid control of the intellect.[57] Congregational and Baptist churches refused communion to those who worshipped in Methodist meeting-houses. In some localities, Dissenters were accused of stirring up mobs against the Methodists and of press-ganging them into the army. Although religious divisions were not as bitter as they had been during the previous

---

[55]Carl B. Cone, *Burke and the Nature of Politics*, Vol. 2 (Lexington, Kentucky: University of Kentucky Press, 1964), pp. 389-90.

[56]David L. Wykes, "'The Spirit of Persecutors exemplified' The Priestly Riots and the victims of the Church and King mobs." *Transactions of the Unitarian Historical Society*, 20 (April, 1991): 24.

[57]Isabel Rivers, "Dissenting and Methodist Books of Practical Divinity" in Isabel Rivers ed., *Books and Their Readers in Eighteenth-Century England* (Leicester: Leicester University Press, 1982), p. 151.

century, old prejudices, though sometimes kept in check, were very much alive.[58]

The Dissenters who suffered restrictions on both their political and religious activities fought to have them removed from their own denominations, but not from other groups. Toleration was only sought out for their own circle of worshipers, and they were, for example, particularly vehement in their hatred of Catholics. In addition, although they spoke about the equality of all men in the sight of God, they nevertheless advocated both economic and religious discrimination for the "others." Men like Thomas Gordon (d. 1750), Richard Price (1723-1791), and Joseph Priestly believed that only those qualified by money and goods should be allowed to participate in public life. Thus, Catholics, as well as servants, paupers, and other landless rabble, were to be considered as second-class citizens.[59]

As the various Protestant denominations fought with one another, or concerned themselves with the dangers of the Papists or the impoverished, the Jews were, for the most part, ignored. This was also particularly true in the relationship of the Anglican Church to the wide spectrum of religious, ethnic, and racial groups in English society – a growing number of outsiders who had many of the undesirable qualities that were classically associated with the Jewish people. They were more numerous, visible, and potentially dangerous to the status quo than the Jews. Therefore, the stock prejudices of the past took new directions and new forms. The radical religious groups of the past century such as the Levellers, the Diggers, and the Fifth Monarchy men virtually disappeared by the early part of the Age of Reason, but religious dissent did not succumb entirely. The Methodists and the Quakers succeeded in transforming its spirit to meet the religious dissatisfactions of the eighteenth century.[60] By doing so, they also became the prime targets of the religious establishment.

The Methodists

Satan's slaves against me rose,
    And sought my life to slay;
Thou hast baffled all my foes,

---

[58]Michael R. Watts, *The Dissenters: From the Reformation to the French Revolution.* Vol. 1 (Oxford: Clarendon Press, 1978).

[59]Carl B. Cone, *The English Jacobins: Reformers in Late Eighteenth Century England* (New York: Charles Scribner's Sons, 1968), pp. 7-8.

[60]John W. Wilkes "The Transformation of Dissent: a Review of the Change from the Seventeenth to the Eighteenth Centuries." in *The Dissenting Tradition,* ed. C. Robert Cole and Michael E. Moody (Athens, Ohio, Ohio University Press, 1975), p. 114.

And spoil'd them of their prey;
Thou hast cast the' accuser down,
   Hast maintain'd Thy servant's right,
Made mine innocence known,
   And clear as noonday light.[61]

See! how those holy, self-abasing souls,
Whom the Blest Spirit with his influence rules,
See! with what watchful industry and care
They labour in salvation's great affair:
Their bodies with what abstinence they tame,
To quench Concupiscence's raging flame....[62]

The Methodists became a growing concern to the Anglican Church soon after they were founded by John and Charles Wesley in Bristol in the early 1730's. These two brothers, aided by a cadre of zealous preachers, attracted a growing number of people who were dissatisfied with the establishment's religious practices, and they did not hesitate to criticize the ecclesiastical power structure. The Anglicans, in turn, were outraged by the emotionalism, the groaning, the shrieking and the hysteria that they believed characterized the Methodist prayer services. They sharply criticized those who violated the order, the decorum, and the solemnity of religious worship. The Anglicans feared that the Methodists' emphasis on salvation by faith would undermine the stability of contemporary society by denying the necessity of good works.

In addition, they disapproved of their primitive superstitions and their strong stand against card playing, theatres, and horse racing. The Methodists, following Wesley's teaching that the devout life is in conflict with the world of property and patronage, did not fit into any approved niche in contemporary society. They were strangers to the whole structure of the Church of England with its tithes and sinecures as well as to the social clubs and friendly societies which centered around the ale and coffee houses.

Methodists could be recognized by their plain, severe dress, and by their detachment from any kind of revelry. They condemned virtually all earthly pleasures as a means of attaining heavenly joy. By attacking the treasured pastimes which made life tolerable for the bulk of the people, they made enemies from a cross section of the population who condemned their "holier than thou "attitude. In addition, their unique regime and rituals seemed to be as mysterious as those of the

---

[61]Charles Wesley, "Afterwards" in *Hyms and Sacred Poems,* 1749. Cited in *Charles Wesley, A Reader.* Ed. John R. Tyson (Oxford: Oxford University Press, 1989), p. 258.
[62]"A Character of the Methodists" *Gentleman's Magazine,* 9 (July, 1739): 377.

Freemasons. The rumors that were circulated about their alleged love feasts were indicative of how they were considered to be a threat to middle class morality. Hatred against the Methodists was as irrational as the classic anti-Semitic charges leveled against the Jewish people. Some of the early followers of Wesley were, like medieval Jews, accused of kidnapping children and practicing sorcery. As outsiders, Methodists were viciously attacked by Catholic mobs in Ireland for being zealous Protestants. They received even worse treatment at the hands of Protestants in England for being Papists. Wesley himself was accused of following both Popery and Puritanism. The Anglicans saw in Methodism the same fanaticism which, in the previous century, had torn the fabric of English life apart and had resulted in a bloody religious war. In this spirit, one critic of the new movement wrote:

> Cromwell like you did first pretend,
> Religion was his only end;
> But soon the Mask away did fling,
> Pull'd down the Church and killed the King.[63]

As Paul Langford points out, "Methodists were staunch defenders of the historic authority of the church against the internal subversion of Unitarians and the external attacks of the Dissenters." However, "this only irritated the Anglicans and made their persecution that much harder to bear."[64] In the eyes of the Establishment, the Methodists were aliens, fanatics, and enthusiasts who were determined to lead the faithful astray. As a means of stemming the growing tide of support for the new group, Anglican bishops prohibited Methodist preachers from conducting services in their churches. Mobs were stirred up by local vicars to disrupt prayer meetings, and magistrates issued warrants for the arrest of Methodist preachers or turned a blind eye when they were beaten and driven out of town. In addition, a steady stream of anti-Methodist sermons and pamphlets accused them of being Papists in disguise, political traitors, religious heretics, and dangerous subversives.

Hogarth captures this prejudice towards the Methodists in his etching, "Credulity, Superstition and Fanaticism." It depicts a church service where the preacher, who resembles the evangelist, George Whitefield (1714-1770), conceals a harlequin's robe under his gown and a Jesuit tonsure under his wig. In place of the traditional church hourglass, there is a thermometer which gauges the emotional level of the

---

[63]Peter Paragraph, *The Methodist and the Mimick* (1767), cited in Arthur Warne, *Church and Society in Eighteenth Century Devon* (New York: Augustus M. Kelley Publishers, 1969), p. 111.

[64]Paul Langford, *A Polite and Commercial People: England 1727-1783* (Oxford: Oxford University Press, 1992),p. 269.

congregation from "madness" and "convulsion fits" to "despair" and "suicide." In addition to a host of distorted figures, in various states of religious frenzy, there is also a Jew in the congregation with a bloody knife over an opened Bible that is turned to a picture of the sacrificial altar. Thus, Methodism, equated with chicanery and Catholicism, is depicted as combining the most violent and primitive aspects of both Judaism and Christianity. George Lavington, Bishop of Exeter(1684-1762), states in the preface of his work, *Enthusiasm of Methodists and Papists Compared*, that the whole conduct of the Methodists is "but a counterpart of the most wild fanaticism of Popery." (p. 3) To show just how similar the two groups really are, he prints in parallel columns passages from Wesley and Whitefield together with similar ones from Ignatius Loyola (1491-1556), the founder of the Society of Jesus.

Since the early period of the establishment of Methodism coincided with the time when the country was fearful of foreign invasion, many of these kinds of accusations were taken very seriously by those concerned with their national security. Anglicans who associated Methodism with a decline of reason and ultimately with the corruption of the entire country, attacked it as vehemently as they did Catholicism. According to Rogal, "If anything, the anti-Methodist writers succumbed in the name of reason and in terms of their own concepts of enlightenment to an enthusiasm far in excess of that which they attacked."[65]

The first publicly written attack that was made against the Methodists appears in *Foggs Weekly Journal* of December 9, 1732. The author of an anonymous letter ridicules their practices and compares them to the Pietists of Saxony and the Essenes of ancient Judea. He notes that:

> They avoid every object that may affect
> them with pleasant and grateful sensation
> ....neglect and voluntarily afflict their
> bodies....keep Wednesdays and Fridays,
> let blood once a fortnight....in short practice
> everything contrary to the judgment of other persons.[66]

The first sermons directed against the Methodists are rather mild, compared to those that would follow, and they deal primarily with doctrinal matters. For example, preachers are critical of the Methodist practice of sprinkling babies and not dipping them during their rite of Baptism. In several sermons, Wesley's doctrine that true faith is

---

[65]Samuel J. Rogal, "Enlightened Enthusiasm: Anti-Methodism in the Literature of the Mid and Late Eighteenth Century," *Enlightenment Essays* 5 (Spring, 1974), p. 13.

[66]Cited in Richard Green, *Anti-Methodist Publications Issued During the Eighteenth Century* (London: C.H. Kelly, 1902), p. 1.

inseparably attended by an assurance of the forgiveness of sins, is challenged.[67] This temperate attitude soon changes, and Methodists are now condemned from the Anglican pulpits as being "restless deceivers of the people" who "fill the heads of the ignorant and unwary with wild perplexing notions." They are viewed by their rivals as being "righteous overmuch" an indication that their severe ways do not fit into the Anglican lifestyle.[68] As Methodist numbers grow, the sermons and pamphlets directed against them become increasingly vitriolic. One Anglican cleric warns that their message is a particularly dangerous one since it was made under the pretense that they were still members of the Church of England. He views them as "snakes in our bosom" who by "neglect or collusion "have crept into the established churches and delude the common people into believing that their doctrines reflect Anglican teachings.[69] William Mason (1724-1797), in his work, *Methodism Displayed and Enthusiasm Detected,* notes on the title page that his book is an "antidote against, and a preservative from the delusive principles and unscriptural doctrines of a modern set of new-light seducing preachers..." He warns the reader not "to be led by them into a maze of anti-Christian errors and a wilderness of unscriptural perplexities." (p. 5) The Anglicans were anxious to emphasize the "otherness" of the Methodists. Preachers, therefore, condemn the "instruction from the mouth of strangers" that corrupted the people.[70] They harp on the fact that they are "strangers and intruders" who are linked to the hated Papists and not to the true practicing Christians.[71] For this reason they have to be kept in check.

Even worse than being considered strangers, the Methodists are also viewed as dangerous enemies who were a physical threat to the Anglicans. John Free, as severe a critic of the Methodists as he is of the Catholics, notes that according to the Dean of Gloucester:

> Some of Whitefield's followers have insulted
> and reviled me in passing along the streets,
> and declared, that they looked upon me as the
> enemy of God and his religion. This was owing
> to Mr. Whitfield's pointing at me so often in his

---

[67]Ibid. p. 4.

[68]Ibid.

[69]John Free, *A Sermon Preached Before the University at St. Mary's in Oxford on Whitsunday 1758* (London: 1759), p. x.

[70]John Tottie, *Two Challenges Delivered to the Clergy of the Diocese of Worcester in the years 1763 and 1766 Being Designed as Preservatives Against the Sophistical Arts of the Papists and the Delusions of the Methodists* (Oxford: J. Fletcher, 1766), p. 13.

[71]Ibid. p. 26.

prayers, and describing me in his harranges to the people....[72]

Free believes that the abuses that the Anglican clergy suffered at the hands of the Methodists could fill an entire book. "In their religious frenzy," he notes, "they set the laws and magistrates at defiance." He describes them as "hell hounds" who pursue those clerics who oppose their cause. Like the Catholics, they are a dangerous threat to the security of the nation.[73]

> I see no reason why people, who wish well to
> the Constitution should so quietly behold the
> increase and turbulent proceedings of the
> Methodists. Since their enthusiasm is in
> many respects similar, in other respects
> worse than Popery, and as capable of
> being heated to attempt any revolution in the state.[74]

Free claims that one Sunday, as he stood on his pulpit delivering a sermon, he "was in continual and most imminent danger of being murdered by the Methodists." There was, he notes, "such continual phrenzy that we could expect nothing but bloodshed every moment."[75]

John Free's prejudices, which were shared by many of his contemporaries, reflect a whole pattern of bigotry directed against all those who did not fit into the Anglican mold of proper and reasonable religious practices. His vitriolic condemnation of enthusiasm is not limited to the Methodists or to any one time or place. In one of his pamphlets, he is also critical of fanatical heathen priests and priestesses, the magical powers of the ancient philosophers, the "superstitious and enthusiastic" founders of the Jesuits and the Jansenists, the Lutherans' "swarm of corrupted pietists," and the Quakers' "inspirations, visions, and dreams."[76] Lastly, he turns to Jewish mysticism and asks:

> The Cabala of the Jews, what is it else
> but a production of disordered brains,
> a medley of imaginations and a chaos
> of dreams, on the different orders of
> spirits and their marvelous operations?[77]

The alleged irrationality of Judaism is but one of his many targets. It is almost an afterthought ; certainly not his major concern. Later in the

---

[72]John Free, *Dr. Free's Edition of the Rev. Mr. John Wesley's Second Letter* (London: 1759), p. 26.

[73]Ibid., pp. 26-7.

[74]Ibid., p. 31.

[75]John Free, *The Whole Speech which was Delivered to the Reverend Clergy of the Great City of London on Tuesday the 8th of May* (London: 1759), p. iii-iv.

[76]John Free, *Dr. Free's Remarks Upon Mr. Jones' Letter* (London: 1759). pp. 45-50.

[77]Ibid., p. 50.

pamphlet, when Free discusses in greater detail the dangers that the enthusiasts pose to English society, the Jews are not even mentioned. Jewish Cabbalists are only a historical curiosity; he is primarily concerned about preserving an Anglican ecclesiastical system by keeping out Christian outsiders.

In another one of his many pamphlets, *A Display of the Bad Principles of the Methodists in Certain Articles Proposed to the Serious Consideration of the Worshipful Company of Salters in London,* Free relates how an "avowed Methodist wanted to secure the position of the Tuesday's Lectureship in an Anglican Church. As a person concerned with the Public good, he has to protest such an appointment since it would bring "blasphemy, impiety, and atheism into the Church." It would also make room for "all manner of vice and villainy by which means the bands of society are dissolved and government is overturned" (p. 10). Such a "crafty enthusiast" is an enemy who can undermine not only the Anglican Church, but also the foundations of all religions.(p. 11)

The attitudes of the Methodists towards other religious groups was often personified by John Wesley (1703-1791) whose life, from the very beginnings of his long career until he died, was filled with controversy. Wesley sincerely believed that he was a special messenger raised up by the Holy Spirit to correct the defects of the Anglican Church. Though he was strongly opposed to separatism, his powerful pulpit oratory was often focused upon the Church's hierarchy and various "outsiders" as well.[78] In his *Treatise on Original Sin,* Wesley surveys ancient and modern religions all over the globe; he concludes that they have few, if any, redeeming qualities. Classical religion, he believes, is Godless, and it is filled with cruel practices and lustful thoughts. Jewish history is nothing but a record of "astonishing wickedness" while heathens are thieves, drunkards and liars. Mohammedans, Catholics, and Protestants (other than his own followers) are not much better.[79] Though Wesley did visit a synagogue in Rotterdam, this description of his experiences shows that the brief encounter with flesh and blood Jews did not change his negative attitudes towards them.

> Having waited until past four in the afternoon,
> we stepped into the Jews' Synagogue which
> was near the water side. I do not wonder that
> so many Jews (especially those who have any
> reflection) utterly abjure all religion. My spirit
> was moved within me at that horrid pageantry,

---

[78]Albert C. Outler, ed. *John Wesley* (New York: Oxford University Press, 1980), p. 19.
[79]John Wesley, *Treatise on Original Sin,* cited in Leslie Stephen, p. 420.

that mockery of God which they call public worship.[80]

Although Wesley may have been sympathetic to Catholic mysticism, his basic attitude to Papists is typical of most Protestants of his day. He is prepared to grant freedom to any group who knows what the word means, but Wesley believes that the Catholics do not deserve freedom because they are not willing to grant it to others. He castigates them for what he believes is their persecuting spirit. In turn, Richard Challoner(1691-1781), one of the most eminent eighteenth century Catholics to answer such charges, accused the Methodists of not truly being people of God; he linked them with the Deists who also departed from the true faith.[81] Wesley was responsible for heightening sectarian rivalries and creating in the Methodist Church a legacy of anti-Catholicism that was to continue into the nineteenth-century.[82] Wesley's attitudes towards the Catholics resemble the classic medieval approach of the Church towards the Jews. That is, they are to be despised, hated, and viewed as pariahs who must be prevented from corrupting their neighbors, but they are not to be physically harmed.[83]

Thus, the Methodists and their leader, victims of persecution and degradation, lashed out at other religious minorities who also occupied the attention of the establishment. The story of each of these "others" demonstrates the complexity of the bigotry of the times; the shifting prejudices that spared the Jewish community from so much of the violence of the age.

The Quakers

The Zeal of the Quakers was often too hard for
their discretion, and they play'd a thousand
extravagant pranks, that savoured more of
lunacy than of religion. They broke into churches
and disturbed public worship, by railing at the
minister and reproaching the congregation: the
spirit moved them to revile all persons that did
not adopt their doctrines and principles. They
uttered blasphemies, and seduced zealots from the army.[84]

But it is a very great and dangerous error in

---

[80]Cohen, *Anglo-Jewish Scrapbook*, p. 276.

[81]David Hempton, *Methodism and Politics in British Society 1750-1850* (London: Hutchinson, 1987), p. 34.

[82]Richard Brown, *Church and State in Modern Britain 1700-1850* (London: Routledge, 1991), p. 125-26.

[83]George Rudé, *Hanoverian London: 1714-1808* (London: Secker and Warburg, 1971), p. 115.

[84]Tobias Smollet, *The Present State of all Nations. cited in Gentleman's Magazine* 41 (May, 1771): 205.

> the Quakers, and lays a foundation for heinous
> Idolatry, as heinous, and as dangerous though
> more subtle, as any Idolatry of the heathens, to
> fancy to themselves that the immediate object of
> their spiritual perception sight or feeling is God himself....[85]

The Quakers, a highly visible and significant minority group, who in the early decades of the eighteenth century numbered about 30,000 or 40,000,[86] were alienated from both the orthodox dissenters and from the Anglican Church. Like the Jews, the Quakers with their distinctive dress and speech set themselves apart from the rest of the population and became the object of caricature and lampoon. In order to avoid attracting additional hostile attention to themselves they tried to keep a low profile and avoid unnecessary contact with outsiders.[87] Nevertheless, as in the case of the Jews, the image of the Quakers, with their wide brimmed black hats and somber clothes was easily recognizable by people from all walks of life.

Quakers carried with them into the eighteenth century a definite feeling of distrust by the masses that was based on the religious and social values that they had formulated earlier. Periodically, they defended themselves by claiming that they believed in God and in Christ and that they were not Deists, Enthusiasts, Heretics or Schismatics.[88] John Wilkes notes that of all of the small religious groups in the country, they were the most devout and obstinate in pursuing their ways and defying authority.[89]

The Quakers rejected the sacraments, trappings, liturgies, and rituals of the Church of England. They saw the church as a society of friends, and they condemned "steeple houses", corrupt clergy, and the tithes that were needed to maintain a religious hierarchy. Though they acknowledged the authority of the state, they refused to fight for their country. Quakers would not take an oath, and they refused the "hat honor." In accordance with the teachings of George Fox (1624-1691), they rejected the notion that there were superiors and inferiors in society. All people, they believed, should be addressed as "thee" and "thou". Like the Jews, they established an efficient system of taking care of their own

---

[85]George Keith, *The Magic of Quakerism or the Chief Mysteries of Quakerism Laid Open* (London: 1707), p. 15.

[86]Rupp, p. 144.

[87]A Neave Bradshaw, *The Quakers: Their Story and Message* (New York: The Macmillan Co., 1938), p. 178.

[88]*Gentleman's Magazine*, 2 (June, 1732): 782.

[89]Wilkes, p. 109. The self-segregation of the Quakers was also a means of preventing young Quakers from marrying out of the faith; a problem for both them and the Jewish people. See, for example, Moses West, *A Treatise Concerning Marriage* (London: J. Sowle, 1707), p. 31.

that was praised by members of other faiths. One writer, in the *Gentleman's Magazine* for February, 1731, notes that they "maintain none of their poor in idleness that are able to work, and suffer none to want that are helpless" (p. 60). Excluded from higher education, the clergy, the professions, and from Parliament, Quakers channeled their energies into trade and Industry, and they almost "colonized the Industrial Revolution."[90] Though they were respected for their business and manufacturing skills, their financial dealings in government contracts and in speculative promotions as well as the fact that they had capital to lend, brought them the kind of publicity that they shunned. For some critics, their close ties to Change Alley ranked them ahead of the Jews and various other undesirables who were involved in stock jobbing. As one observer of the contemporary scene notes:

> Within this precinct, to the everlasting honour
> of stock Jobbing, stands that Den of thieves,
> vulgarly call'd Change-Alley. A foreigner
> told me, that when he came first into England,
> he apprehended it might be a place appointed
> for the holding of religious controversies in,
> on seeing such numbers of Quakers, Jews,
> Priests, Turks, and Infidels assembled.[91]

Like the stock jobbers in general, and the Jews in particular, the Quakers were viewed as cunning traders who, often at the expense of the general public, used their international contacts to their own advantage. These stereotypes were reinforced by articles like the following one that appeared in *Mist's Weekly Journal* for July 1,1727.

> We hear a noted Quaker at Norwich,
> having an express directly from Holland.
> with the first news of the King's death, kept
> it a secret, and did his business before the news
> was brought from London, and by that means
> got above a thousand pounds.

In the November 4, 1727 issue of *Mist's Weekly Journal,* it is noted that "Whigs, Jews and Quakers," who are "the most considerable traders, "are often blamed for London's periodic financial difficulties.

Because Quakers were middlemen in various essential commodities, in times of shortages both the central government and the local authorities found them to be a convenient scapegoat for the people's hardships.[92] At such times, Quakers experienced both prejudice and

---

[90]Rupp, p. 149.
[91]*A View of London and Westminster,* p. 46.
[92]John Stevenson, *Popular Disturbances in England 1700-1870* (New York: Longman, 1979),p. 30.

physical violence. For example, in August, 1756 there was a rise in the price of wheat in the West Midlands. Blame was placed on the millers as well as those who had a monopoly on the grain. Since some of the wheat dealers were known to be Quakers, mobs, who were incensed over the rising cost of bread, attacked and nearly destroyed three of their meeting houses.

Unlike other nonconformist groups in England, the Quakers developed a very efficient national body to deal with the persecution that they suffered at the hands of the majority faith. This strong central organization provided both legal services and support for those in need of help. In addition, a very elaborate intelligence system was set up in England and Wales to warn individual Quakers of impending danger.[93] This separate system of government, viewed by many of their critics as subversion, was another source of suspicion and distrust that was to affect their relations with the world around them. In a broadside printed at the beginning of the century, the author asks in words similar to those that Haman directed against the Jewish people in the *Book of Esther*, "How can they call themselves dutiful subjects when they neither obey his majesties laws, nor observe his lawful commands."[94]

The dislike of the "unlike" in Quaker beliefs, practices, and religious community structure was a source of prejudice and persecution that was so similar to what the Jews and other minorities experienced. A sampling of some of the anti-Quaker literature of the time reveals how this "other "fit into a familiar pattern of bigotry.

Francis Bugg (1640-1724?) begins his work, The *Picture of Quakerism Drawn to Life*, with an attack upon the Quakers' claim that they are the "Elect People of God." He calls them an "Erronious Sect", and he believes "that the Gangrene of their heresie shall prevail no further"(p. 2-3). The association of the Quakers with contagion, disease, and vermin, is a recurring theme in anti-Quaker tracts of the period[95] just as it was part of anti-Semitic literature during the Nazi era. Fortunately for the Quakers, it did not lead to extermination, but it did portray them as pernicious human beings worthy of persecution. Bugg also associates

---

[93] Arnold Lloyd, *Quaker Social History 1664-1738* (Westport, Connecticut: Greenwood Press Publishers, 1979), p. 104.

[94] *Some Remarks on the Quakers address to His Majesty* (London: 1701) : first side.

[95] Bugg, in his tract, *A Brief History of the Rise Growth and Progress of Quakerism* (London: 1697) also referred to the Quakers who encroached upon the livelihood of other clergy as "flies and mice who feed upon others' provisions." (p. 9) See also *The Snake in the Grass or Satan Transform'd into an Angel of Light* (London: Printed for Charles Brome, 1697) where the author claims that, "Quakerism is but one branch of enthusiasm, tho' the most spread and infectious of any now known " (preface, p. i).

them with both the Catholics and the Pharisees, two particularly despised groups. Although he is not certain that the "Jesuits had a hand in their (Quaker) forming," he does believe that if "one may guess the father by the child's likeness, Ignatius Loyola, the founder of the Jesuits, was at least the grandfather of the Quakers"(p. 4). Bugg also believes that "Quakers are not the Church of the First Born, of which Christ Jesus is head; but the Synagogue of the Self Righteous and Pharasaical Church" (p. 29). Perhaps his strongest condemnation is leveled against what he perceives to be their dual loyalty.

> ....you the leaders of the Quakers do not only
> disobey the law of the land yourselves, but you
> hold your yearly meetings in London a week or
> ten days together; and there you make laws.
> orders and decrees, against the known laws
> made at Westminster and therein and thereby
> absolve the King's subjects of their obedience,
> so far as they adhere to you as the higher powers(p. 83).

Bugg believes that Quakers are guilty not only of seducing the people from the Christian religion, but from their allegiance to the government as well (p. 101). Therefore, they must open the locked doors of their general councils to the public so that everyone can see exactly what they are doing.

Bugg, a prolific writer of anti-Quaker tracts, continually harps on the similarities of the Quakers to the Catholics, and he often refers to them as the "New Rome." In his eyes they are not to be taken lightly. The New Rome, he writes, "is as fatal and as dangerous to the Protestant interest as her elder sister."[96] He also criticizes the Quakers for allowing women to play a role in their religious organization. He is shocked that "women should hold a court or synod distinct by themselves, have a clark, a book, a purse, and the management of the church government once a month."[97] Finally, Bugg, like the modern day revisionists who deny that the Holocaust ever took place, scoffs at the Quaker claims of persecution. Their tales of suffering, he claims, are exaggerated in order to gain sympathy. In many cases they are not nearly as serious as the alleged victims portray them.[98]

Equally vituperative, Charles Leslie (1650-1722), in the preface of his work, *A Parallel Between the Faith and Doctrines of the Present Quakers and that of the Chief Hereticks in all Ages of the Church and also a Parallel Between Quakerism and Popery*, accuses the Quakers of being "proud, haughty and

---

[96]Francis Bugg, *The Pilgrims Progress From Quakerism to Christianity* (London: Printed by R. Janeway, 1700), p. 82.
[97]Bugg, *A Brief History*. p. 86.
[98]Bugg, *The Picture of Quakerism*, p. 110.

high minded (as) if to exult themselves and debase the rest of mankind."
They are "blasphemous against God and injurious to men," and they
ridicule organized religion and disturb the peace of civil societies. He
particularly condemns "their enthusiastic madness", their belief that the
"Light Within" is a higher power than the Scriptures as well as the laws
of the State. Quakers, therefore, are nothing more than the disciples of
the heretics of all ages who challenged true Christian beliefs. He
concludes his preface with a stock conversionist prayer where, as
heretics, the Quakers are joined together with the Jews, Turks, and
infidels in the hope that they "may be saved among the remnant of the
true Israelites, and be made one fold under one shepherd, Jesus Christ
our Lord."

Throughout the book, Leslie repeats many of the standard criticisms
leveled against Quakers, and he also puts special emphasis on the
Quaker-Catholic connection. He notes that Popish emissaries are
suspected to have been the first to establish and to promote the Quaker
faith in the country. The hated Jesuits were sent by the Pope to divide the
Protestants, and they have been found to be among the Quaker
preachers. In addition, some Quakers were educated in Catholic
seminaries on the Continent.(p. 58). The contradictory nature of Leslie's
bigotry is demonstrated in his work, *Primitive Heresie Revived in the Faith
and Practice of the People Called Quakers,* where he scathingly compares the
Quakers to the Deists who were on the other side of the religious
spectrum. Here, he condemns the Quaker emphasis on the Inner Light
which he feels is very similar to the Deists' belief in the Divine light of
reason(p. 28). Like the Deists, the Quakers also deny the incarnation of
Jesus, the truth and reality of his death and suffering, and his
resurrection and future judgment (p. 2-7).

On the title page of his pamphlet, *Seasonable Advice Concerning
Quakers,* Stillingfleet notes that it was written "for the benefit of the
unlearned members of the Church of England who have any Quakers or
Quaker-nestings amongst them, or in their neighborhoods." The image
of the Quakers as some kind of vermin that are a threat to the well being
of good Protestants sets the tone for all that follows. In the preface, the
author notes that he has written about Quaker beliefs and practices to
arm the reader "against the cunning craftiness of men who lie in wait to
deceive" (p. A2). He views their distinctive appearance and speech as a
means of being superior to the rest of humanity and to enslave the
English people "with the Jewish bondage and Mosaical severities under
the pretense of Christian liberty"(p. 10). Not only does he compare the
Quakers to the Jews, but he also lumps them together with the Deists as
well. "How can the Quakers," he asks, "call themselves Christians and
yet think the light within to be sufficient to Salvation without anything

else? This, he believes, is "downright Deism" and not Christianity (p. 43). Stillingfleet also attacks them for not believing in Baptism or in the Lord's Supper, and for denying the Holy Scriptures while, at the same time, not hesitating to call their own writings the word of the Lord (p. 91).

Edward Cockson (fl. 1703-1711), in *Quakerism Dissected and Laid Open*, reinforces old hatreds, and he adds some new ones as well. In addition to the Quakers' blasphemies against God and their invectives against the government, he condemns them for their injustices against property. If they could ever achieve power, they would, he believes, convert church and government property into alms houses or sell it and give the money to the poor. Cockson not only condemns the Quakers for having been the enemies of Charles I, but he views them as subversives who are a continual threat to the nation. William Penn's conspiracy "to procure an invasion from abroad" was but one example of their treachery (p. 11). Cockson believes that "they would have the Church of Rome and their Mass tolerated rather than the Church of England and their service" (p. 60).

Just as the Jews and other undesirables of the time were often described as having a dark and sinister complexion, Cockson writes the following about the Quakers:

> And now you have seen the men, their
> nature and their Negro Features and
> complections: I will now hasten to rip
> them open....(P.14).

Other criticisms made by the author that resemble those traditionally leveled against the Jews are the Quakers' rejection of the first day of the week as the true Sabbath and their disinheriting and disowning of children who leave the fold (p. 56). Cockson notes that they generally limit their charity to their own poor. They are also opposed to the toleration of any other sect but their own – two stock anti-Semitic allegations (p. 59).

Since the early centuries of Christianity, Jews have been subjected to those who would convert them to "the true faith." At various times they were involved in disputations with Christian clerics with the hope that superior arguments would help those who reject Jesus to see the error of their ways. Quakers too, were targets for such attempts to "bring them into the fold." In a work, *A Letter to the Right Reverend The Lord Bishop of London: Occasioned by Disputing With a Quaker*, the author notes in the Preface that just as the Lord Bishop of London was concerned about "the many learned and ingenious detections of the errors of the Romish Church," he should also direct his attention to the Quakers. "For," the author notes," the industry of these people seems not all equaled by the defenders of our church, our best writers being wholly silent on that head" (pp. 1-2). He shares some personal experiences he had with a Quaker friend whom he calls his "Apostate Kinsman," and he believes that there is a need for a confutation of Quakerism that is free from "heat and impatience." Instead of invectives against them, he urges a calm reasonable approach to reclaim the "misled "so that hopefully, "their increase will speedily cease"(pp. 58-9).

The end result, the conversion of the apostate, had not changed. Only the means of bringing about this transformation were now more in keeping with the spirit of the Age of Reason. Thus, for example, after William Whiston lists in his *Friendly Address to the Baptists* all of the Quakers' errors of belief and of worship and notes how they have earned the contempt and disgust of the Christian clergy, he concludes his work with the prayer:

> May God Almighty in his due time, so reform
> all that is amiss in the sacred functions and render
> all their conduct and ministrations so Christian,
> pious, edifying, and unquestionable, as may recall
> those wandering sheep again into Christ's sheepfold;
> and take away all future occasions of ofference from
> them, and from their adversaries for ever (p. 57).

Those unique Quaker attributes of dress, language, pacifism, anti-clericalism, single price bargaining, refusal to take an oath as well as collusion with the Catholics which attracted serious criticism, was also integrated into the more popular literature of the period. The title page of the following anonymous work shows how the Quaker, like the Jew of the eighteenth century, became more a buffoon than a villain. The sexual prowess of the "other", as previously noted, is in keeping with the prejudice directed against virtually any religious, ethnic, or racial group. Now it is the Quaker's turn to be the object of such barbs. It reads as follows:

> *A Yea and Nay Mouse-Trap:* or, The
> Quaker in Darkness, Being a true, but
> comical Account of an eminent Quaker
> in Southwark, who being mov'd by the
> Spirit to lye with a Merchant's Maid, was
> taken in Bed with her in the very sporting
> Minute, by the Merchant himself, with a
> pleasant Account of the cunning, sly Tricks,
> and Intrigues the light Quaker made us of to
> tempt the poor dark Wench to sin, which he
> perform'd by giving her ten Guineas to bribe
> her thereto. The particulars of which being
> taken from the Injur'd Maid's own confession to her Master.

This all-inclusive title is followed on the page by an additional lengthy comic barb at the moral hypocrisy of the Quakers whose earthy passions are hidden behind their austere dress and demeanor.

> Although ye look demure, and cant,
> With broad brim'd Hat, and Cravat scant;
> Yet now and then, it seems ye rutt on,
> And slyly Love to run at Mutton,
> To impart that light, ye so much brag on,
> To a poor Wretch with scarce a Ragg on,
> Makes it appear 'tis soon put out,
> By any nasty female-Clout.[99]

Quaker hypocrisy is a recurrent theme in the Chap Books of the period. In one of them, *A Good Husband for Five Shillings: or a Lottery for Ladies*, the author claims that behind the austere facades of their homes, Quakers enjoy life's pleasures. Their "humdrum sanctity" is a cheat: their God is Mammon. Though they appear to be fasting and praying, in reality they are feasting and carrying on with their friends (p. 6).

Another anonymous writer was able to combine comic slurs against Quaker morality with some equally farcical anti-Semitic innuendoes concerning circumcision and the Jewish aversion to eating pork products. In a brief work, *The Quaker turn'd Jew being A true Relation, how an eminent Quaker in the Isle of Ely on Monday the 18th of April 1675 Circumcised Himself, out of Zeal for a Certain Case of Conscience, Renounced his Religion, and Became a Prosolited Jew*, the author describes how a Quaker seduced his neighbor's wife in a pig stye. In addition to society's punishment, he "dissembled" himself so that in the future he would not "perpetuate any such crime" (p. 7). Unfortunately, in spite of his penance, he was not forgiven by his neighbors, and he was forced to remain an outcast known as "The Apostaliz'd Quaker: or, the Proselyted Jew." The author further notes that he "has resolved never more to eat swines flesh, because of the unhappy adventure of the hogg-stye"(p. 8).

These images of the devious, threatening, immoral, and comic Quakers, were carried to the theater as well. More than any other religious group, they were viewed as the successors to the hated Puritans of the prior century; true disciples of Oliver Cromwell. Ezra Maxfield believes that, as in the case of the stage Jew, the playwrights made the most of the Quakers' more obvious beliefs, speech patterns, dress, and means of conducting business that set them apart from the rest of society. They did not know or care to know very much about them as real flesh and blood people, and playwrights usually used stereotypical Quakers to

---

[99]Cited in Joseph Smith, *Bibliotheca Anti-Quakeriana* (London: 1873 Kraus Reprint, New York, 1968)p. 31.

provide amusement as "ranting canting hypocrites."[100] They also created stage figures who occupied the financial world that was usually associated with the Jews; by doing this, they furnished alternative objects of ridicule and hatred. For example, in Thomas Durfey's *Two Queens of Brentford* the author notes:

> The Quaker quaint, that bustling Babe of Grace
> That buys and sells and spreads each odious thing
> With such a sound he makes Change Alley ring.[101]

Gradually, as their seventeenth century backgrounds faded from memory, the Quakers became a more tolerated minority in England. Perhaps one reason for their acceptance was that they appeared to be much more reasonable in their demands than their co-religionists in the American Colonies. It is noted in Hooker's *Weekly Miscellany* for Friday, April 8, 1737 that those across the sea "use a little less reserve" in dealing with the authorities. In England they will not take off their hats, but they allow others to uncover "their stubborn heads." Quakers in the colonies, on the other hand, are not so obliging. By having brothers and sisters abroad who were so firm in their "otherness," the English Quakers did not seem so unreasonable. For those who are objects of prejudice, more prominent targets, even if they are related, can draw off some of the bigot's venom. In English society, and in the Colonies as well, there was obviously an abundance of such groups.

The Sabbatarians

> These Sabbatarians are so call'd, because
> they will not remove the Day of Rest from
> Saturday to Sunday....Were it only for this one
> opinion or belief of theirs concerning the
> absolute necessity of keeping the Sabbath on
> Saturday without paying any regard to the next
> day, which is the first day in the week, and which
> we call Sunday with the author of the Revelations;
> that alone would be enough to make them unavoidably
> a society by themselves.[102]

---

[100]Ezra Kempton Maxfield, "The Quakers in English Stage Plays Before 1800" *P.M. L. A.*. 45 (March, 1930): 272.

[101]*Ibid.*, p. 269. The close association of Quakers with Change Alley was, of course, not limited to the theatre. In the anonymous work, *A View of London and Westminster: or the Town Spy*, the author notes that a foreign visitor to the exchange thought that it was "a place appointed for the holding of religious controversies in, on seeing such numbers of Quakers, Jews, Priests, Turks, and Infidels assembled." p. 48.

[102]John Ozell (tr.) *M. Misson's Memoirs and Observations in his Travels over England* (1719), p. 235 cited in Bryan W. Ball, *The Seventh-Day Men: Sabbatarians and*

> William Henry Black, the Victorian shepherd of
> the Seventh-Day Baptists, was convinced that
> if only the history of the Saturday-Sabbatarians
> might one day be written, it would "serve to show
> that we are not the simpletons, or hypocrites, or
> Jews, or nobodies" that they had often been painted.[103]

In addition to the relatively large and well-established "religious others" who continued to grow and evolve through our own day, there were those who did not continue to practice their faith in any significant way beyond the confines of the eighteenth century. Nevertheless, they too proved to be a challenge to the status quo. Perhaps the most prominent of these Nonconformist denominations, who, like the Quakers, were carry-overs from the previous century, and who were still a thorn in the side of the religious establishment, were the Sabbatarians. They, too, were spiritual heirs of the Puritans who were deeply committed to the Protestant cause – determined to remove all Papist influences from church doctrine and practices. To do so, they believed that it was necessary to restore a pure biblical faith which was free from later-day accretions that were not in the spirit of the teachings of Jesus and his disciples. Because their members participated in various practices associated with the Jewish Sabbath, which they believed were an integral part of the rituals of the early Church, they were scorned by the religious establishment. These Seventh Day Men, Sabbatarians, Fifth Monarchy Men or Anabaptists, as they were called, vigorously defended their doctrines.

Between 1600 and 1750 Sabbatarians established over sixty identifiable congregations all over the country where they kept Seventh-day observances alive for several generations.[104] Their influence went beyond their own church membership, and it attracted the attention of a diverse group from all walks of life. The great number of tracts, sermons, and articles in the press which condemned them as Judaizers, are testimony to their leaders' ability to disseminate their views and to stir up the ire of their more traditional Christian neighbors.

Benjamin Keach (1640-1704), in his tract, *The Jewish Sabbath Abrogated*, which was written at the beginning of the century, notes in his preface how he met a person with "an unsettled and waivering spirit and aspiring temper who suk'd in the notion of the Jewish Sabbath and laboured to corrupt many others of the younger sort" (p. A2). As a result,

---

Sabbatarianism in England and Wales, 1600-1800 (Oxford: Clarendon Press, 1994), p. 9.
[103]David S. Katz, *Sabbath and Sectarianism in Seventeenth-Century England.* (Leiden: E.J. Brill, 1988), p. 178.
[104]Ball, p. 2, p. 6.

some of them refused to do any business or work for their masters on the first day of the week. The writer notes that when the story was made public, "it had almost put the whole congregation into a flame" (p. A2). It is not clear if it was the matter of theology or the loss of a day's labor that was the greater concern. In any event, such doctrines, an obvious challenge to the status quo, were a threat to the power of the Church and the civil authorities to regulate the lives of the people.

The real core of the Sabbatarian controversy, whether Saturday or Sunday should be kept as a sacred day of rest and spiritual reflection, is addressed in a variety of religious tracts. These works are directed at erring Protestants. However, to prove their point, the authors of these works often challenge Jewish practices by reinforcing traditional Christian theology. In one such tract, *Thoughts on the Jewish Sabbath Occasion'd by Some Gentiles Observation of that Day,* the pseudonymous author notes that the Saturday Sabbath was limited only to the Jewish people. It was "outdone and superseded by that which is universal and has greater reason in it "(p. 71). He continues a tradition of earlier clerics who tied the seventh day observance of the Sabbath to a covenant which God had made with the Jewish people and which He later had broken in favor of a new one with the Christians.[105]

The Sabbatarian controversy is illustrative of yet another aspect of the lingering religious animosities from the past century. In time, many of these hatreds diminished, but others, like those directed to the Catholics, were coupled with a fear and a distrust of foreigners who came from other parts of the British Isles or the Continent. Through the course of the century, these diverse ethnic and religious groups invariably served as important distractions for the hate-mongers of the time – a buffer against anti-Semitism.

---

[105]Richard Baxter, *The Divine Appointment of the Lord 's Day Proved* (London: Printed for Nevil Simmons, 1671), p. 225.

3

Ethnic "Others"

The Irish

The whole kingdom (is) a bare face of nature,
houses or plantations; filthy cabins, miserable,
tattered half-starved creatures, scarce in human
shape....every meadow a slough, and every hill
a mixture of rock, heath, and marsh: and every male
and female, from the farmer inclusive to the day-
labourer, infallibly a thief, and consequently a
beggar, which in this island are terms convertible.[1]

To conclude, he's a coward in his own country, a
lusty stallion in England, a graceful footman in France,
a good soldier in Flanders, and a valuable slave in
our Western Plantations, where they are distinguished
by the ignominious epithet of White Negroes.[2]

....a fire broke out in Mr. Hydes livery....an honest
Irishman, who lived in the yard where the fire began,
willing to save a looking-glass for which his wife had
a great value, threw it out of the window into the street,
and broke it all to pieces.[3]

For centuries, the English quest for national identity fostered both a sense of superiority and also a deep animosity towards the peoples of the other nations of the British Isles.[4] However, in the eighteenth century,

[1]Swift, *Correspondence*, ed. Williams, IV, 34. cited in David Nokes, "The Radical Conservatism of Swift's Irish Pamphlets," *British Journal for Eighteenth-Century Studies*, 7 (Autumn, 1984): 171-72.
[2]*The Character of an Irishman* in Edward Ward's *London-Spy* (ca. 1700) cited in Edward D. Snyder, "The Wild Irish: A Study Of Some English Satires Against the Irish, Scots, and Welsh," *Modern Philology*, 17 (April, 1920):160.
[3]*London Morning Post* (January 23,1740).
[4]Debby Banham, "Anglo-Saxon attitudes: in search of the origins of English racism," *European Review of History* 1 (No. 2, 1994): 155. The author views this

London needed a large supply of immigrant labor to make up for the ravages of its exceptionally heavy death rate. As a result, the Metropolis attracted, along with those English people who came from the countryside, the best and the worst of the scores of immigrants who were driven out of their own countries for either economic or political reasons.[5] The most conspicuous and the most numerous of them were the Irish.

Throughout the eighteenth century, approximately three quarters of Ireland belonged to English or to Anglo-Protestant families. The economy, which was based on the raising of sheep for wool and cattle for beef, encouraged the growth of vast grazing lands at the expense of the native population who lived in constant fear of starvation. Irish Catholics were viewed by the English as racially inferior human beings who were living in a country that was a cultural margin of Britain and which was open to exploitation.[6] Often, they were used as a foil to show the supposed superiority of the British way of life. A contemporary writer claims that one of the advantages of a union of Great Britain and Ireland would be the opportunity to "reduce the natives by gentle and wise means, from Popery and idleness, to our religion and method of living."[7]

Tragically, the Irish people were brutalized by those who were sent to "civilize" them. The Irish bard, of the seventeenth century, Eamoun an Duna, records the very first English words that would become part of an Irish-speaking person's vocabulary;

> Transport, transport, *mo mheabhair ar Bhearla*
> Shoot him, kill him, strip him, tear him.
> A tory, hack him, hang him, rebel,
> A rogue, thief, a priest, a papist.[8]

British rule in Ireland was based upon the premise that conventional political norms were not applicable to such an unstable and

---

animosity towards the Welsh, Scots, and Irish and the need to politically dominate them as a form of continuous racism that goes back to the Anglo-Saxon landings.

[5]Dorathy George, *London Life in the Eighteenth Century* (New York: Alfred A Knoff, 1925), p. 116-7.

[6]Nicholas Canny, "The Marginal Kingdom: Ireland as a Problem in the First British Empire" in *Strangers in the Realm: Cultural Margains of the First British Empire*, ed. Bernard Bailyn and Philip D. Morgan (Chapel Hill: University of North Carolina Press, 1991), p. 38. Paul Johnson, *A History of the English People* (New York: Harper and Row, 1985), p. 105.

[7]*London Magazine* 1 (July, 1732):182. For an attempt to "reform the Irish Papists" and to bring them into the Presbyterian Church see *The British Journal* for June 6,1724.

[8]Peter Linebaugh, *The London Hanged: Crime and Civil Society in the Eighteenth Century* (Cambridge: Cambridge UP, 1992), p. 290.

ungovernable country.[9] Contemporary articles about Irish life that appeared in English publications created stereotypes to justify their oppression. For example, according to Hooker's *Weekly Miscellany* for May 13, 1737, instead of building up their domestic industries, the Irish squander their money on foreign luxuries. "The matrons of this forlorn country," he notes, "send out a greater proportion of its wealth for fine apparel than any other females on the whole surface of the terraqueous globe"(p. 1). Other English critics claimed that the Irish themselves are to blame for the neglect of their country's arable land. They are too lazy to turn their lush grass into hay, and they burn their oats to save themselves the bother of threshing. The Irish are so ignorant of farming, that they tied their plows to their horses' tails rather than devise some sort of a harness. Their knowledge of religion is not much better than that of tiling the soil. As the *Gentleman's Magazine* for January 1753 notes: "Ask many of them what was the name of the Virgin Mary and 'tis ten to one, but they answer Jane or Susan, and that St. Patrick was her godfather"(p. 54). In the *London Magazine* for August, 1760, even a sympathetic observer of the contemporary scene who is impressed with the Irish people's music and their gaiety in the face of the harsh realities of their daily lives, notes that along with their rustic simplicity, they are mostly "illiterate and uninstructed"(p. 464).Stories of Irish drinking also abounded in the English Press. The *Gentleman's Magazine* for August, 1753 claims that more people in Ireland died from alcohol than from "small pox, fever, broken limbs, accidents, and all other distempers put together" (p. 391). .According to Hooker's *Weekly Miscellany* for May 13, 1737, the Irish imbibe each year 1000 tons of French wine – which is more than the inhabitants of either Sweden or Denmark consume. It is claimed in the same issue, perhaps with tongue in cheek, that the Irish are partly Spaniards and partly Tartars. From their Spanish roots they have developed a sense of false pride, and their Tartar ancestry has influenced them to pursue such idle occupations as the of tending flocks. Irish Laborers are urged to stay at home and perform honest labor on their undeveloped land rather than migrate to England.

In spite of such admonitions to stay at home, insurrections against English rule were invariably followed by harsh retribution, and each year thousands emigrated from their poverty-stricken and strife-torn homeland to England. They carried with them their pitiful belongings, a reputation for rebellion, and an alien religion and culture. Virtually all strata of society regarded this Gaelic way of life with abhorrence, and they considered it to be vastly inferior to their own Englishness. To be

---

[9]Canny, p. 61.

called a "Hibernian" was to be labeled a "rowdy" by the majority culture. As Paul Langford notes :

> Irish eccentricities and Irish tempers were
> inexhaustible topics of conversation. The
> stereotypes were so firmly established that
> no individual could hope to overcome them,
> though he might nurse the hope of Anglicizing
> his sons and daughters so completely that
> their origins would never be suspected.[10]

Most of Irish immigrants who flocked to London came as unskilled laborers who were employed as porters, milk sellers, street hawkers, laborers, boarding house keepers, and weavers. In addition, there were many, known as "Spalpeens, "who provided migrant labor during the harvest season for the farmers in the vicinity of London. Small colonies of skilled and semi-skilled bricklayers and weavers were also part of this labor force. The Irish, desperate for work, were willing to undercut the native laborers by working for half of their regular wages. As a result, fights between them and the English were common in the countryside as well as on the streets of London. Out of ethnic loyalty and solidarity, the Irish, like the Jews, hired people from their own group which created in the English mind the image of a secret trade union and a closed shop. Even where Protestants were employed by the Irish, when hard times came, these workers were the first to go. In the London riots of 1780, the mob took vengeance for these economic deeds.[11]

In London, where a significant number of the Irish joined the ranks of the professional beggars and the lower classes of the city, they were often viewed as the crude, boisterous, quick-tempered troublemakers of English life. The press, in the very way that it covered the activities of the Irish, encouraged this image. The following St. Patrick's Day incident is reported in the *London Daily Post* of March 19, 1740 as follows:

> The same day there happened an extraordinary
> riot in Clare Market, occassion'd by some butchers
> boys hanging up an Irishman in effigie, being St.
> Patrick, their tutelar Saint's Day; which the Sons of
> Hibernia justly taking to be done in derision of their
> country, were so provok'd at, that a bloody battle
> ensued, and one or two lives were lost; nor could the
> mob be suppressed till some files of musketeers were
> sent from Whitehall, who had the trouble of conducting
> one of the rioters, an Irishman, to Newgate.

---

[10]Langford, p. 326.
[11]Hibbert, p. 127.

Perhaps the most popular columns of the newspapers of the time were those devoted to listing the individuals apprehended, convicted, and executed for various crimes. The Irish, like the Jews, are invariably singled out for special mention. For example, *The Weekly Miscellany* for February 17, 1733 reports that "On the 9th of October last one Patrick Ralph, an Irish boy about 17 years of age and William Gander, were committed to Hereford Gaol." When two petty thieves, John Jenkins and Patrick Murphy were hanged, it is noted in The *London Morning Post* of April 16, 1740 that "they were young fellows both born in Ireland."

The Irish were also linked together with the Jews as the criminal element in society. Sir John Fielding (1721-1780), in a letter to the Secretary of State concerning the condition of the Jews in England, raised the question of Irish immigration. He suggested that by limiting the number of both of these groups who could settle in the country, many robberies would be prevented. Fielding was convinced that there were already more Jews and Irish in London than the labor market could possibly absorb.[12] Actually, the Irish were disliked more than the Jews because they posed a greater threat to native labor. Since it was extremely difficult for Jews to be apprenticed to Christian masters, Jewish opportunities for competition were much more limited. In addition, the Jewish Community had a long tradition of maintaining their own poor, and they did not tax the resources of the local charities.

The Irish insurrections in their native land added to their troublemaker image in the minds of the English. It is noted in the *Gentleman's Magazine* of September, 1734, that "the cause of Jacobitism hath taken its flight among the wild Irish"(p. 496). This stereotype became progressively worse through the last decade of the century. In one Chap Book, *An Account of the late Insurrection in Ireland,* the Irish are accused of committing atrocities which range from the shooting of prisoners to the massacre of those innocent Protestants who fall into their hands. It claims that the rebel spear men take pleasure "in piercing the victims through with their spears, even licking their blood in exaltation "(p. 29). The stereotypical image of the Jew thirsting for Christian blood now had competition with that of the vengeful Irish.

Ireland, as well as Scotland, was also viewed as a potential staging area for an assault on England and the restoration of the Stuarts. In addition, a significant number of the Irish emigrated from their country and joined foreign armies rather than live under British rule. Although it is difficult to determine just how many joined with the French, there were enough of them to form an independent Irish Brigade that, during the War of the Austrian Succession, defeated the British at Fontenoy. For

---

[12]George, p. 126.

a time, they were poised on the other side of the Channel for an invasion of England where they hoped to link up with Charles Edward's thrust from Scotland.[13]

During the period of the French Revolution, the United Irishmen, an organization formed in October 1791, corresponded with the French Republicans. In 1795 they decided to seek assistance from across the Channel for their rebellion against English rule in Ireland They also realized that their ultimate success was dependent upon political subversion in England; an armed insurrection would tie down large numbers of British troops and the government would be forced to grant concessions to the Irish radicals.

These Irish revolutionaries wanted to establish a union of similarly minded people in Ireland, France, and England. As tensions mounted in Ireland, there was a considerably closer contact between Irish activists and the English radicals. Irish expatriates were leading social protesters among the impoverished English and Irish workers and artisans in the growing metropolitan areas. In 1799, the Committee of Secrecy, which the British Government had established to investigate subversive activities, reported that the Irish connection had been an important dimension of popular radicalism since 1792. The fact that they exported a revolutionary spirit to England at a time when the country was at war with France did not endear the Irish, both at home or abroad, to the Establishment. They created in the British psyche a reputation for establishing a militant brand of radicalism and for supporting political subversion which would remain with them for the next two hundred years.[14]

The Scots

The genius of the Scotch is mutiny, they scarcely
want a guide to move their madness. Prompt to
rebel on every weak pretense, blustering when
courted, crouching, when oppress'd, restless
in changes and perjured to a proverb.[15]

They write from Edinburgh, May 19, that
12 ministers, 21 preachers, and 18 Catechists
had been sent to the Highlands, and Islands of

---

[13]Frank Mclynn, *The Jacobites* (London and New York: Routledge and Kegan Paul, 1988), p. 131.
[14]Alan Booth, "Liberty or Slavery: Irish Radicalism in the 1790s," *Irish Studies Review*, (no. 2 Winter, 1992): pp. 26-7.
[15]*A Political and Satirical History Displaying the Unhappy Influence of Scotch Prevalency in the Years 1761, 1762, and 1763* (London: Published by M. Darly, n.d.), Caption for Plate 117.

> Scotland to reform the inhabitants thereof....and
> that these missionaries had already had good
> success in places where ignorance and superstition
> do most abound.[16]

> But what a nation is Scotland; in every reign
> engendering traitors to the state, and false and
> pernicious to the kings that favour it the most!
> National prejudices, I know, are very vulgar; but,
> if there are national characteristics, can one but
> dislike the soils and climates that concur to produce them.[17]

Scotland, like Ireland, was also identified in the English mind with rebellion and political chaos. The country was divided into two separate and very distinct areas. There was the Presbyterian, English-speaking Lowlands, and in contrast, the Catholic or Episcopalian and Gaelic-speaking Highlands. The Lowlanders, conscious of their poverty and provincialism, were anxious to improve their lot not only by importing English agricultural methods and technology, but by imitating their social customs as well. They purchased London periodicals, Anglicized their names, and took elocution lessons to remove their distinctive accent. In their desire to pass as English, they were resented by those whom they tried to imitate. The Highlanders, on the other hand, though occasionally romanticized as chivalrous brigands, were viewed by many of the English and urban Scots as belonging to a different, more primitive and barbaric race.

> They go naked from below the knee to
> mid thighs; wear a durk and a pistol at
> their girdle, and a target at their shoulder.
> They are desperate in fight, fierce in
> conversation, apt to quarrel, mischievous,
> and even murderers in their passions[18]

It was generally believed that they inhabited a land of poverty, violence, superstition, witchcraft, ritual executions, and cattle raiding. It was also a place which possessed a stubbornly persisting Gaelic civilization.[19]

In 1709 the Scottish Society for the Propagation of Christian Knowledge was established to control these unruly elements, to uproot their ancestral language and culture, and to instill within them true

---

[16]*Penny London Post* June 1, 1726.

[17]Letter from Horace Walpole to Sir Horace Mann June 14,1780. Cited in Snyder p. 719.

[18]*The Highlander Delineated: or the Characters, Customs and manners of the Highlanders* (London: J. Roberts, 1745),p. 3.

[19]Eric Richards, "Scotland and the Uses of the Atlantic Empire" in Bailyn and Morgan, p. 80.

religion and morality. After the crisis of 1745-6, when the Young Pretender's armies had successfully overrun Scotland and a good part of England before their final defeat, the Highland Society was dismembered, the use of certain surnames was forbidden, and the kilt and the bagpipe were banned. The uprisings in the Highlands, coupled with the alliances that its inhabitants had made with the Jacobites, also required that England maintain troops in that rebellious part of country which was the weak spot in its defenses and the scene of severe repression.[20]

The Lowlanders and the Highlanders, two very different kinds of people, offered both the stereotypes of eager, ambitious, hard working, aggressive individuals who wanted to "out-English the English" as well as barbaric, unassimilating, unmanageable, unbending, and inferior human beings who would have nothing to do with their betters. The Scots were perfect objects of English bigotry: when both these elements of their society were viewed together, they ran the whole gamut of contradictory prejudices that, as previously noted, are invariably part of group hatred.

Daniel Defoe appreciated the depth of the English prejudice against the Scots. In his work, *An Essay at Removing National Prejudices Against a Union with Scotland Part I,* he writes:

> National prejudices are some of the worst sort of
> humane antipathies, and, as they may be applayd,
> have frequently very bad effects. And I cannot clear
> the English from the just charge, of being the nation
> in the world the most addicted to them, and when
> once they have entertained such unhappy notions,
> are the hardest of any nation in the world to be brought
> off them again (p. 11).

Defoe wonders why two nations who are natives of the same island, who have been allied through intermarriages both of nobility and common people, and who have traded together and possess the same Protestant religion should have such deep animosities between them (p. 11).

On May 1, 1707, to mark the union of England and Scotland, William Talbot, Lord Bishop of Oxford, preached a sermon before the Queen at St. Paul's Cathedral where he expresses the hope that :

> Our two kingdoms are this day united, let our
> hearts from this time be so too: The names of
> England and Scotland are lost in that of Great
> Britain; let all the names of parties and characters

---

[20]S.J. Connolly, "Varieties of Britishness: Ireland, Scotland and Wales in the Hanoverian state." *Uniting the Kingdom? The making of British History,* eds. *Alexander Grant and Keith J. Stringer* (London: Routledge, 1995),p. 195.

> of distinction, be buried with them: Let there be
> no other contentions between us, but those kind
> ones who shall do each other the most friendly offices (p. 16).

Unfortunately, pious platitudes do not end deep-seated prejudices that separate peoples. Mutual hatreds existed since the eleventh century, and border villages in both countries had memories of atrocities committed by plundering armies. According to Jacob Vilner, "Scotland even after the Union remained largely another country, different substantially in its social thought, its legal system, its political and economic structure, its educational and religious institutions and principals.[21] English travelers to Scotland wrote of the extreme poverty of the country; beggary along with rebellion and political chaos became synonymous in English minds with Scotland. In various prints, the natives are portrayed as undernourished, thin-faced, backward people who are afflicted with an itch that came from the lice found in their coarse clothing. In the words of one English observer of the land and its people:

> Had Cain been Scot God had revers'd his Doom,
> Not forced him wander, but confin'd him Home.[22]

Those Scots. who came to London to seek their fortune were subject to severe prejudice which was as much a part of the nativism of the middle and lower classes as the traditional English hatred of the French. Satirists mimicked the Scots' speech patterns as they did of the Jewish peddlers and petty merchants, and they poked fun at all of their provincial character-weaknesses.[23] In a print that depicts a country road with a sign post marked "To London," two ragged Scots, dressed in their native plaids, trudge along towards the metropolis. The caption at the bottom reads: "From barren lands by famine led the Scotchmen fly to us for bread."[24] Another satirical print has a stronger message which reads, "Englishmen beware and Scotchmen's power dread, or theyl deprive you of liberty, life and bread."[25] According to John Brewer, they "enjoyed the dubious distinction of being marginally more unpopular

---

[21]Jacob Vilner, "Man's Economic Status" in *Man versus Society in Eighteenth-Century Britain: Six Points of View*, ed. James L. Clifford (Cambridge: Cambridge University Press, 1968), p. 22.

[22]Verses on the title page of *An Exact Description of Scotland With a True Character of the People and Their manners* (London: n.d.).

[23]Herbert M. Atherton, *Political Prints in the Age of Hogarth: A Study of the Ideographic Representation of Politics* (Oxford: Oxford University Press, 1974), pp. 210-12.

[24]*A Political and Satirical History*, Plate 187.

[25]Ibid., Plate 142.

than the Jews."[26] To the English of virtually every social class, the people of Scotland were contemptible creatures who were poorly fed, spoke in an unintelligible manner, and were afflicted with the itch. In addition, although they appeared to be subservient by nature, they were, in reality, completely untrustworthy.[27]

A major source of prejudice against the Scots was their ambition to succeed in spite of the obstacles that were placed in their path. Any out-group that manages to be more successful than many of the natives becomes a prime candidate for prejudice; the Scots were no exception to this rule. As they entered areas like the diplomatic corps or the medical and the legal professions that were regarded as a strictly English preserve, they paid a price for their successes. In *Stat Nominis Umbra Part I*, the pseudonymous author, Junius, comments upon their "characteristic prudence, the selfish nationality, the indefatigable smile, the persevering assiduity, the everlasting possession of a discreet and moderate resentment "that is part of their make-up (p. xxvi). He is convinced "that the Scots, transplanted from their own country, are always a distinct and separate body from the people who receive them." Furthermore, "In other settlements, they only love themselves; – in England, they cordially love themselves, and as cordially hate their neighbours" (p. xxvi). A particularly conspicuous group of Scots who became the object of scorn and ridicule were those, who, following the backlash of prejudice against them in England after the conflict in 1745, went to India to seek their fortunes. On their return, the successful ones were often condemned in England and at home for being typical nouveaux riches who were trying to imitate their betters.[28]

When Lord Bute, the royal favorite, achieved power, he became the target of the hostility that was directed against all of the too pushy and too successful Scots who were achieving fame in England. In addition, there was the fear that swarms of Scots would come to the new "Promised Land" in search of financial gain and preferment. Opposition writers noted that not only did Bute lack administrative experience, but they wondered if, as a Scot without a single drop of English blood in his veins, he had any natural interest in the affairs of the country. In an anonymous pamphlet, *A Serious Address to the Vulgar in which the Character and Abilities of a Certain Nobleman, and the Prejudice against the Place of his Birth are impartially Considered,* the writer challenges the notion

---

[26]John Brewer, "The Misfortune of Lord Bute: A Case Study in Eighteenth-Century Political Argument and Public Opinion," *The Historical Journal* 16 (No. 1, 1973):19.

[27]Ibid., pp. 19-20.

[28]G.J. Bryant, "Scots in India in the Eighteenth Century," *The Scottish Historical Journal* 64 (April, 1985): 38.

that Bute was regarded by many as a foreigner. "With what colour of justice then, or upon what pretense of self interest," he asks, "can we deny the natives of Scotland a share in the government of a kingdom, of which they form so considerable a part" (p. 28)?He was definitely in the minority as any number of accusations were made against Bute's competence as well as his morality. *The Whisperer*, a journal that ran for two years (1770-1771), continuously reinforced anti-Scottish stereotypes through personal attacks upon Bute who is referred to as "a prostituted Earl of the House of Stuart." Its editor, William Moore, delighted in writing about "necessitous Scotchmen", and how the King is the dupe of his mother and these "creatures."[29]

The most scurrilous accusation that was made against Bute was that he was having an affair with George III's mother. Linda Colley believes that this was not simply an attack upon immorality in high places. She feels that, "The accusation that one Scottish minister was penetrating the mother of the King of England was symbolic shorthand for the real anxiety: namely, that large numbers of Scots were penetrating England itself, compromising its identity, winning access to its riches and cutting out English men."[30]

The presence of an "other" in high places often does not help to overcome the prejudice against outsiders. In fact, it may worsen the situation. Criticisms of the minority person who has achieved a position of power can actually generate negative attitudes towards his entire group. At the same time, ingrained prejudices against them can be further used to denigrate the individual who has tasted success. Thus, as Brewer notes:

> The tactic of fanning hostility to the Scots with hatred of Bute, and *vice versa*, very swiftly produced results. Anti-Caledonian clubs were formed in London's taverns and the Scots (like the Jews before them) were booed and jeered in the theater....anti-Scottish toasts including those condemning the favourite were drunk openly in the streets of London and the provinces.[31]

When Lord Bute established his position at court, and his countrymen came in greater numbers to England, a more complex stereotypical image of the Scots began to emerge. The Scot who travels to London to seek a livelihood no longer appears on the stage as a simpleton with a distinctive dialect who plays the bagpipes, wears a blue hat, practices the Presbyterian religion, and possesses little valued

---

[29]*The Whisperer* 15 (March 3, 1770):97.
[30]Colley, p. 122.
[31]Brewer, p. 21.

Scottish currency. He is now an arrogant person who is prepared to teach the English proper elocution. He is also mean, reflecting the alleged spirit and values of his native land.[32]

Edward Snyder believes that the English idea of the typical Scot can best be expressed by the words "bigoted Ignorance."[33] Unfortunately, the same could be said of their perception of other "domestic foreigners," the Welsh.

The Welsh

This nation conceives it right to commit
acts of plunder, theft, and robbery, not
only against foreigners and hostile nations,
but even against their own countrymen.
When an opportunity of attacking the enemy
with advantage occurs, they respect not the
leagues of peace and friendship, preferring
base lucre to the solemn obligations of oaths and good faith.[34]

We the poor remnants of ancient Britons are
confin'd in the mountains of Wales cultivating
an ungrateful soil, whose production is
insufficient to support its occupier. The tendency of
our boasted constitution to accumulate property
into few hands, and the present wretched mode
of taxing the produce of labor, and the necessaries
of life has of late increased the number of our poor
into an alarming degree....and if we happen to
complain of our hardships, we are immediately
told in a true Aegyptian phrase ' that we are idle.'[35]

Last Wednesday a Welch Porter, being intrusted
to receive at the Bank, a bill belonging to a noble
lord at St. James's is gone off with the money.[36]

The people of Wales, like those of Scotland and Ireland, differed significantly from the English in both customs and language. During the twelfth and thirteenth centuries there was, in Wales, the development of a sense of national identity. At that same time, when the Welch adopted

---

[32]J.O. Bartley, "The Development of a Stock Character II. The Stage Scotsman; III. The Stage Welshman (to 1800)," *The Modern Language Review* 38 (Oct. 1943): p. 279-84.

[33]Snyder, p. 184.

[34]Giraldus de Barri, *The Itinerary of Archbishop Baldwin Through Wales A.D. MCLXXXVIII*, Vol. 2 translated and annotated by Sir Richard Colt Hoare Bart (London: Printed for William Miller, 1806), p. 339.

[35]William Jones cited in Geraint H. Jenkins. "A Rank Republican (and) a Leveller: William Jones Llangadfan," *The Welsh History Review* 17 (June, 1995): 382.

[36]*London Penny Post* June 3,1726 p. 4.

the term *Wallia* to identify their country, outside observers also created a stereotyped image of their alleged characteristics which was to last for centuries.[37] Archbishop Theobald of Canterbury (1139-61) considered them to be a barbaric, primitive, and fierce undisciplined people who lived like animals in a strange country. High mountains, deep forests and difficult paths added to the image of "wild Wales" and to the brutishness of the natives. The Church, anxious to impose a uniform standard of morality on European society, found the Welsh customs of marriage, legitimacy etc. to be unacceptable.[38] By condemning these practices, medieval clerics contributed to the "otherness" of the Welsh just as they did to the Jews. In the next centuries, in the eyes of the Anglican Church, the Welsh language continued to be considered as an inferior tongue, the very symbol of the backwardness of the people who spoke it, and a barrier which prevented the bringing of English standards of enlightenment and civilization to the primitive people of Wales.[39] By the last decades of the eighteenth century, for many of the Welsh, the Anglican Church was becoming an alien institution. None of the appointed bishops were Welsh nor could they speak the native language. English bibles and prayer books were used in church services, and clerics were encouraged to promote the use of the English language.[40] This prejudice was to continue for many years, beyond the Age of Reason.

The inhabitants of the eighteenth century Welsh counties were divided into two classes. There were English-speaking landowners who were in touch with their counterparts in England who shared their values, and the illiterate tillers of the soil who spoke the Welsh language of their ancestors unaffected by the intellectual movements of the prior two centuries.[41] Many of these Welsh, on their upland farms, were trapped in an abject poverty which sent them to England to seek a better life. Because of the close proximity of Wales and England, there were more Welsh in London than either Irish or Scots. By Stuart times, they were already an integral part of the Metropolis' population; like the Jews, they could live wherever they wished in the capital. The Welsh did not compete for space with other immigrants, and they could be found not

---

[37]Davies, R.R." Buchedd A Moes Cymry" ("The Manners and Morals of the Welsh "), *The Welsh History Review* 12 (December, 1984):174.

[38]Ibid. pp. 174-75.

[39]Jenkins, H. Geraint, "Horrid Unintelligible Jargon: The Case of Dr. Thomas Bowles," *The Welsh History Review* 15 (December, 1991):511.

[40]Jenkins, Geraint H. "A Rank Republican (and) a Leveller" p. 374.

[41]John Rhys and David Brynmor-Jones, *The Welsh People: Chapters on their Origin, History and Laws, Language, Literature and Characteristics* (1906; rpt. New York: Haskel House Publishers, 1969) p. 470.

only in the Strand and Solo, but in Bloomsbury and St. James as well.[42] During the eighteenth century, these newcomers suffered few of the economic disabilities that are common among most ethnic or religious immigrant groups. Perhaps the best reason for their relative good acceptance into English life was that, unlike the Irish and the Scots, swarms of them did not descend upon England to compete with the natives in the professions or as laborers. However, they were not fully trusted by the populace. The following article that appears in *Mist's Weekly Journal* of March 2, 1728 shows just how much these "others" are suspected of committing various crimes without any real proof.

> We hear from Gloucester, that a gang of
> Welch folks of both sexes, who would give
> no good account of themselves, were taken
> up on the borders of that country; they had about
> them all manner of shop goods, a description of
> which, and of the goodly possessors was made
> publick, in order for a discovery (p. 2).

The fact that nothing further appears in subsequent issues of this weekly suggests that they were innocent of the charges brought against them.

Although a high proportion of the Welsh were in the poorer classes, there were also those who achieved affluence. Yet, many who were among the elite of society, remained very visible as outsiders; they were ridiculed for their accent, physical appearance, and habits. Most of them were viewed as being devious and dishonest. Border cattle raids of previous years were remembered in such ditties as:

> Taffy was a Welshman
> Taffy was a thief;
> Taffy came to my house
> And Stole a leg of beef.[43]

The rabble, always looking for some kind of a diversion, openly provoked the Welsh by hanging a "Taffy" in effigy on St. David's day. The chapbooks of the time were filled with tales of dishonest Welsh drovers, vagrants, and tinkers who were ridiculed for their backwardness in unfamiliar English surroundings. The following title of one of these Penny Books summarizes not only its contents, but many of the popular anti-Welsh prejudices as well.

---

[42]Jones, Emry. "The Welsh in London in the Seventeenth and Eighteenth Centuries," *The Welsh History Review* 10 (December, 1981):475.

[43]Ibid., p. 469. According to Patrick Ford, "The phrase 'Taffy (for Welsh Dafydd) was a Welshman, Taffy was a thief' goes back to about the 14th century, a time when, after the loss of Welsh independence, Welsh people were streaming into England. "See *Boston Globe* (August 26, 1995)" Letters to the Editor.

The Welsh Wedding. Shewing, How Shon-ap-
Morgan rode up to London upon a Goat to get a
Wife, with his comical Courtship and Marriage.
And how he was married to a Cotton-Twister, by
an old Smallcoal-Man in a Barn, poor Taffy
thinking it an English Church. Also, the comical
Wedding-Dinner, three score Dishes of butter'd
Leeks, three Hundred Red herrings, some bak'd,
some boil'd some stew'd and some fry'd; with twenty
Gallons of Leek Porridge, and three Tubs of Butter-
Milk and Whey, with a Sack-posset for Taffy. And
how he was bury'd in Tom Turd's Fields. With
Taffy's Last Will, wherein he leaves something to every Body.

English travelers, imbued with a sense of arrogance towards the natives of Wales, added to the popular stereotypes through accounts of their journeys through the countryside. One of them, William Bingley, an Anglican cleric, who first visited the country in 1798, notes in his work, *North Wales including its Scenery, Antiquities, Customs,* that those Welsh who lived on the main roads took pride in their expertise in "over-reaching their Saxon neighbors in any of their little bargains." it is a common practice for them to ask double the price they will take for their goods, and "those persons who are acquainted with these practices never give them the full price of what they purchase" (II p. 265). He also notes that the Welsh are a superstitious people who have a "greater inclination to credulity than what at least an Englishman can discover among our own people" (II p. 268). The lower class of the Welsh continue to believe in witches, convinced that certain old women "possess the power of inflicting disorders both on men and cattle" (II pp. 275-76). The traveler was particularly disturbed by his visit to a religious meeting of "Jumpers." He notes the "noise of their groaning and singing or oftimes rather bellowing, the clapping of their hands, the beating of their feet against the ground" that stupefied the senses. It had, he believes, "more the appearance of heathen orgies than of the rational spirit of Christian devotion" (I p. 209). Bingley's two volume work showed the best of Wales' rugged landscape and the worst of its people; it reaffirmed the image of the Welsh that the English had nurtured for centuries.

The stage Welsh also perpetuated the stereotype of those individuals who were fond of the harp, kept goats, loved cheese, leeks and onions, drank metheglin (a form of fermented honey) were proud that they were descended from the Greeks or the Trojans, were inclined to thievery, called people from their country cousin, and had distinctive Welsh speech patterns.[44] Behind this stereotypical figure there was the clear

---

[44]Bartley, pp. 286-87.

message that to be accepted and to achieve a measure of success in this new society meant to become "English". It required that those who sought to become part of the ruling class become "Anglicized" and accept the social, political, religious, and linguistic practices of the "superior culture".[45] As Richard Brown notes:

> Accent was important. English may have been
> spoken in the Scottish Lowlands but with a
> distinctive regional flavour. "Scottish" was
> a synonym for rudeness in England and the
> leading sectors of Scottish society hastened to
> educate their children in English schools. After
> the 1750s elocutionists visited Edinburgh to
> give lessons in English pronunciation. Being
> seen to be "English" opened up career possibilities
> which being "Scottish", Welsh or Irish did not.[46]

Though the privileged few Welsh gentry of London maintained a Welsh school and a Society of Ancient Britons to foster a sentimental attachment to their native land, they, like the Sephardic Jews, wanted to blend in as much as possible with the majority culture. There were some Welsh, however, like the political radical, William Jones, who were very much concerned about the plight of their people's culture and self-image. Jones believed that the French Revolution had ushered in a new era for the small oppressed European nations. The early successes of these revolutionaries across the Channel encouraged him to champion the cause of the Welsh language and culture. In addition to collecting ancient Welsh manuscripts and encouraging the preservation of Welsh folk music and customs, he also spoke out about the plight of the poor farmers and the laboring class.[47] For the authorities in London, he was another potential source of unrest during a troubled time in British history.

The Huguenots

> We forbid our said subjects of the pretended
> Reformed religion to assemble themselves
> together for religious exercises in any place or
> private house, under any pretext whatsoever,
> the same in bailiwicks and otherwise, even if
> the said exercises may be sustained by decrees
> of our Council....We enjoin all Ministers of the
> said pretended Reformed religion, who are not

---

[45]Richard Brown, *Society and Economy in Modern Britain 1700-1850* (London: Routledge, 1991), pp. 359-60.
[46]Ibid., p. 361.
[47]Jenkins, "A Rank Republican (and) a Leveller" pp. 378-79.

willing to be converted and to embrace the
Apostolical Roman Catholic Religion, to depart
from our Kingdom and Territories within fifteen
days....We make express and reiterated
declarations, that none of our subjects of the said
pretended Reformed religion, they, their wives
or children shall be permitted to take away with
them from our Kingdom and Territories any of
their property or possessions under the penalty
of the galleys for men, and confiscation and
imprisonment for women.[48]

Here lies the body of Lewis Galdy, Esq. who
departed this life at Port Royal, the 22d of
December, 1739, aged 80. He was born at
Montpellier in France, but left that country for
his religion, and came to settle in this island
where he was swallowed up in the great
earthquake in the year 1692, and by the
providence of God was by another shock
thrown into the sea, and miraculously saved
by swimming until a boat took him up. He liv'd
many years after in great reputation, belov'd
by all who knew him, and much lamented at his death.[49]

In addition to the Irish, Scots, and Welsh who came to England from other parts of the British Isles to improve their lot, there were others from abroad who settled in the country not only for financial reasons, but also to escape religious persecution. The presence of a sizable immigrant community has been an important aspect of London life since medieval times. By the fifteenth century, over two thousand foreigners, some five percent of the population, made their homes in the Metropolis. They were mostly crafts people and traders from France and the Low Countries who were attracted by the need for their skills in the busy capital. By and large, they settled outside the walls of the city to escape the animosity of native workers as well as the regulations of the various guilds. Occasionally, outbursts of hostility from English artisans turned into anti-foreign riots, but a steady stream of immigrants seeking new opportunities continued to pour into the city. Catholic persecution in the 1540s and 1550s brought the first waves of religious refugees to London where they received a warm welcome from the French and Walloon communities as well as from Edward VI. By his royal grant of 1550, the

---

[48]Revocation of the Edict of Nantes by Louis X IV in 1685. Cited in Abraham D. Lavenger, *French Huguenots : From Mediterranean Catholics to White Anglo-Saxon Protestants*. (New York: Peter Lang, 1990) American University Studies, Series IX History Vol. 80. pp. 212-13.
[49]*London Morning Post* (September 8, 1740).

first independent foreign churches were established to cater to the needs of both the older and newer immigrants.[50]

The most significant group to come to England during the Age of Reason was the Huguenots, a highly skilled group of French Protestants who had proven their worth as traders, professionals, and skilled artisans to the kings of France. Like the Jews of Angevin England, they had enjoyed royal protection and they were permitted to practice their faith as long as it was not offensive to the general population. Unfortunately, as in the case of medieval Anglo-Jewry, this special status that they enjoyed in France was to come to an end. By 1685 the Huguenots faced more than three hundred decrees which challenged both their religious freedoms and their right to be members of the professions or masters of trades Their schools and houses of worship were closed, and royal troops were forcibly quartered in many Huguenot homes. When Louis XIV officially revoked the Edict of Nantes, there were mass conversions to Catholicism that resembled the Jewish experience in Spain at the time of Ferdinand and Isabella. These new converts were labeled *Nouveaux Convertis*, a term of scorn and ridicule that was similar to the Spanish use of the word, Marranos, for Jewish converts to Catholicism.[51]

Many Huguenots who wished to remain true to their Protestantism fled to England. In the first waves of immigration, during the 1680s, some 80,000 of them landed in the country. Although a large number of these refugees ultimately settled in America, approximately 40,000 remained.(They were more numerous than the Quakers and fewer than the Catholics.) By 1700 there were approximately twenty-five French congregations that met regularly in London and Westminster including one that was made up of Sabbatarians. Cunningham believes that it was the general feeling of indignation towards the French Catholics who had oppressed the Huguenots that overcame, to some degree, the initial jealousies of the trade corporations and the religious suspicions of the Anglicans.[52] Lurid tales of torture and murder at the hands of the French Papists were circulated after the refugees landed, and the Huguenots became a graphic example of what would happen to English Protestants if they would ever allow a Catholic monarch to rule over them.

---

[50]Andrew Pettegree, "The French and Walloon Communities in London, 1550-1688," *From Persecution to Toleration: The Glorious Revolution and Religion in England*, eds. Ole Peter Grell, Jonathan I. Israel and Nicholas Tyache (Oxford: Clarendon Press, 1991), pp. 78-9.

[51]Hillel Schwartz, *The History of a Millenarian Group in Eighteenth-Century England* (Berkeley: University of California Press, 1980),pp. 12-14.

[52]W. Cunningham, *Alien Immigrants to England* (London: Swan Sonnenschein & Co., 1897),pp. 230-31.

In addition to a certain amount of charity and compassion for the less fortunate and a sense of national pride for caring for the oppressed, English pragmatism was a dominant factor in welcoming these newcomers. Advocates of immigration saw the arrival of the Huguenots as an opportunity to repopulate the country with foreign settlers who would turn France's loss into England's gain. Daniel Defoe, argued that it was to the advantage of a country to take in industrious refugees. He felt that trade and numbers of people are the true riches and strength of a nation.[53] Actually, the bulk of the Huguenot refugees were people of modest means; some of them were in need of financial assistance when they landed in England. As in the case of the Jews, there were also some well to do Huguenots who were able to transfer at least some of their liquid capital to their adopted country. Though their contemporaries exaggerated the amount of wealth they brought over, and modern historians have overstated their role in the Bank of England, they were a definite factor in the economy of England.[54]

As Protestants, the Huguenots welcomed English liberty, but as French they looked down upon England's lack of culture. Nevertheless, like the members of other immigrant groups, they Anglicized their names and they ceased to speak in their native tongue. They were a highly skilled and educated group who quickly found an important place in the intellectual world of their adopted country. Between 1680 and 1720, sixteen Huguenots were elected fellows of the Royal Society which was far out of proportion to their percentage of the population.[55] In addition to being cultural and scientific intermediaries between England and the Continent, they were skilled in various crafts.[56] Unfortunately, their talents as gold and silversmiths were not always appreciated by the natives of England who viewed many of these newcomers as a threat to their livelihood. Like the Jews, the Huguenots were the victims of the traditional closed-shop attitude of the English craft guilds. Their capacity for hard work, their ability to sell goods at a lower price than the English, and their total commitment to succeed in their adopted country also stirred up the jealousies of the local

---

[53]Daniel Defoe, *A Brief History of the Poor Palatine Refugees* (Dublin: E. Waters, 1710), p. 15.

[54]F. M. Crouzet, "Walloons, Huguenots and the Bank of England." *Proceedings of the Huguenot Society* 25 (2) 1990: 176.

[55]Graham C. Gibbs, "Huguenot Contributions to England's Intellectual Life and England's Intellectual Commerce with Europe, c. 1680-1720," *Huguenots in Britain and their French Background 1550-1800*, ed. Irene Scouloudi (Totowa, New Jersey: Barnes and Noble Books, 1987), pp. 27-28.

[56]*The London Morning Post* of January 24,1740 notes the passing of Mr. James Du Beck, "one of the most eminent Snuff-Box-Makers in England."

manufacturers. Their mercantile success prompted a popular saying that "A drop of Huguenot blood in the vein was worth a thousand ponds a year."[57] Another expression used to describe their ability to move quickly to achieve their goals was: "As keen as a Huguenot just landed from France."[58]

Like the Jewish people in many countries on the Continent, the Huguenots, while in France, had experienced forced conversion, compulsory attendance at Catholic religious services, and discrimination in employment. Their suffering and oppression led them to believe that they, too, were indeed a chosen people.[59] As a result, when they first came to England they clustered together in their own communities, and they discouraged inter-marriage with the natives and other immigrant groups.[60] They were considered to be "a separate body in the nation"[61] since they maintained, like the Jewish people, their own charity system and created social organizations and burial societies that were based on regional ties. To strengthen group solidarity in the Huguenot Diaspora, these groups were placed under a French national umbrella. At first, they clung to their Calvinistic traditions, and they were reluctant to join the Anglican Church. However, unlike the Jews, their Protestantism was an important contributing factor to their ultimate assimilation into English society.

Huguenot leaders, like those of the Jewish community, realized that their members were very vulnerable to the criticisms of the masses. They, too, urged the refugees to maintain a low profile and to avoid creating negative public opinion. In 1706, when three prophets came to England from Languedoc, the communal elders were concerned that their ecstasy, so out of place in a society that paid lip service to moderation and reason, would reflect poorly upon the Huguenots as a whole. They were disturbed by the fact that the three had to stand in the pillory for their false prophesies and that their enemies also saw them as a polluting influence on of the social body. (The French prophets were accused of

---

[57]Robin D. Gwynn, "Patterns in the Study of Huguenot Refugees in Britain: past present and future," *Huguenots in Britain*, p. 219.
[58]*A Second Part of a View of London*, p. 24.
[59]Miriam Yardeni, "Huguenots and Jews in Seventeenth and Eighteenth Century Brandenburg and Prussia," in *Studies in Judaism: Anti-Jewish Mentalities in Early Modern Europe* (Lanham, Maryland: University Press of America, 1990), p. 241.
[60]This did not continue for very long. For an overview of their assimilation into English life, see Abraham D. Lavender, *French Huguenots: From Mediterranean Catholics to White Anglo-Saxon Protestants* (New York: Peter Lang, 1990) American University Studies Series IX Vol. 80, pp. 140-42.
[61]*A Letter to the French Refugees Concerning their Behaviour to the Government* 1710 cited in Robin Gwynn *Huguenot Heritage: The history and contribution of the Huguenots in Britain* (London: Routledge & Kegan Paul, 1985),p. 168.

committing unnatural sexual acts, and they were linked to the detested Sodomists.)[62] The communal heads sighed with relief when the message of these charismatics failed to take root among the French and when finally, by 1715, it had lost most of its intensity.[63] The Huguenot leaders were particularly concerned about the moral image of their immigrant constituency; the French churches agreed that when necessary they would deny communion in order to "suppress profanity and the dissolute morals of the people."[64] Yet, like the Jews, they were not entirely successful. In fact, the two immigrant groups were occasionally linked together as the causes of some of England's ills. For example, the *London Morning Post* of March 31,1740 reported that:

> The people in Exchange Alley give out that
> the lottery is full, tho' the bill is not yet passed,
> and we hear, some French brokers have
> subscribed for upwards of thirty thousand tickets,
> and there has been three shillings advance
> given to fix the price; so that by suffering the
> tickets to be engrossed, the publick is liable to
> be bubbled every year by Jews or Foreigners.
> – No wonder trade decays and shop-keepers are undone (p. 1).

In Bristol, during the period of agitation over the passage of the "Jew Bill", mobs chanted "no general naturalization, no Jews, no French bottlemakers, no lowering wages of labouring men to four-pence a day and garlic."[65] Because England was so often at war with France, additional pressure was put upon the Huguenots to affirm their loyalty to the Crown. This was a far greater problem for them than for the Jews who, though associated with the Iberian Peninsula, were usually considered to be a nation in exile that did not have strong ties to any of England's traditional enemies.

The story of the Huguenots, like that of the arrival and the settlement of the Jews, is part of the broader picture of England's immigration and naturalization policies which span the hundred years or so from the time of the Restoration to the middle of the eighteenth century. The General Naturalization Act of 1709, a high water mark in this endeavor, was the result of lengthy debates and considerable soul searching concerning the benefits of encouraging newcomers to settle in the country. It was soon

---

[62]Schwartz, p. 111.

[63]Lavender, p. 113.

[64]Bernard Cottret, *The Huguenots in England: Immigration and Settlement c.1550-1700* trans. Peregrine and Adriana Stevenson (Cambridge: Cambridge University Press, 1985), p. 263-64.

[65]Daniel Statt, *Foreigners and Englishmen: The Controversy over Immigration and Population, 1660-1760* (Newark: University of Delaware Press, 1995), p. 193.

to be tested by the arrival of a horde of refugees from what is now Germany.

The Palatines

I think our charity ought to begin at home,
the Palatines may be poor enough,
but their coming hither can never make us
rich (as has too often been learnedly worded)
when we had so many before we could not
tell what to do with them.[66]

They write from Newport in Rhode Island,
Sept. 26, that they had advice there from
Philadelphia, that some weeks before 100
Palatines, men, women, and children, were
arrived; and a great many more were expected in a short time.[67]

The second largest immigrant group to arrive in England were the Germans who had visited English ports as early as the second half of the twelfth century. They obtained the special protection of Henry II and other important privileges as well. Through the years, the Germans established mercantile colonies in the port cities of the east coast; they also journeyed inland where the major fairs were held. Their largest settlement was at London, a city that was a magnet to so many immigrant groups. There the Germans became active in a host of fields that varied from crafts to manufacturing.[68] Like the Sephardic Jews, they found a relatively secure place for themselves in English life. With the arrival of a horde of poor refugees from their former homeland during the first part of the eighteenth century, this sense of acceptance would be challenged.

Following the passage of the General Naturalization Act of 1709, thousands of Germans from the area of the Rhine valley poured into England. These "poor Palatines", many of whom were on the brink of starvation, had been led to believe that Queen Anne would pay for their passage to the American colonies. They had also been encouraged to come by those who were concerned about the depopulation of England. Within the space of several months some 13,000 of them, with the help of the Whig government, entered the country. They soon became an

---

[66]*The Pallatines Catechism; or, A True Description of their Camps at Blackheath and Camberwell. In a Pleasant Dialogue between an English Tradesman and a High Dutchman* (1709). Cited in Statt, p. 149.

[67]*British Journal* December 7, 1723 p. 3.

[68]Hermann Kellenbenz, "German Immigrants in England." *Immigrants and Minorities in British Society*, ed. Colin Holmes (London: George Allen & Unwin, 1978).pp. 63-66.

embarrassment to their benefactors who were simply overwhelmed by the sheer number of refugees. It soon became apparent that these newcomers were virtually penniless and that many of them were physically unable to work. Funds were raised to take care of their immediate needs. However, as with the case of the Huguenots, this compassion was short-lived. When, for example, the city of Canterbury was asked to receive some of the "persecuted Protestants," the mayor responded that due to the difficult economic times, there was not enough work to employ the city's own poor let alone any newcomers in need. All over the country, this became the typical response to the government's plan to settle the Palatines.

Though, at first, the Whig ministry had encouraged their immigration, the presence of so many destitute foreigners made government officials rethink their policy and initiate plans to stem the flow. In spite of attempts to discourage their migration, thousands of Palatines continued to pour into the country; tent cities were set up around London to receive them. In a letter patent issued by the Queen, as well as in the correspondence between several of the bishops and the clergy to raise funds, the Palatines were portrayed as victims of French persecution. In addition, the bishops claimed that these refugees were attracted to the superior freedoms that the English Constitution and Government offered its subjects. By helping them to settle in the land, not only would the natives receive rewards from heaven, but the newcomers would also increase the prosperity of the entire populace.[69]

Unfortunately for the Palatines, such inducements brought only temporary relief. English attitudes towards them began to harden when it appeared that they had come to England not so much for religious freedom, but to seek a better livelihood. At a time of economic depression, native tradesmen and laborers began to view the newcomers as competitors. Tensions mounted, threats were made against the Palatines, fights broke out between them and the English, and mobs invaded the refugee camps looking for Catholics who were allegedly in their midst. People from all walks of life were resentful that the government had brought such poverty-stricken, diseased refugees to England without knowing what to do with them. In spite of financial inducements by the authorities, few of the English were willing to settle the Palatines in their parishes. The sight of impoverished Germans begging on the streets of London hurt the Whig government. In the general election of 1710 the Tories attained a substantial majority in the in the House of Commons; a virulent xenophobia characterized the new

---

[69]Statt, pp. 138-40.

administration.[70] Through the years, foreigners, so often stereotyped in the public imagination, would continue to feel this "otherness" most keenly. This prejudice would affect all newcomers to England. The Jewish community and other ethnic and religious groups would especially feel its sting in the 1750's when, due to economic issues, anti-foreign sentiment was particularly bitter.

---

[70]Ibid., p. 163.

4

Racial "Others"

The Blacks

The Negro is possessed of passions not only
strong but ungovernable; a mind dauntless,
warlike and unmerciful; a temper extremely
irascible; a disposition indolent, selfish and
deceitful; fond of joyous sociality, riotus mirth
and extravagant show....As to all other fine
feelings of the soul, the Negro, as far as I have
been able to perceive, is nearly deprived of them.[1]

If the benefits of foreign commerce are so great,
and so essentially necessary to the support of
Great Britain and her colonies, and the
improvements therein so restrictive of our
enemies power, if disposed to hurt us, how vast
is the importance of our trade to Africa, which is the
first principle and foundation of all the rest; the
main spring of the machine, which sets every
wheel in motion.[2]

The Abolition of slavery is a god-like act: to confess
that we have long been in the wrong; to
renounce our errors, perhaps at the expense of a
certain quantity of wealth would distinguish us from
those barbarians whom we are taught to abhor: and
would be worthy of a reign favourable to mercy....[3]

Yet, was I born, as you are, no man's slave,
An heir to all that lib'ral nature gave;

---

[1]*Gentleman's Magazine* 58 (1788): 1093-94.
[2]African Merchant, *A Treatise Upon the Trade From Great-Britain to Africa; Humbly Recommended to the Attention of Government* (London: Printed for R. Baldwin, 1782), p. 4.
[3]*The General Magazine and Impartial Review* 2 (January, 1788): 83.

My thoughts can reason, and my limbs can move
The same as yours; like yours my heart can love;
Alike my body food and sleep sustain;
And e'en like yours – feels pleasure, want, and pain.
One sun rolls o'er us, common skies surround;
One globe supports us, and one grave must bound.[4]

The above citations reflect the wide spectrum of attitudes towards the Blacks during the eighteenth century. They range from a crass commercialism, cloaked in patriotism, that supported their transport and sale on the auction block, to an awareness of past wrongs and the beginnings of an appreciation of their human qualities. The arguments for and against the slave trade brought Blacks into public view and called them to the attention of many English people who had previously ignored their presence. However, this was only part of the history of the prejudice that people of color had experienced in the country.

The presence of Blacks in England, like that of the Jews, can be traced back to Roman times. It was, however, In 1555 when the trader, John Lok, brought the first group of African slaves to England that Black immigration really began. Their presence in the country was not really noted until the later part of the sixteenth century when Blacks became numerous enough to have Elizabeth I issue an edict in 1596 to expel them from the country. When this, and another equally ineffectual edict failed to change the status quo, she commissioned, in 1601, a Lubeck merchant, Casper van Senden, to deport them. By this time, the Blacks were so much a part of the English scene and such an economic asset that this attempt to expel them also failed.[5] The English slave trade, as well as returning planters from the colonies who brought their servants home with them, added to the Black population of England.

In seventeenth century London, Blacks became everyday sights on the streets, in the craft shops, at the marketplace, and on the stage. By the early part of the eighteenth century, there were more than 10,000 of them in the capital ; about two percent of the city's total population. Another 5000 Blacks could be found in the provinces, particularly in the slave trading seaports of Bristol and Liverpool. This number was augmented by Black sailors and musicians as well as by refugees who had fought on

---

[4]Epilogue to "The Padlock," in Africanus, *Remarks on the Slave Trade and the Slavery of the Negroes* (London: Printed by J. Phillips, 1788), p. 56.
[5]Gretchen Gerzina, *Black London: Life Before Emancipation* (New Brunswick, New Jersey: Rutgers University Press, 1995), pp. 3-4.

the loyalist side in the American Revolution and who came to England to be granted their promised freedom.[6]

The Blacks, even more than the Jews, were a very visible minority on the urban scene. As in the case of other "outsiders", attempts were made to prevent them from competing with the native workers. In 1731 the Lord Mayor of London issued a proclamation that forbade "Negroes or other Blacks" to become apprentices to any freeman in the city. Although London did not have racial ghettos, poverty forced many of them to live together in the city's slums. Known as St Giles black birds, they were conspicuous among the beggars on the streets of London. Black servants, dressed in ornate liveries and wearing silver collars that were engraved with their master's initials, a status symbol for the wealthy, were a common sight in the Metropolis. They were seen accompanying women of means who often pampered them like exotic pet dogs, and who cherished their black skin (the darker the complexion the more valuable the servant) which accented their own whiteness.[7] There was a certain mystery attached to their blackness which attracted artists and writers as well as white members of the opposite sex.[8]

About two thirds of the Blacks were young males. Edward Long, a Jamaican planter, feared that in the course of a few generations English blood would become contaminated, and the whole nation would resemble "the Portuguese and Moriscoes in complexion of skin and baseness of mind."[9] However, interracial marriages, which were quite common, did not raise any serious issues for the general public since they usually occurred among the lower classes.[10] In a sarcastic description of one such wedding ceremony that appears in *Mist's Weekly Journal* of May 4, 1728, the reporter's remarks are focused on the low status of the couple and not on the interracial aspects of their union. The groom is described as "a Negro gentleman who has the honour to serve his Majesty in the capacity of chimney sweeper." The bride is "a Lady belonging to a very noble family, she being one of the kitchen maids to

---

[6]Philip D. Morgan, "British Encounters With Africans and African Americans, *circa* 1600-1780," in *Strangers Within the Realm,* eds. Bernard Bailyn and Philip D. Morgan, p. 159.

[7]See, for example, Plate II of Hogarth's series of etchings, "Harlot's Progress," where the Black servant is equated with his mistress's pet monkey.

[8]Edward Scobie. *Black Britannia: A History of Blacks in Britain* (Chicago: Johnson Publishing Co., 1972),p. 9 and Folarin Shyllon, *Black People in Britain 1555-1833.* (London: Oxford University Press, 1977), pp. 102-103.

[9]Edward Long, *Candid Reflections upon the judgment lately awarded by the court of the King's bench in Westminster Hall on what is commonly called 'the negro case.'* Cited in James Walvin, "Black Caricature: The Roots of Racism," in *'Race' in Britain: Continuity and Change.* ed. Charles Husband (London: Hutchinson, 1987), p. 68.

[10]Gerzina, p. 21.

his Grace of Montague." Furthermore, "the bride upon the wedding day had twelve pages to attend her, all in the bridegroom's livery beside other domesticks."

The Age of Reason was also a period of growth for racism. The accession to the throne of William, Prince of Orange, was viewed by many as a triumph of Gothic freedom that had been inherited from England's glorious ancestors. By mid-century, belief in the Germanic genius of the nation's early founders was so pervasive that it was rarely questioned.[11] Coincidental with this sense of racial superiority and a growing Anglo-Saxon myth, was the expansion of the slave trade. Although the Spaniards and the Portuguese were the first European powers to be engaged in this nefarious practice, it was the British, with their vast maritime power and their growing colonial empire, who turned it into a very profitable undertaking. Consequently, those who opposed such practices were often viewed as working against the best interests of the nation. An anonymous merchant noted:

> In what light then but in that of enemies
> to their country can we look on those, who,
> under the specious plea of establishing
> universal freedom, endeavour to strike at
> at the root of this trade, the foundation of
> our commerce, the support of our colonies,
> the life of our navagation, and the cause of
> our national industry and riches.[12]

In order to justify this very lucrative commercial practice that placed the national economy above human rights, a writer in the *Scots Magazine* for June, 1772 argues that putting Blacks in chains saves these unfortunates from the cruel slaughter numbers of them could expect at the hands of their own people in Africa. Thus, they are actually "redeemed" by the European traders who sell them in the English colonies where "their lives, estates, and properties are safe under the protections of the laws of each country." In addition to "being fed and clothed at a great expense to their masters," it is noted that they are allowed to raise livestock and maintain their own gardens from which "they make a considerable profit." In regard to what we today would call job security, medical, and retirement benefits, It is argued that their lot is better than that of the common laborers in England (pp. 299-300).

Other advocates of slavery portrayed the Blacks as subhumans, members of an inferior race. In the *London Magazine* for June, 1760 a

---

[11]Hugh Mac Dougall, *Racial Myth in English History: Trojans, Teutons, and Anglo-Saxons* (Montreal: Harvest House Ltd., 1982), pp. 73, 81.
[12]African Merchant, p. 7.

traveler to Morocco, describing the population of the country, notes the presence of "wooly headed blacks" who had been taken prisoner and brought there from the western coast (p. 335). This demonstrates their obvious physiological inferiority; they are not as fully developed as the Caucasians who had real hair. There are also those who believe that other parts of their anatomy were overdeveloped; this too diminishes their humanity. For example, John Hippisley feels that the increase in the population of Africa was due to their lack of restraint in "the indulgence of desire."[13] For the supporters of slavery, they are simply brutes; a nameless, faceless, commodity needed to support a triangular trade that enriched shipping, banking, and other commercial interests. In a typical pro-slavery tract of the period, *Some Further Objections Humbly Offer'd to the Consideration of the Legislature, Against the Bill, For Establishing the Trade to Africa in a Regulated company*, the author claims that the natives "have no more humanity or justice than mere brutes" and that they are "wholly guided by their natural inclinations to abuse and impose whatever is in their power"(p. 1). For the Jews, commercial connections were important for their acceptance in English society. The Blacks, on the other hand, found that the trading world kept them in chains, and it encouraged the worst prejudices against them.

Like the Jews, the Blacks were a popular target of the eighteenth century cartoonists who reduced their physical features, alleged natural abilities or inabilities, and speech patterns into grotesque caricatures.[14] These stereotypes were perpetuated throughout the century by the commercial classes who believed that the blessings of Christianity and the "civilization" of the white plantations justified their exploitation of the Blacks. The Chap Books of the time, which drew lurid portraits of satanic blacks, also supported the notion of their innate depravity. The full title of one of these popular penny histories, *The Blackamoor in the Wood: Or A Lamentable Ballad on the tragical End of a gallant Lord and virtuous Lady; together with the untimely Death of their two Children wickedly performed by a heathenish and blood-thirsty Villain, their Servant. The like of which Cruelty was never heard of.*, is sufficient to show how the Blacks were portrayed in the tabloids. Shakespeare found that Shylock, the Jew, made a recognizable villain. For the authors of cheap thrillers, the Blacks served the same purpose.

Unfortunately, they did not fare much better in the works of such enlightened philosophers as David Hume (1711-1776) who considered Blacks to be naturally inferior to Caucasians. Hume had the highest

---

[13]John Hippisley, "On the Populousness of Africa," in *Essays* (London: T. Lownds, 1764), p. 6-7.
[14]Walvin, p. 59.

regard for the ancient Germans who, he believed, were superior to the rest of humanity in their ability to cultivate qualities of liberty, valor, honor, and equity. In his "Essay on National Characters," Hume notes that in all of human history "there never was a civilized nation of any other complexion than white, or even any individual eminent in action or speculation." He believes that Blacks, by their very nature, are incapable of making any contribution to the arts, sciences or the world of commerce and industry. [15] When Francis Williams, a Black, studied at Cambridge University and became a noted Latin poet, Hume remarked that he is to be admired "for very slender accomplishments, like a parrot who speaks a few words plainly."[16]

Hume's racism was in keeping with the general attitudes of many of the English of the time who believed that the mental capabilities of Blacks were significantly different from whites; that skin pigmentation was a definite sign of degeneracy. Furthermore, they viewed Blacks as being low on the chain of being and, in many ways, they were not fully human. For example, in an account of the capture of a Dutch ship by pirates that appears in the *Weekly Miscellany* for April 12,1735, it is reported that the Dutch Consul in Algiers "obtained the liberty of the crew, consisting of fourteen men and a Black" (p. 3). Obviously, for the writer of this piece, the fifteenth member is in a separate category of humanity form the rest of the crew. These subhuman qualities attributed to Blacks are discussed at length by Edward Long in his *History of Jamaica* where he presents some vivid descriptions of their bestial features. "When we reflect on the nature of these men, and their dissimilarity to the rest of mankind," he writes, "must we not conclude that they are a different species of the same genus?" (p. 356)

The Jews, on the other hand, were not viewed as being by nature mentally inferior. It was their religious tradition and practices which deadened their minds and which prevented them from knowing and appreciating the achievements of modern thought.[17] The Jewish people, therefore, were a step above the Blacks because they had the human potential to overcome their narrow thinking and to channel their abilities into what the thinkers of the age thought were the right directions. Thus, David Hume could refer to his talented friend, Isaac de Pinto, as a "good

---

[15]David Hume, "Of Natural Characters" in *Philosophical Works* Vol. III ed. by T.H. Green and T.H. Gross (London: 1882), p. 252.
[16]Folarim Olawale Shyllon, *Black People in Britain* 1555-1833 (London: Oxford University Press, 1977), p. 199.
[17]Richard Popkin, "The Philosophical Basis of Eighteenth-Century Racism" in *Studies in Eighteenth-Century Culture: Racism in the Eighteenth Century*, ed. Harold E. Pagliaro (Cleveland: Case Western Reserve University Press, 1973), p. 250.

man tho a Jew."[18] He would not have said the same thing about a person of color.

There were Blacks who did manage to overcome the prejudices against them and achieve prominence in English society. Francis Barber was Samuel Johnson's manservant, trusted confidant and heir. Job Ben Solomon translated Arabic manuscripts and could write out the Qur'an from memory. He was idolized by polite society – wined and dined by those who were fascinated that a black could excel as a scholar. Ignatius Sancho, an admirer of Laurence Sterne, became a familiar figure in London's literary and political circles. Philip Quaque was born in Africa and educated in England. Following his ordination as a priest by the Bishop of London, he returned to the Gold Coast as an Anglican missionary. He was praised for his efforts by the Society for the Propagation of the Gospel in Foreign Parts; his learning and devotion to his calling was used as proof of the weakness of Hume's racist theories.[19] Olaudah Equiano, who had been kidnapped into slavery and who heroically regained his freedom, was deeply involved in the abolitionist cause and the quest for racial justice. His very popular and widely acclaimed autobiography, which was published in 1789, gave the English people a painfully realistic portrayal of the Black experience.

Talented people, who are members of despised minority groups, tend to elicit a certain amount of wonder from members of the majority culture. Obstacles may often be placed in their paths to keep them out of the mainstream. Yet, when these barriers are overcome, those rare few find a very special place for themselves in a normally hostile society. The honors, of course, are invariably reserved for them alone, and not for their group as a whole. They are simply the exception that proves the rule. By the same token, in eighteenth century England, Black clerics, literary figures, and scholars may have become prominent in their particular fields. However, this adoration was rarely translated in any meaningful way into respect for Black abilities in general.

Elisabeth Young-Bruel stresses the differences between racism and anti-Semitism, and she warns of the dangers of over-generalizing prejudices against people of color.[20] Certainly, many of the London poor who made up the anti-naturalization mobs of 1753, and who chanted slogans against the Jewish people often befriended Black fugitives. Nevertheless, there are certain parallels between these two "isms." For

---

[18]Ibid., See also Richard Popkin, "Hume and Isaac de Pinto." *Texas Studies in Literature and Language* 12 (1970): 417-30.

[19]*Gentleman's Magazine* 41 (Supplement, 1771): 596.

[20]Elisabeth Young-Bruel notes: "Antisemites will tend to become, as it were, all-purpose bigots. But racism, more rooted in conflicts with the id, does not have this generalizing dynamic: it is more single-minded, single focused" (p. 55).

example, the English admiration for the biblical Jews that was accompanied by a general disdain for their modern flesh and blood descendants had certain parallels with their attitudes towards the Blacks prior to their arrival in the country. Though, as previously mentioned, individuals concerned about maintaining the Africa Trade did portray them as subhumans, there were many Britons who viewed the African natives as being noble and virtuous savages who were on a higher moral plane than "civilized" people. Not only did these sentiments appear in the tracts that condemned slavery, but on the stage as well.

In Archibald McLaren's (b.1755) play, *Negro Slaves; or the Blackman and Blackbird,* the plot centers around Quako, a noble slave on a plantation in the United States, who is badly mistreated by his master, Racoon. Quako's goodness and concern for others constantly provokes Racoon who exclaims: "The Savage has the impudence to think, nay even speak like a Christian" (1.1.). When the slave sets one of his master's caged Blackbirds free, he is told that for such a deed his beloved wife Sela will be taken from him and sold to another master. Ultimately, through the kindness of an Englishman who himself had been enslaved by the Indians, both Quako and Sela are set free. In the preface to the play, McLaren notes that when he served with the British Army in Philadelphia, he met a "Black man who, far from being ignorant, could read, write, speak, sing and dance in a stile far superior to many of the common rank of White People." He was amazed to learn that he had acquired this knowledge through his own diligence and the kindness of a genuinely caring Englishman.(p. 2). The farther away in time that the Jews were, the more they were admired by the majority culture. For the Blacks, the greater the distance they were from England's shores, the more praise and compassion they received.

The Blacks, like the Jews, were also prime candidates for conversion to Christianity ; the motives behind such activity are patently clear in many of the missionary tracts of the period. Samuel Davies, in his work, *The Duties of Christians to Propagate their Religion among Heathens,* claims that "A black skin, African birth or extract, or a state of slavery, does not disqualify a man for the blessing of the Gospel; does not cast him out of the charge of its ministers"(p. 15). However, the flaws in his sense of humanity become quite apparent in the way that he views the Blacks. He notes, for example, that Jesus' death upon the cross was for Africans as well as for the British people. It was for the "contemptible Negroes" as well as for the Whites (p. 17). However, their conversion has practical value for "there never was a good Christian yet, who was a bad servant. To be a Christian....is to be obedient to superiors." Furthermore, conversion to Christianity, he believes, "will make them better servants than the terror of the lash" (pp. 27-28). Other missionary literature, though more humane, perpetuated the stereotype of the basic inferiority of the Blacks while praising the efforts of those who tried to convert them to Christianity. For example, in the tract, *The Black Prince, a True story; Being an Account of the Life and Death of Naibanna, An African King's Son*, there is a glowing account of how a young Black, who was sent to England to learn the ways of the country, becomes convinced of the need to bring Jesus into his life. Though the author praises the African's decision, his general attitude towards the innate qualities of the Blacks is in keeping with the spirit of the times. He notes:

> May we not conclude, from the above story,
> that God has given the most rude and savage
> people, minds capable of knowing, loving, and
> serving him. And may we not learn hence, to
> cherish sentiments of kindness and affection
> towards all men, what ever be their colour, or
> however low they may stand in the scale of
> human beings (p. 14)

It is, after all, with a "child like simplicity" that the Black Prince comes to embrace Christianity.

Though much was written about the need to convert the Blacks (as it had been about the Jews), this does not mean that they were readily accepted into the fold. There were those who were skeptical that the baptismal fount could change them into true Christians. This cynicism and prejudice is quite evident in an account of an "uncommon christening" of a Black baby at the Parish Church of St. Giles's Cripplegate that appears in *The Penny London Post* of March 23, 1726. The reporter notes that in the procession the "reputed father, a Guiney Black, a very well-drest fellow" came first along with the Godfather. They were followed by "the midwife, or rather her deputy, a white woman, carrying the little footy Pagan, who was to be metamorphosed into a Christian." Following them came the mother "who was also a Black, but not of the Guiney Breed, a well shap'd. well dress'd genteel woman." Finally, the Godmother appeared, "attended by six or eight more, all Guiney Blacks, as pretty genteel girls, as could be girt with a girdle, and setting aside the complexion, enough to tempt an old frozen Anchorite to have crack'd a commandment with any of them." The reporter concludes his account of this event by noting that it caused a great hubbub in the church, but finally "things were so order'd that the young town-born Negro was carr'd home as staunch a believer as any of the European complexion of the same age ever was" (p. 4).

In addition to such stories of conversion to Christianity, newspapers also featured other dimensions of the Black experience at the hands of good Christians that were much more sobering. For example, Hooker's

Weekly Miscellany of March 25, 1737 features a letter from Antigua which describes in gory detail the punishments meted out to blacks who tried to rebel against their owners. The hangings, burnings and other means of execution that "destroyed sixty-nine sensible Negroe men, most of them tradesmen as carpenters, masons, and coopers" sickens the writer who wishes that he could leave the island and find employment in England (p. 4). Those Blacks who took part in a slave insurrection in South Carolina were treated slightly better. Hooker's *Weekly Miscellany* of March 22, 1739 notes that :

> Such as were taken in the field also,
> were after being examined, shot on the spot;
> and this is to be said of the Carolina Planters,
> that not withstanding the provocation they had
> received from so many Negroes they did not torture
> one Negroe, but only put them to an easy death (p. 3).

The story of the growth of anti- slavery sentiment in late eighteenth century England, and its ultimate success in the nineteenth is beyond the scope of this book. There is, however, one dimension to this movement that should be considered within the context of protean prejudice. It is possible for truly noble causes that have already gained significant support to be spurred on by false pride and also by negative feelings directed towards new objects of prejudice. Linda Colley believes that the anti-slavery movement in England became so prominent in the 1780s and not sooner, because it was at that time that the nation had to reaffirm its unique commitment to liberty after an unsuccessful colonial war had called it into question. The fact that the newly created United States of America still used slave labor provided the English people with a reason to show their moral superiority. She believes that the Black slaves were the beneficiaries not only of humanitarian zeal, but also of the need to redeem a sense of national honor and to put some of England's former and present enemies in their places.[21]

The debates concerning whether or not slavery and the slave trade would be tolerated, and the vast amount of literature that was generated by both sides kept the Blacks in the public eye. Images of the over-sexed subhuman came into conflict with those of the noble savage who had been wronged by "civilized" society. There were those who argued that the Negroes' defects in form and complexion made them a lower order of human beings than the Europeans. On the other hand, public figures like Joseph Spence (1699-1768), Sir Joshua Reynolds (1723-1792), and William Hogarth (1697-1764) maintained, through reasoned discourses, that definitions of beauty were relative; that black and white were

---

[21]Colley, p. 354.

equally beautiful. These were more than an intellectual exercises, but arguments for the common humanity of both races.[22]

For any number of reasons, slavery would be abolished in the early part of the next century, but for the free Blacks of England and other people of color, the real struggle for social equality was just beginning. "Caricature rather than truth" continued to be the hallmark of the English impression of the Blacks.[23] As the twentieth century writer, Salman Rushdie, notes:

> You talk about the Race Problem, the Immigration
> Problem, all sorts of problems. If you are liberal,
> you say that black people have problems. If you
> aren't, you say that they are the problem. But the
> members of the new colony have only one real
> problem, and that problem is white people. British
> racism, of course, is not our problem. [24]

The Gypsies

Our horses they take,
Our wagons they break,
And us they fling
Into horrid cells,
Where hunger dwells
And vermin sting

When the dead swallow
The fly shall follow
Across the river,
O we'll forget
The wrongs we've met,
But till then O never:
    Brother, of that be certain.
(Sorrowful Years)[25]

Along with those who emigrated to England from lands of economic and religious oppression or who came as slaves, there were the Gypsies, who, in their unique way, added to the ethnic and racial stereotypes of the time. In the medieval world, religious aliens who did not conform to Church teachings were not tolerated. In more modern times, this prejudice was extended to those who appeared to be foreign in customs,

---

[22]David Dabydeen, "References to Blacks in William Hogarth's Analysis of Beauty," *British Journal for Eighteenth-Century Studies* 5 (No. 1 Spring, 1982): 94-95.
[23]Walvin, p. 71.
[24]Cited in Helga Quadflieg, "Across Borders; Beyond Borders: Perspectives of a Multicultural Society," *Journal for the Study of British Culture*, 1 (1994): 153-54.
[25]George Borrow, *Word Book of the Romany: or English Gypsy Language* (London: John Murray, 1874), p. 211.

dress, speech, and language.[26] In each of these areas, the Gypsies could easily compete with the Jews for the attention and the distrust of the masses.

The original Gypsy exodus was probably out of India some time in the tenth century. Their very name suggests, however, that it was generally believed that they originally came from Egypt. Various folk tales were created to explain the origins of this mysterious group of wanderers whose dark complexion, strange language, and exotic customs set them apart from the indigenous population. Early legends connect them with the crucifixion of Jesus. In the most popular of these stories, a Gypsy blacksmith was the only person willing to forge the nails that were used on the Cross. Of the four that he made, three were used by the Romans in the Crucifixion while the fourth, which remained red hot, pursued the Gypsy blacksmith to the ends of the earth. It reappears in the tents of his descendants when they find a comfortable place to settle, and it causes them to flee in terror and to continually move from place to place.[27] Gypsy migrations were also explained as a punishment of exile for their failure to give help to the Holy Family during its flight to Egypt.[28]

The similarity of these stories with the Legend of the Wandering Jew demonstrates how both the Jews and the Gypsies were bound together by a common theological hatred which provided a religious pretext for persecution and degradation. This shared prejudice, which continued with additional embellishments through the centuries, was perpetuated by both groups' very marked differences from the world around them. In medieval times, both Jews and Gypsies were accused of bringing the Bubonic plague to Europe. As pariah peoples, both were forced to live apart from the native population; Gypsy settlements were often found next to the Jewish Ghettos. In Spain, they were both subjected to Ferdinand and Isabella's decree of expulsion in 1492.[29]

The Gypsies are, in the words of Isabel Fonseca, the "quintessential strangers."[30] Driven from country to country, they have refused to give up their distinctive way of life, and in many instances their suffering parallels that of the Jews. They became the object of the scorn of all strata of society and of both the Catholic and Protestant churches. Among the

---

[26]Rosemary Reuther, "The Theological Roots of Anti-Semitism" in *The Persisting Question: Sociological Perspectives and Social Contexts of Modern Antisemitism* ed. Helen Fein (Berlin, New York: De Gruyter, 1987), pp. 42-43.
[27]Marlene Sway, *Familiar Strangers: Gypsey Life in America* (Urbana: University of Illinois Press, 1988), pp. 39-40.
[28]Angus Fraser, *The Gypsies* (Oxford: Blackwell Publishers, 1992), p. 86.
[29]Ibid., p. 41.
[30]Isabel Fonseca, *The Gypsies and Their Journey* (New York: Alfred A. Knopf, 1995).

many accusations leveled against them were those of child stealing, cannibalism, and witchcraft. In addition, these "others" were often viewed as sorcerers and practitioners of black magic – members of a sect who had made a pact with Satan and who cursed God. Like the Jewish people, they were often viewed as being less than human. Prejudice against them was often more severe than anti-Semitism, and both physical and cultural genocide plagued them throughout their history.[31]

It is generally accepted that the Gypsies first came to the British Isles around the year 1490. One band crossed over to Ireland while the other went north to Scotland. At first, they were regarded as Christian Pilgrims in need of alms. When their true identity was discovered, they were scorned by the local populace. Perhaps the earliest mention of Gypsies in England appears in *A Dialogue of Sir Thomas More* where one of the witnesses at an inquest into the death of Richard Hunne is referred to as an Egyptian woman who could tell marvelous things by simply looking at a person's hands.[32] In 1530, an official report gives a more detailed perception of the Gypsies describing them as follows:

> Diverse and many outlandish people calling themselves Egyptians, using no craft or feat or merchandise....have gone from shire to shire and place to place in great company and used great and subtle means to deceive the people, bearing them in hand that they by palmistry could tell men's and women's fortunes, and many times by craft and subtlety have deceived the people of their money and have also committed many heinous felonies and robberies to the great hurt and deceit of the people they have come among.[33]

England followed the pattern of persecution that was prevalent on the Continent. In 1530, when there were now about 15,000 Gypsies in the country, the first anti-Gypsy act was passed which threatened the confiscation of all goods of any such person entering the country. Later, in 1547, Edward VI instituted a law which required that any Gypsies found in the country were to be branded with a "V" and enslaved for two years to a master who might put them to use "by beating, chaining, or otherwise, in such work and labour as he saw fit." If they attempted to escape, Gypsies were to be branded with an "S" and made slaves for life. It was too difficult to effectively enforce these laws; two years later they

---

[31]Walter Starkie, *In Sara's Tents* (New York: E.P. Dutton & Co., 1953), p. 42.

[32]Sir Thomas More, *A dyalogue of Syr Thomas More, knt.* (London: 1529), book 3, ch. 15. in Fraser, pp. 113-14.

[33]Nebojsa Bato Tomasevic and Rajko Djuric, *Gypsies of the World: A Journey into the Hidden World of Gypsey Life and Culture* (New York: Henry Holt, 1988), p. 260.

were repealed. During the reign of Elizabeth, Gypsies were persecuted for allegedly harboring in their midst priests and emissaries of Rome who had come to England to stir up a rebellion against the Crown. By the seventeenth century it was a hanging offense to even associate with them. During the second half of the century, Parliament dealt with the "Gypsy Problem" by deporting them to the British plantations in Virginia, Jamaica, and Barbados where they were placed in servitude along with beggars, debtors, and criminals. In 1714, British merchants and planters applied to the Privy Council for permission to ship Gypsies to the Islands of the Caribbean to be used as slaves.[34]

For obvious reasons, Gypsies tried to maintain a low profile and avoid the authorities. Yet, their dark complexions, their seemingly unintelligible language, and their nefarious ways of earning a living, kept them in public view. They also attracted the attention of writers who used them, as they did the Jews, for various literary purposes. Ben Jonson (1573?-1637)in his masque, *The Gypsies Metamorrphos'd*, has them serve as a mirror to reveal some dangerous truths about contemporary society. Yet, at the same time he also perpetuates the stereotype of their roguish cunning, their love of the dance, and their fortune telling skills. In the masque, their songster, the Jackman, sings a ballad of a Gypsy captain who held a banquet in Derbyshire for the Devil. Like Jews, they have magical and supernatural powers that set them apart from society. In *The Adventures of Joseph Andrews*, Henry Fielding (1707-1754) describes a death bed confession of a woman who "had formerly traveled in a company of gipsies who had made a practice of stealing away children "(Book IV Chapter 12). This theme of using Gypsies to account for lost children who were stolen from their parents also appears in the first chapter of Daniel Defoe's novel, *The Fortunes and Misfortunes of the Famous Moll Flanders*. In *The History of Tom Jones*, Fielding's hero and his companions come across "a company of Egyptians, or, as they are vulgarly called, Gipsies," celebrating a wedding. It is noted that "it is impossible to conceive a happier set of people than appeared to be met together." In addition, "These people are subject to a formal government and laws of their own, and all pay obedience to one great magistrate, whom they call king." Here, the author contrasts simple, Gypsy life with the false trappings of civilized society. The Gypsy King speaks to them in a broken English, similar to that of the fictional Jew.

> Me doubt not, sir, but you have often
> seen some of my people who are what
> you call de parties detache, for dey go

---

[34]Ian Hancock, *The Pariah Syndrome* (Ann Arbor, Michigan: Karona Publications, 1987), pp. 89-92.

> about everywhere; but me fancy you
> imagine not we be so considerable body
> as we be, and maybe you will surprise
> more when you hear de Gipsy be as
> orderly and as well governed as any upon
> face of de earth (Book XII: Chapter 12).

It also becomes quite evident that he is part of a pariah people when he tells Jones: "For me know and hears good deal of your people, dough me no live among them. "The Gypsy King appears to be a likable rogue rather than a villain when he makes the observation: "How de difference is between you and us. My people rob your people, and your people rob one another" (Book XII, Chapter 12).

Articles in the popular press are less charitable. One of them that appears in the *London Daily Post* for September 11,1740, resembles modern accounts of street gangs fighting over the control of their turf.

> We hear that last week, a large body of
> strolling Gypsies, that had got beyond
> Sitingborn in Kent, were met with by a
> company of others, who call themselves
> Gypsies of Kent, and insisted, that the
> others had no right to incroach on their
> liberties; Beacking -Hill was the place fixed
> on for a meeting the next day, where a
> battle ensued, and after a very obstinate fight
> on both sides, the Kentish heroes, put the
> others to flight.

Mist's Weekly Journal for March 12, 1726 also warns of the dangers posed by these "idle vagabond people called Gypsies" who, by pretending to tell fortunes, cheat the young, ignorant, and unwary. Those who had been victims of their fraudulent schemes are urged to help the authorities to prosecute them.

Chap Books, printed by societies concerned with religious and moral values, describe how the Gypsies swindle honest people and, at the same time, undermine the authority of both the Church and the State. In one of them, *Tawney Rachel; or The Fortune Teller: With Some Account of Dreams, Omens, and Conjurors*, the reader is advised:

> Never fancy that you are compelled to
> undo yourself, or to rush upon your own
> destruction, in compliance with any
> supposed fatality. Never believe that
> God conceals his will from a sober
> Christian who obeys his laws, and
> reveals it to a vagabond gipsey, who
> runs up and down breaking the laws,
> both of God and man (p. 16).

In January, 1753 an incident occurred which focused unprecedented public attention upon the Gypsies of England. Elizabeth Canning, an eighteen year scullery maid, was missing from the sixth to the twenty-ninth of the month. When she finally returned home, she claimed that she had been carried off by two men who had beaten her near Bedlam Wall and then dragged her ten miles to a secluded house in Enfield Wash. There, an old Gypsy woman and her accomplice had robbed her of her stays – a crime punishable by death – and tried to force her into prostitution. When she refused, she was locked in a room and fed only bread and water to induce her to change her mind. After several days, she managed to break a window and escape her captors.. During her questioning by the authorities, it was deduced that she had been taken to the house of a certain Mother Wells and that the Gypsy woman in question was Mary Squires. Canning identified the alleged culprits who were subsequently tried and convicted. The Gypsy was condemned to death, and her accomplice was to be branded and imprisoned.

Arthur Machen believes that nothing during the reign of George II equaled the "furious and ferocious folly" that was generated over the Canning Trial. All semblance of common sense and common justice was lost as the hideous vice of Mary Squires and the superhuman virtue of Elizabeth Canning was bandied about.[35] Passions were so inflamed by the Canning Trial, that the City of London was divided into "Canningites" and "Egyptians". Fighting frequently broke out in the streets; a mob gathered outside the court house to prevent anyone from entering the building who might give favorable testimony for the defense. In addition, papers were handed out during the trial that were designed to stir up prejudice against the accused as well as Gypsies in general. However, the mob did not need the printed word to excite them. They "responded vigorously to a stark story of good and evil; of wicked gypsies, an old bawd and a poor innocent girl who defended her virginity."[36]

The trial had all the ingredients of a medieval mystery play with the Gypsies replacing the wicked Jews. Even those who tried to be impartial in their reporting of the proceedings did not refer to Mary Squires by name, but wrote about "the Gypsy" just as they used the pejorative term, "the Jew," to refer to Jewish criminals.[37] Henry Fielding (1707-1754) turned the trial into a contest between the forces of light and darkness. He claimed that Elizabeth Canning was a young girl who had no motive

---

[35]Arthur Machen, *The Canning Wonder* (London: Chatto and Windus, 1925), p. 13.
[36]John Treherne, *The Canning Enigma* (London: Jonathan Cape, 1989),p. 157.
[37]*Gentleman's Magazine*, 23 (March, 1753): 107-11. This is the first time that the complete story is told in the magazine.

to ruin other lives while the defendants were "street robbers and gipsies who have scarce even the appearance of humanity." They were sub-humans who were capable of committing crimes of "wanton cruelty" against their innocent victims.[38] John Hill, who along with Lord Mayor of London, did not believe Canning's story, notes in his account of the affair, that "it was immediately resolved that nothing less than a human sacrifice could expiate the flagitious assault upon her (Elizabeth Canning's) chastity."[39] In addition, publicity about the trial brought up other alleged Gypsy crimes which afforded "a good opportunity for an invective against the Gipsies." [40] He claims that to prevent a pardon, stories were spread that the witnesses for the prosecution had been intimidated and that the whole neighborhood of Enfield was threatened with a "general conflagration."[41]

Ultimately, Mary Squires provided an alibi which exonerated her of any wrong doing. Elizabeth Canning, on the other hand, was now found guilty of perjury, and she was sentenced to transportation to the American Colonies. Unfortunately, for the Gypsies as a group the trial had a negative effect upon their place in English society. It brought up, for example, the whole issue of their right to live in the country. In an article that appears in the *Gazetter* of April 3,1753, it is noted that according to several statutes Gypsies are not permitted to enter the country. If they violate the law, they are to be treated as felons, their property is to be confiscated and they, and anyone seen in their company, is to be put to death. Negative stereotypes abounded in the press where accounts of their brutality and their cunning accompanied by scathing denunciations of their alleged crimes were duly reported. In the *Daily Advertiser* of February 16, 1753 it is noted that during the trial "the old Gipsey behaved as a person traditionally and hereditarily versed in the ancient Egyptian cunning." On February 28, 1753, there is an account in this newspaper of a man who had been beaten by two Gypsy men and three of their women. The writer concludes his reporting of the incident with the statement: "This is a further instance of their barbarity to our subjects and shews the immediate necessity of rooting these villains out of their dens." The public's reaction to the trial also shows how the old prejudices against witches had now shifted to the Gypsies. In a contemporary cartoon, Mary Squires appears in witch's

---

[38]Henry Fielding, *A Clear State of the Case of Elizabeth Canning* (London: 1753), p. 21.
[39]Hill, John. *The Story of Elizabeth Canning Considered* (London: 1753), p. 60.
[40]Ibid., p. 62.
[41]Ibid., p. 66.

garb flying on a broomstick.[42] In another, she and Sir Crisp Gascoygne, walking hand in hand, are on the shoulders of four witches.[43]

The uproar over the Canning Trial and its aftermath also drew some attention away from the controversy over the naturalization of foreign Jews. On page 246 of the *Gentleman's Magazine* for May 1753 it is noted under the events of Monday, the twenty- second, of the month that a royal pardon was granted for Mary Squires. For Tuesday, the twenty-third, there is a notice of a bill entitled, "An Act to Permit Persons Professing the Jewish Religion to be Naturalized by Parliament." In the *Scots Magazine* for July 1753, under the heading of new books, two titles appear. The first, *The Jew Naturalized or the English Alienated: A Ballad*, is immediately followed by *The Devil Outdone A Contest between Elizabeth Canning, Mary Squires, and Dr._____ A Ballad.*

Even after the furor over the trial had died down, Gypsies continued to appear in the press. A poor command of the English language and a dark complexion, part of the stereotypical image of the Jew, continued to be used to identify them. For example, *The London Chronicle* of January 24, 1761 mentions the presence of a band of Gypsies at Norwood who spoke a very bad English and who were "blacker than those who formerly used to be there."

For the great bulk of the English people, religion was a stabilizing element in life, and those who professed atheism were not to be trusted. When the Gypsies first appeared in Europe they claimed to be Catholic penitents. In time, their deception was uncovered, and they had the reputation of being unbelievers who possessed no moral code. This intensified the usual distrust of strangers and resulted in strong anti-Gypsy prejudice that continued into the modern period.

The first European thinker to concern himself with the Gypsies' religious and moral convictions is Heinrich Grellman, whose book, *Dissertation on the Gypsies*, printed in London in 1787, is a translation of an earlier German work that was popular on the Continent. Grellman shows little sympathy either for their spiritual beliefs or their ethical practices. Not only are the Gypsies unbelievers, but they have an aversion to everything that is related to religion, and they are even lower than the heathens(p. 60). Grellman advocates force to reform them into useful citizens; calling for missionaries to go out and to bring them the knowledge of God. Since the adults are already set in their ways, he believes that Gypsy children should be separated from their parents and

---

[42]Treheme, p. 138.
[43]George Paston, *Social Caricature in the Eighteenth Century* (1905; rpt. New York : Benjamin Bloom, 1968), pp. 101-102.

given a thorough training in Christian beliefs and practices. Grellman rejects banishment and slavery because it is too difficult and too expensive to carry out (p. 85). In the whole context of eighteenth century anti-Gypsy sentiment, Grellman's ideas were not that extreme. Attempts were made in both Austria-Hungary and in Spain to take Gypsy children away from their parents and to educate them in government schools so that they would lose their distinctive dress, language, culture, music, and nomadic way of life.

From the beginnings of their experience in England, the Gypsies were subjected to much harsher persecution than the Jews. They did not have the wealth or the connections abroad that would give the English any reason to find them to be potentially useful or productive members of society. Not only were they strangers, but they were poor, "rogues and vagabonds" who upset the orderly social structure that the English prized so highly. Jews were perceived, at least by some of the English, as willing to send their children to Christian schools and to be part of the Christian world. This was not a possibility for the Gypsies nor was it considered to be very desirable. If Jews were not in the Christian fold, they could be shown the truth by example and by love. For the Gypsies, there was only the rod and the whip.

5

Secret and Sinful "Others"

The Masons

That noe p'son shalbe accepted a Free
Mason, or know the secrets of the said
Society until hee hath first taken the oath
of secrecy hereafter following : I, A.B. doe
in the presence of Almighty God, and my
fellowes, and brethren here present, promise
and declare, that I will not at any time hereafter,
by any act or circumstances whatsoever,
directly or indirectly, publish, discover, reveale,
or make knowne any of the secrets, priviledges,
or counsells, of the fraternity or fellowship of
Free Masonry, which at this time, or any time
hereafter, shalbee made known unto mee soe
helpe me God, and the holy contents of this booke.[1]

On Monday last the Ancient and Honourable
Society of Free and Accepted Masons met at
Mercer's Hall in Cheapside, where there was a
great appearance of nobility and gentry.... three
Dukes, three Earls, four Barons, four Baronets,
and several other gentlemen of distinction.....the
Right Honourable the Lord Inchequin was chosen
Grand Master for the ensuing year.[2]

Another group who, to a lesser degree, was considered to be a threat
to the establishment on both religious and patriotic grounds was the
Masons. Like the Jews of Europe and the Huguenots of France, they were

---

[1]Article 31 of "The New Articles." Cited in Edward Conder, *Hole Crafte and
Fellowship of Masons* (London: Swan Sonnenschein & Co., 1894), p. 226.
[2]*Mist's Weekly Journal* March 4, 1727 p. 2.

branded as "a state within a state."[3] Nevertheless, they offered the educated elite a kind of sociability normally associated with religious organizations, but without the unique claims to salvation and the enthusiasm that was scorned by so many of them.[4]

The Masons, with their secrets, signs, passwords, symbolic rituals, and exotic initiation ceremonies, stressed the need for strong bonds of loyalty among the brethren that went beyond national ties. Their presence made many of the English very uneasy, particularly during periods of national emergency when the country was threatened with invasion. Because the Masons shrouded themselves in mystery and kept their meetings closed to the public, it is not surprising that stories of sodomy and flagellation were circulated about them in the press and by word of mouth.[5] Secrecy encouraged in the public mind a definite feeling of suspicion and hatred. In an article on Freemasonry in the London Magazine of April, 1737 the author feels that "this mysterious society hath too much the air of an inquisition, where everything is transacted in the dark." He urges the government to keep a close watch on their activities and to take action against them if necessary (pp. 200-201). "Coming out of the closet," however, did not solve the problem. For example, it was the custom at annual assemblies for all the Masons of London to gather in their ritual costumes and parade through the streets before attending an election banquet for their new Grand Master. Because of public prejudices that were directed against these secret "others", Masonic processions were jeered and mock ones were often organized. This forced the Masons, like other targeted groups, to suspend any public display of their rituals and to keep a low profile.[6]

Prejudices against the Masons were as contradictory as any that were historically directed against the Jews. For example, though English Freemasonry was created by Huguenots and Dissenters, in *The Grand Mystery of Free Masons,* a book printed in 1723, they were accused of being Jesuits in disguise. In a typical anti-Masonic article in the *Gentleman's Magazine* for February, 1733, one of their critics speculates

---

[3]Jacob Katz, *Jews and Freemasons in Europe 1723 -1939* (Cambridge, Massachusetts: Harvard University Press, 1970), p. 223.

[4] Harry Payne, "Elite Versus Popular Mentality" in *Studies in Eighteenth Century Culture* Vol 8, ed. Roseann Runte (Madison: University of Wisconsin Press, 1979)p. 15. A Masonic "creed" of the 1720's only required following "that religion in which all men agree, leaving their particular opinions to themselves, that is, to be good men and true, or men of honour and honesty, by whatever denominations or persuasions they may be distinguished." See J.M. Roberts, *Mythology of the Secret Societies* (London: Secker and Warburg, 1974), p. 38.

[5]Roberts, *Mythology),*p. 60.

[6]Bernard Fay, *Revolution and Freemasonry 1680-1800* (Boston: Little Brown & Co., 1935), p. 144.

about the origin of their name. He does not believe that it is derived from the word, "Mass," "because," he notes, "so many zealous Protestants nay, even Jews, the constant enemies to transubstantiation, are accepted brethren"(pp. 68-9). Later, at the time of the French Revolution, when anti-Masonic sentiment was at its peak, they were condemned for joining with the radicals across the channel to abolish all religion and to overturn governments.

In 1794, the events in France heightened the fears of international subversive activities that would ultimately destroy the cherished English way of life. Abbe Augustin Barruel, a refugee priest, arrived in England filled with venom against those who had directed the course of the French Revolution. Three years later, in his work, *Memoirs Illustrating the History of Jacobitism,* which appeared in both French and English, he views the origins of the Revolution as a double conspiracy against both the Church and the monarchy. He believes that it was aided by Free Masons and other secret societies who were in alliance with the subversives at the forefront of the upheaval in his native land. The works of Voltaire(1694-1778), Rousseau (1712-1778), and Montesquieu(1689-1755) had inspired the Masonic lodges to subvert the existing order in France and throughout Europe. No nation, not even England, he believes, is safe from the teachings of atheism and subversion that has been initiated by the Jacobins and reinforced by their followers.[7] John Robison, the secretary to the Royal Society of Edinburgh, in his work, *Proofs of a Conspiracy Against all the Religions and Governments of Europe,* believes that both the Church and the State are now the targets of the Masons whose secret meetings have become "the rendezvous of innovations in religion and politics and other disturbers of the public peace" (p. 10). He is convinced that this once fraternal organization, "under the specious pretext of enlightening this world by the torch of philosophy," was determined to destroy British standards of morality, root out the religious establishments, and subvert the existing governments of Europe as well (p. 11).

Why then, considering the fears of the people, were the Masons not hunted down by the authorities? J.M. Roberts claims that England, unlike other countries on the Continent, did not have a legal tradition of prejudice against voluntary organizations. The fact that many of the Masons came from the leading families of the country also removed the taint of treason from them.[8] In addition, there were any number of other

---

[7]Abbe Augustin Barruel, *Memoirs Illustrating the History of Jacobitism* p. 399. Cited in Bernard Schilling, *Conservative England and the Case Against Voltaire* (New York: Octagon Books, 1976),p. 259.
[8]Roberts, p. 59, p. 207.

secret clubs and organizations with even more disturbing practices that drew attention away from them. Like the Jews, the Masons found that there were certain benefits for living in a society where there were so many other clandestine groups – objects of different kinds of prejudice

Revelers and Sodomists

On Monday night, a gang of twenty five persons
in masquerade habits, suspected to be Sodomists,
were apprehended in a house in Mart Street
near Covent garden, and secur'd in several
prisons, in order to examination, some of whom
we hear have before been convicted, and stood
in the pillary for that crime.[9]

Thomas wright, woolcomber, aged 32 years,
was convicted for committing Buggery on the
body of Thomas Newton: he was born at Newberry,
was an Anabaptist; he said also that Newton swore
falsely against him, but could not deny that he follow'd
these abominable courses, but would not make a
particular confession. He said he lov'd the Church of England.[10]

The history of sodomy in the eighteenth century is not
simply the history of repression. It encapsulates the
history of all society. It can provide a key to unlock the
mysteries of the history of gender, sexuality, individual
identity, human society's relationship to the physical world,
and even (it has been claimed) the mysteries of
the rise of modern capitalism.[11]

Many clerics believed that it was the "infamous clubs of Atheists, Deists, and Socinians" who were leading the people astray and which encouraged swearing, cursing, and "prophanation of the Lord's Day." They made it mandatory for "the children of light" to form their own societies to combat such evil influences.[12] These "clubs and confederacies" that propagated so much wickedness were viewed by these clerics as challenging the very foundations of society. It was in such secret settings that people gathered both to scoff at religion by "loose atheistical discourses" and to "debauch and abuse themselves by those

---

[9]*British Journal* January 2,1725.
[10]*The Penny London Post* May 13, 1726.
[11]Randolph Trumbach, " Sodomitical Subcultures, Sodomitical Roles, and the Gender Revolution of the Eighteenth Century: The Recent Historiography," *History of Homosexuality in Europe and America* vol 5. eds, Wayne R. Dynes and Stephen Donaldson. (New York & London: Garland Publishers Inc., 1992), p. 109.
[12]*A Short Account of the Several Kinds of Societies Set Up of the Late Years for Carrying on the Reformation of Manners, and for the Propagation of Christian Knowledge* (London: Printed by J. Brundell, 1700), pp. 1-3.

beastly acts of lust and intemperance."[13] The prosecution of those who were a part of such groups was not considered to be persecution, but "the duty of the magistrate from the word of God."[14] Those who claimed to be on the side of religion and virtue formed such organizations as the Society for the Reformation of Manners. They could take pride in the fact that thousands were punished for disorderly and lewd conduct by being imprisoned, fined, and whipped, and that many of the streets of London had been purged of
prostitutes."[15]

Defenders of public morality attacked the Masquerades, a form of secret behavior, which provided people with the "opportunity to say and do there, what virtue, decency, and good manners will not permit to be said or done in any other place." [16] In such a setting, to the disgust of many clerics, luxury, immodesty, and extravagance in word or deed could be practiced freely without any sense of personal responsibility.

Sodomitical Clubs were important targets of these moralists. In the May 4, 1726 issue of *The Penny London Post*, there is a lengthy article on these reputed dens of iniquity. The author claims that at least twenty houses have been discovered. In addition, there are numerous "nocturnal assemblies" at the Royal-Exchange, Moorfields, Lincoln's Inn, St. James Park, and the Piazzas of Covent-Garden. Here these sinners "make their bargains and then withdraw into some dark corners to indorse, as they call it, but in pain English to commit Sodomy." The reader is reassured that "strict care will be taken to detect them," in order to avert the judgments from heaven which destroyed Sodom and Gomorrah whose "sons of perdition" resembled the English Sodomites in their "aversion to the female sex" and who "lusted after the angels, believing them to be men" (p. 3). Judging from the following verses of a street Ballad, The *Long Vocation* (1700), Sodomy was not always a clandestine practice.

> When Sodomites were so impudent to ply on th' Exchange And by *Daylight* the Piazzas of Covent Garden to range.[17]

---

[13]Thomas Penn, *A Sermon Preach'd Before the Society For Reformation of Manners* (London: Printed for J. Humfreys, 1708), p. 27.

[14]*An Account of the Societies for Reformation of Manners in England and Ireland* (London: 1700), pp. 1 -2.

[15]*Ibid.*, p. 17. Charles Mitchen, Deputy City Marshall, a man described by the press as "an active fellow for promoting the reformation of manners," was himself convicted of committing "the detestable crime" of sodomy. See *Mist's Weekly Journal* May 20, 1727.

[16]Edmund Gibson, *A Sermon Preached to the Societies for Reformation of Manners at St. Mary-Le -Bow* (London: Printed for John Wyat, n.d.), p19.

[17]Burford, p. 32.

In the May 13, 1726 issue of *The Penny London Post* the editor notes that: "The following proposal is sent to be inserted in this paper as an expedient humbly propos'd to the Legislature, for suppressing a crime which is the most shocking debasement of human nature." Following this, there is a suggestion for certain methods to be used to "blot out the names of the monstrous wretches under heaven." They include:

> When any are detected, prosecuted, and
> convicted, that after sentence pronounc'd,
> the Common Hangman tie him hand and foot
> before the judge's face in open court, that a
> skillful surgeon be provided immediately to
> take out his testicles, and that then the hangman
> sear up his scrotum with an hot iron, as in cases
> of burning in the hand (p. 4).[18]

Both the zeal in which these defenders of morality hunted down those who violated the norms of English society, and the severity of the punishment is reminiscent of the witch hunters of the prior centuries. In fact, Trumbach believes that the sodomy paranoia that took place in the eighteenth and early nineteenth centuries came about when the English elite no longer believed in witches.[19] Prejudices that had formerly been directed at "supernatural others" were now directed at those who were considered to be "unnatural others," the sodomites. They filled in what might be called the "hate gap" and offered numerous opportunities to be the new objects of persecution.

Prejudice against sodomites, like that against the Jew, had a long history in the country, and in some instances they were linked together. In about 1290, the year of the expulsion of the Jews from England, it was stated in the *Fleta*, a treatise composed by a jurist in Edward I 's (1239-1307) court that:

> Those who have dealings with Jews or Jewesses,
> those who commit bestiality, and sodomites, are to
> be buried alive, after legal proof that they were
> taken in the act, and public conviction.
> (Fleta, xxxvii. 3)[20]

In 1376 Parliament petitioned Edward III (1312-1377) to banish foreign artisans and traders, particularly Jews and Saracens, because they had

---

[18]This is remarkably similar to the punishment for Catholic Priests. It shows either a lack of imagination or that both groups were equal objects of violent hatred.

[19]Randolph Trumbach, "Sodomical Subcultures," p. 391.

[20]*Fleta, seu Commentarius Juris Anglicani* (London: 1735), p. 84. Cited in Derek Sherwin Baily, *Homosexuality and the Western Christian Tradition* (Hamdon, Connecticut: Archon, 1975), p. 145.

introduced "the too horrible vice which is not to be named" into the realm.[21] Throughout the Middle Ages, sodomites were regarded in the same way as sorcerers and heretics, and the general attitude of seeking them out and destroying them, often in the name of religion, continued into the Age of Reason as well.

The fear of these outsiders, their origins, the reasons for their growth, as well as the need to prevent their way of life from spreading, appear in an anonymous tract, written in 1749, Satan's *Harbest Home: or the Present of Whorecraft, Adultery, Fornication, Procuring, Pimping, Sodomy, at the Game at Flatts*. The author believes that the increase in effeminacy is due to overindulging of young men, sending them to girls schools, and from an early age, putting them in the company of women (pp. 47-49). He is particularly disturbed by the effeminacy of men's dress and the "Judas like practice," brought over from Italy, "the mother and nurse of sodomy," of men kissing each other. This foreign influence upon good Britons extends to the French who copy from the Italians. The author notes that in their country "the cantagion is diversify'd and the ladies (in the nunneries) are criminally amorous of each other, in a method too gross for expression" (p. 51).He believes that because of these foreign sins, this "abominable practice gets ground ev'ry day" and that it is time to put a stop to it (p. 53).The author follows the contemporary trend of using the word "Italian" as a synonym for Sodomite. He also uses sodomy to contrast the effeminate and corrupt European nations with manly and virtuous England, a nation that is in danger of being corrupted by these imported vices.[22] Restoration drama, by alluding to its practice in exotic locales, supports the notion of placing the blame on foreign countries for initiating and influencing this sodomitical behavior. Thus, it is Catholic Italy and Moslem Turkey and not Protestant England who spawned and spread this vice.

Severe and often violent punishment was a key component of the exercise of power in eighteenth century England. Penalties were expected to be in accordance with both the severity of the crime as well as the character of the offender. [23]

It is not surprising, therefore, that the emergence of a sodomite subculture and its Mollies brought on severe reprisals by both the

---

[21]Rictor Norton, *Mother Clap's Molly House: The Gay Subculture in England 1700-1830*. London: GMP Publishers Ltd., 1992), p. 15.
[22]Lawrence Senelick, "Molies or Men of Mode? Sodomy and the Eighteenth-Century London Stage," in *History of Homosexuality in Europe and America*, eds. Wayne R. Dynes and Stephen Donaldson (New York and London: Garland Publishers, 1992),p. 316.
[23]Susan Dwyer Amussen, "Punishment, Discipline, and Power," *Journal of British Studies* 34 (January, 1995):19.

authorities and the populace. By the middle of the eighteenth century judges were often reluctant to make buggery a capital crime, but emotions ran so high that anyone who was sent to the pillory even for a relatively short time for attempted sodomy received a virtual death sentence at he hands of the mob. The following article that appears in Hooker's Weekly *Miscellany* of September 23,1737 shows both the harshness of the punishment meted out to sodomites and the intensity of the anger that was directed towards them.

> Last Saturday Thomas Hull, from Leicester, and
> Robert Rawlins, a soldier, stood in the Pillory in
> Wine Street, persuant to their sentence for
> Sodomistical Practices; but never were two
> wretches worse pelted, especially old Hull, who
> was stunn'd several times, and so depriv'd of his
> senses, that he hung some time by the wrists in
> iron handcuffs of the Pillory: after which the mob
> continued pelting with such fury, that had not the
> Pillory broke down, tumbling them backward over
> head and heels on the street, and the magistrates
> with some constables interven'd, they certainly would
> have been killed on the spot. Hull was carried away on
> a man's back to Newgate, where lay speechless and
> thought past recovery till the Monday following (p. 4).

The Sodomites, considered to be subhumans by all strata of society, were, as Senelick points out, "reviled as monstrous sinners and beastly wretches, creatures so like dogs that even the most inhuman treatment of them could be tolerated."[24] Furthermore, it was generally believed that their crime was very different from all others; that it merited severer punishment than murder or rape.[25] The *Penny London Post* of August 1, 1776 notes, for example, that of those prosecuted for sodomy. "three have been lately executed at Tyburn, three stood in the pillory last week, and three have died under prosecution before tryal, viz one in Newgate, one in the Compter, and a third who was out upon bail" (p. 4).

The military reflected the general attitudes and practices of civilian society, and the punishments that were meted out to convicted sodomites were as harsh as those of the civil courts. The Navy treated sodomy among the officers as a more serious crime than homicide; in the minds of the admirals it was closely related to the general breakdown of military order and discipline.[26] Following the catastrophic mutinies at Nore and Spithead in 1797, the execution of sodomites began in earnest.

---

[24]Senelick, p. 129.
[25]Ibid.
[26]Arthur N. Gilbert, "Buggery and the British Navy, 1700-1861," in *History of Homosexuality in Europe and America,* pp. 144-45.

Psychologically, the British navy equated the rebellion of lower class sailors against the command structure with the revolt of the lower elements of the body against its higher faculties. Sodomy, which they believed released the beast in man, "threatened to destroy the principles on which naval performance and survival depended – discipline, self-control, order, and devotion to duty, manliness and honor."[27]

The wearing of ornate, effeminate clothing was also viewed as a threat to the moral order and to the strength of the nation. For example, after the bubble burst, the press characterized the directors of the South Sea Company, as a troupe of eunuchs who dress in women's clothes and who promote "effeminate and sodomitical tastes" in order to weaken the power of the nation.[28]

Interestingly enough, lesbianism is rarely mentioned in contemporary literature. Known as "the Game of Flats," it was generally believed that it was only practiced by upper class women in private and in very select houses. Because women were trivialized by males in positions of power, lesbianism was not viewed as a serious threat to the stability of the country. By and large, it was considered to be an aberration of little consequence that was below the level of a misdemeanor.[29]

---

[27]Ibid., p. 148.
[28]Norton. p. 41.
[29]Burford, p. 166.

6

National "Others"

The French

The French, in Land Armies, are far our Superiors:
They are making large and dreadful Strides towards
us, in *naval Power*. They have more *than disputed*
with us the Empire of the Mediterranean. They are
driving us from our Forts and Colonies in *America*...
Thus by a gradual and unperceived Decline, we seem
gliding down to Ruin. We laugh, we sing, we feast, we
play: We *adopt* every *Vanity*, and catch at every *Lure*,
thrown out to us by the *Nation* that is planning our
Destruction....in our *Fondness* for *French* Manners,
(we) resemble the *Lamb* described by the *Poet* (which)
licks the Hand that's *raised* to *shed his blood*.[1]

(at the Guillotine)....children of ten years old were
slaughtered, as well as old men and women of eighty.[2]

Of all the major European powers, France was perceived to be the
greatest physical and spiritual threat to England's cherished way of life.
There was a long tradition of anti-French sentiment that was nourished
and reinforced through the country's educational system and its press.
Certainly, the awareness of France as England's major military,
commercial, diplomatic, and cultural enemy, was a key ingredient of the
national mentality. Hatred of the French was also one of the few
fundamental beliefs that could be readily accepted by all classes,
religious denominations, and political groups.[3] J.F. Bosher is correct in
his assessment that French foreign policy in the early part of the

---

[1]John Brown, *Estimate of the Manners and Principles of the Times* (London: 1757) pp.
143-45. Cited in Gerald Newman, *The Rise of English Nationalism* (New York: St.
Martin's Press, 1987), p. 83.
[2]*Anti-Jacobin or Weekly Examiner* January 15, 1798.
[3]Newman, p. 75.

eighteenth century posed a greater threat to England than many historians are willing to accept.[4] But beyond this physical danger, which continued to occupy the attention of the people for a good part of the century, France also represented the antithesis of everything that Britons held to be sacred. The stereotypical French person was a liar and a cheat, an artful conniver who resembled the monkey in both appearance and mannerisms.[5]

Not only were French arms a danger on the battlefield, but throughout the century, many believed that the values of this degenerate country would infiltrate England's moral superiority and destroy the country from within. In an article that appeared in the *London Magazine* of July, 1760, the writer begins with the words:

> What at present provokes my pen, is, the
> general madness after French fopperies,
> at a season when that fantastic people are dying
> their robes in the blood of our countrymen, and
> leading all ranks and sexes captives by the
> witchcraft of their luxurious vanity in every excess (p. 335).

He concludes with a plea for a speedy restoration of "ancient virtues and simplicity in manners and apparel, which would be a greater conquest than to possess all France, and the rich mines of all the Indies" (p. 336).

These sentiments were echoed by a countless number of Britons who were concerned about the effect of French luxuries on the solid citizens of the country. One fear, in particular, was that of effeminacy, "foreign foppery", which was perceived to be a threat to English manhood and to the vigor of the nation. Occasionally, in the "Letters to the Editor" columns such fears were shared with the reading public. In The *Weekly Miscellany* of April 19, 1735 a writer expresses dismay that "French and dancing" have become the essential parts of a "British masculine education." He is shocked that boys must have a richly laced waistcoat, play at Quadrille and go to the playhouses so that they can behave as men. In reality, such training simply turns them into Frenchmen. The "Grand Tour," which many felt was an important part of a true gentleman's education, was condemned by those who saw it as a drain on English finances as well as a corrupting influence upon young men. On the front page of *Mist's Weekly* for July 8, 1727, it is noted that:

> Some of the greatest men have laid the foundation
> of their fame in a domestick education only....Let
> us not unbalance the whole solidity of the British

---

[4]J.F. Bosher, "The Franco-Catholic Danger, 1660-1715," *History: The Journal of the Historical Association.* 79 (February, 1994): 13.

[5]Newman, pp. 231-2.

> genius, and lose the critereon of its characters in
> the affection of French accomplishments. We are
> the greatest and richest and freest of all nations;
> let us also be the wisest.

The author believes that the only results of this exposure to the French way of life are "a finical effeminacy, the monkey of dress, the refinement of folly, and the ingenuity of vice."

Sam Foote, in his plays, *The Englishman in Paris* (1753) and *The Englishman Returned from Paris* (1756), portrays the adventures of John Buck who, like many of the young aristocrats, was sent to Paris to polish his manners and to refine his taste. When he returns to England, he is a caricature of French fashion and manners. The hero's outlandish dress and mannerisms reinforced the audience's sense of their own superior British values and virtues. For the average Briton, the very low opinion of the sexual morality on the other side of the Channel was reflected in the popular name, "the French Disease," that was indiscriminately used to label venereal infections.

The middle decades of the eighteenth century were a time for the growth and development of a strong sense of nationalism that was often based on this feeling of British moral superiority. During this period there was a proliferation of processions and country- wide celebrations; the equivalent of our modern media events. The periodicals kept the reading public aware of national politics, and their cartoons of John Bull confronting Nick the Frog and the Russian Bear were an important factor in creating and sustaining national stereotypes.[6] It was a potentially dangerous time for the Jews; a perfect opportunity to unify a nation by purging the "others" from society or by officially denigrating them to a lower social level than the true Britons.

Fortunately for the Jews, the English defined themselves as a nation not by attacks upon them, but through their ongoing conflict with their oldest and bitterest enemy, France. One could be a true "free-born Englishman", a free person living in a free country, simply by not being French. To a great degree, It was this national rivalry and prejudice that raised British self esteem, and which was the basis of their heightened sense of national self-worth.

Hogarth portrays this perception of a superior English way of life, in contrast to that of the French, in his etching, "O the Roast Beef of Old England, Or the Gate of Calais." It depicts a cook staggering under a huge sirloin of beef that he is delivering, from a recently arrived ship, to an English eating-house in the city. A greedy friar, two ragged French

---

[6]Roy Porter, "Georgian Britain: An Ancient Regime," *The British Journal for Eighteenth-Century Studies* 15 (No. 2 Autumn, 1992): 144.

soldiers, and some miserable exiles look on with envy. The beef is the symbol of British vigor and independence; the food of a prosperous and free people. It stands in contrast to the poverty, starvation, and suppression of the French and their unfortunate allies. The Catholic cleric, who has fattened himself at the expense of the people, represents the corruption of the French religion compared to the virtues of the Anglican Church. Both the theme and content of Hogarth's etching appears in an article in the *British Journal* of June 1, 1723 which compares the two cities of Dover and Calais. The writer notes that although they are only eight leagues from each other, they are world's apart.

> In one liberty, plenty and prosperity;
> in the other abject slavery, misery and
> poverty. The very beasts look like their
> masters, and their masters like them. and
> both like the picture of famine....ecclesiasticks
> ....all fat, brisk, and Jolly; but the hungry laity
> mere shadows or skeletons(p. 5).

Perhaps the most bizarre testimony to the superiority of the British way of life over that of the French can be found in a confession made by a condemned prostitute, Mary Stanford, that appears in the *Penny London Post* of August 5, 1726. The writer notes that after admitting her lewdness, wickedness, whoring, and drinking, she "preferr'd hanging at home to transportation abroad, and she was of the opinion, that her living in foreign Paris was worse than a disgraceful and shameful death at home" (p. 4).

The English reactions to the French Revolution, which went through several different stages, highlight some of the shifting prejudices of the times both within and beyond the borders of their country. When the news of the storming of the Bastille reached the English public, the first thought of many of them was that the French, their old and bitter enemies who had recently aided the American colonies in their rebellion, deserved to be consumed by revolution.[7] Soon afterwards, several of the English reformers rejoiced in the hope that some of the spirit of tolerance that was being generated across the Channel would affect the status of the dissenters in their own country. For William Blake (1757-1827), it was a time of hope and of regeneration. In his poem, "A Song of Liberty," he writes:

> Look up! look up! O citizen of London, enlarge
> thy countenance! O Jew, leave counting gold!
> return to thy oil and wine. O African! black African!

---

[7]Philip Anthony Brown, *The French Revolution in English History* (London: George Allen & Unwin Ltd., 1965), pp. 28-9.

Go, winged thought, widen his forehead![8]

Others, fearful of the religious reforms in France that were a potential threat to the English way of life, advocated new internal alliances within the country. George Colebrook, in his *Six Letters on Intolerance,* urges the toleration of all religions and he advocates the right of all citizens who are civically qualified to hold office. It is necessary, he believes, "to connect in a general league all grave, sensible, and religious persons against the increasing and common enemies to their faith."[9] He looks for support from the dissenters, who like the Jews, have been unjustly persecuted.[10]

Until the Revolution entered into its violent stages, there were no significant feelings of revulsion in England. However, after these excesses took place, public opinion shifted against the revolutionaries; there was now considerable antagonism against those in England who felt that the citizens of their country could learn from the French. Events on the other side of the Channel lent plausibility to the often expressed fears of the Church and state being in danger. For a while, the Dissenters were silenced in an overwhelming tide of reaction and repression.[11]

Allport notes that stereotypes wax and wane with the intensity and the direction of prejudice. They also adapt to the prevailing temper of prejudice or to the needs of the situation. For example, during World War II the Russian people were portrayed in the media as being rugged, brave, and patriotic. A few years later, after the Iron Curtain had descended, they became fierce, aggressive, and fanatical. [12]

For many of the English people, the French revolutionaries' attack upon the Catholics now turned the hated Papists into objects of compassion. For example, in the *Edinburgh Magazine or Literary Miscellany* for February, 1797, there is an eyewitness account of the indignities suffered by twenty-three English nuns at the hands of the French authorities who demanded that they remove the crosses from their convent, take down their bell, and throw off their habits. The writer describes the nuns' "angelic purity" and how their "veils which were to be cast off were bathed in tears" (pp. 122-23). Another writer, in the *Gentleman's Magazine* for March, 1797, comments on the arrival in England of Catholic priests who were fleeing from the atheistic French authorities. He urges Britons to welcome them

---

[8]Ibid., p. 28.
[9]George Colebrook, *Six Letters on Intolerance* (London: 1791), p. 212.
[10]Ibid.
[11]Ursula Henriques, *Religious Toleration in England 1787-1833* (Toronto: University of Toronto Press, 1961), p. 98.
[12]Allport, p. 198.

"in the hour of their distress like fellow creatures and like guests, as the children of one common father and as the disciples of one common Master." They have been driven to England, he notes, "by fire and sword" on account of their religious practices and they are deserving of Christian charity.

The French Revolution and the subsequent upheavals on the Continent created new objects of scorn that took some pressure off the Catholics and, to some extent, the Jews as well. No longer, for example, does the Pope appear to be evil incarnate. He is replaced by the revolutionaries across the Channel. The *Gentleman's Magazine* for July, 1796 notes: "The Papal system in the Christian church cannot be so great an usurpation as the harlot of Liberty and the genius of Reason, which have supplanted God himself in his temple" (p. 566). In the June, 1799 issue of the *Gentleman's Magazine*, the seven headed and horned beast with a blasphemous name upon its head that is described in Revelation (13:1) is no longer associated with Papal power, but with the seven republics established by Napoleon's armies (464). The verses in Mathew, "So when you see the desolating sacrilege spoken of by the prophet Daniel, standing in the holy place (let the reader understand), then let those who are in Judea flee to the mountains..." (15:15-16) which had traditionally been interpreted to be a reference to the destruction of Jerusalem for the sins of the Jewish people, is now applied, in the July, 1796 issue of the *Gentleman's Magazine*, to the French Revolution (pp. 566-67). Condemnation of the French is often expressed in theological terms that had formerly been reserved for medieval Jewry. In the *Gentleman's Magazine* for October, 1797, a writer claims that, in one of his portraits, Voltaire looked like an "odious devil" (p. 821). Another, considered him to be the anti- Christ.[13] The Philosophes are referred to as "those children of hell," and preachers take delight in condemning them and their compatriots to death and damnation.[14]

Fears of the subversion of the English way of life that would result from the revolution in France appear in the sermons of the time that are often reviewed in contemporary publications. In one of these, the preacher, William Agutter, warns that the violence in France is not a spontaneous outbreak, but a deliberate plan to "inculcate atheism and to propagate vice." The reviewer adds to these words his own fears that the British, by being indifferent spectators, will assist in such diabolical work. He admonishes them with the words:

> Britons beware! you have the example of France;

---

[13]Seamus Deane, *The French Revolution and Enlightenment in England* (Cambridge, Massachusetts: Harvard University Press, 1988) p. 32.
[14]Ibid.

> ye have now the plot discovered; ye may, as it
> were, see behind the scenes, and discover
> the chief actors and the moving springs.[15]

The popular press, citing the translated works of Abbe Barruel, turned the Jacobins of France into monsters whose conspiracy against Christianity had been going on for over 150 years. Their hatred of religion had spread to that of the monarchy and then to those governments which enforced the moral order and restrained the passions of the people. As a result of the teachings of deism and atheism, a goodly number of Jacobins could be found in every country in Europe including England.[16]

The threat of such godless people to the well being of England was often highlighted in the press. In one such article found in the *Gentleman's Magazine* for June, 1798, the author notes:

> At this present critical period, when England is
> not only alarmed by the threats of an invasion
> from a foreign enemy, but likewise from the intestine
> brawls of which we daily have but too frequent
> accounts; when, above all, religion bleeds at every
> vein from the repeated wounds she has received;
> when in our neighbouring hostile nation her altars
> are thrown down, her priests reviled, and the same
> horrid perturbation which Atheism has caused there
> seems impending over our heads; should not every
> true lover of Christianity and his country stand forth
> and endeavour, as far as lay in his power, to impede
> the progress of so erroneous and so horrible a doctrine
> as Atheism (p. 473).

These sentiments are common in such publications as The *Anti-Jacobin or Weekly Examiner* which, for example, in its issue for November 20, 1797, views the French Revolution not simply as the overturning of a government, but the subversion of the whole order of society. It warns its readers that "the vindictive spirit of Jacobinism is carried to its highest pitch" against Great Britain. In the November 30, 1797 issue of this weekly, it also claims that the Paris journals contain a "thundering proclamation" to the French armies to march on London where they are to be joined by those who support Parliamentary reform and by the "whole Irish Nation" as well.

---

[15]William Agutter, "A Sermon preached on the Day of general Thanksgiving December 19, 1797, in the Chapel of the Asylum for Female Orphans" in *Gentleman's Magazine*, 68 (February, 1798): 148.
[16]See, for example, A review of *Memoirs, Illustrating the History of Jacobinism* in *Gentleman's Magazine* 68 (January, 1798): 38-39.

Edmund Burke (1729-1797), in his *Reflections of the Revolution in France,* sees the danger of the Revolution not only in France itself, but in the kinds of attitudes and actions it fosters that could bring about a similar upheaval in England. He believes that the authorities need to censor treasonable books and maintain a close watch of subversive groups and their contacts with revolutionaries in other countries. Those members of the Jewish community who either read or learned of the contents of his book had every reason to fear the repercussions of his attacks upon the Jews. Although Burke does not single them out as a dangerous minority in the same way that he views the Unitarians, they are clearly undesirables. He notes, for example, that the next generation of the French nobility who would survive the Revolution "will resemble the artificers and clowns, and money-jobbers, usurers and Jews who will be always their fellows, sometimes their masters" (p. 46).

Burke also has some choice comments to make about Lord George Gordon (1751-1793), the eccentric Protestant proselyte to Judaism. He believes that this poor soul should be incarcerated for his libel. He tells the French:

> Let him there meditate on his Thalmud until
> some persons from your side of the water, to
> please your new Hebrew brethren, shall ransom
> him. He may then be enabled to purchase, with
> the old boards of the synagogue, and, a very
> small poundage on the long compound
> interest of the thirty pieces of silver, the lands
> which are lately discovered to have been usurped
> by the Gallican church (p. 81).

Burke criticizes the new clergy of France who have "thrown the children's bread to dogs; and, in order to gorge the whole gang of usurers, peddlers, and itinerant Jew-discounters at the corners of the streets, starved the poor of their Christian flocks" (p. 254). They should not be trusted "so long as Jews have assignats on ecclesiastical plunder, to exchange for the silver stolen from churches"(p. 254). Hitting closer to home, Burke admits that there are in London some respectable Jews who should remain in the country. However, there are also among them numerous housebreakers, receivers of stolen goods, and forgers, "men well versed in swearing "who would be just right for the new ecclesiastical positions in France (pp. 254-55).

The first part of Thomas Paine's (1737-1809) *Rights of Man,* which appeared in March, 1791, was a reply to Burke's work; it made him a symbol of the forces of sedition in the country. Though the two men were at opposite ends of the political spectrum, they both shared a deep prejudice against the Jewish people. Burke saw them as despised money lenders and stock jobbers while Paine hated them because of their influences upon early Christianity. The first two parts of his work, *Age of Reason,* caused a furor in England because of his bitter attack upon revealed religion. No doubt, his vehement hatred of Christianity distracted his readers from his caustic tirades against Judaism and the Jewish people, and it neutralized any potential serious anti-Semitic reactions. This was very fortunate for the Jews of England; unlike the previously mentioned Deists, he was a skillful demagogue who directed his words to the common people.

In his work, Paine displays a very low opinion of Hebrew Scriptures. Except for the Book of Job, which he believes was actually a translation of a text originally written by a Gentile, he finds it difficult to read the Bible without "indignation or disgust" (p. 155). By the same token, Christian Scriptures are nothing more than a forgery "without even the apology of credulity." They were "written by a sort of half Jews." He believes that the frequent references that are made to "that chief assassin and impostor, Moses," proves his point (p. 227). Paine views the ancient Hebrews as butchers; since Christianity's roots are in Judaism, it too is a bloody faith. He mocks both religions, and he condemns the way that they view God. Paine claims:

> The Jews have made him the assassin of
> the human species to make room for the
> religion of the Jews. The Christians have made
> him the murderer of himself and the founder of a
> new religion, to supersede and expel the Jewish religion (p. 255).

Though the Jews were attacked by Burke on the Right and Paine on the Left, it was the radicals, the British Jacobins, who ultimately bore the brunt of the anxieties of the time. The country was bracing itself for a French invasion. In numerous pamphlets and articles in the popular press, that are remarkably similar to those that appeared in the 1930's and early 1940's, instructions were given to the English people on how to resist the invaders once they had landed on English soil.[17]

In 1797 after naval mutinies had threatened the effectiveness of British sea power, a bill was rushed through Parliament which made it a capital offense to encourage such practices. Two years later, radical societies were banned by law, and in 17999 and 1800, legislation was passed by Parliament which made all combinations of workers and trade unions illegal. Although this was not implemented very often, a very real threat hung over the radicals and trade unionists. There were no mass

---

[17]*Gentleman's Magazine* 68 (May, 1798): 420-22. This is a review of a pamphlet, *Thoughts on a French Invasion and the Proper Means of Resisting it By Haviland Le Mesurier Commissary-general for the Southern District of England.*

arrests. However, leaders were harassed, intimidated, and prosecuted; many of the rank and file abandoned the reform movement.[18] Little thought was given to the relatively insignificant Jewish minority that posed no threat to national security. More pressing matters were at hand.

The Spanish

> In the year 1706 the French and Spaniards
> gave us a remarkable instance of their fear
> and superstition – for an eclipse of the sun
> falling upon the day that our troops landed
> to relieve Barcelona, our enemies retired in
> great confusion, taking it an ill omen to see
> the sun obscured.[19]

> There was a time when the Spaniards bore
> the reputation beyond all nations, for bravery
> in war, and not longer ago than the time of Charles
> the fifth, Europe was in dread of a universal
> monarchy, from the Spanish discipline and valor,
> yet this mighty fame dwindled away, and in less
> than a century after, a Spanish army gave little
> more terror than an unarm'd militia would have done.[20]

For a significant part of the eighteenth century, Spain was another real or potential enemy of England. As in the case of France, its repressive Catholicism added to the normal distrust that the Britons had for foreigners. The dreaded Inquisition, with its graphic, frightening tales of torture, imprisonment, and death in the name of religion, not only blackened the Image of the Catholics, but it also portrayed the Spaniards as a particularly cruel and inhuman people who lacked the fundamental traits of common decency and honor that the English believed were an integral part of their own way of life.

During times of actual conflict or at the approach of war, the Spanish were referred to in news dispatches as "hen hearted cowardly dogs" or "haughty dons who wanted courage."[21] The public was also encouraged to read stories of British bravery and loyalty to duty that stood in contrast to the arrogance, cowardice and perfidy of the Spanish. Sometimes these works were serialized and sold in sections for a penny each by the publishers of the daily newspapers. The title of one of these serials, *England's Triumph; or Spanish Cowardice exposed. Being a complete*

---

[18]H.T. Dickinson, *British Radicalism and the French Revolution* (Oxford: Blackwell, 1985), pp. 41-42.
[19]*The Grumbler* April 19, 1715.
[20]*Mist's Weekly Journal* May 20, 1727.
[21]Hooker's *Weekly Miscellany* March 15, 1739 and Hooker's *Weekly Miscellany* April 19, 1740.

History of the many signal Victories gained for 400 years past by the Royal Navy and Merchant Ships of Great Britain over the Insulting and Haughty Spaniards, conveys the spirit and the content of these works which contrasted England's gallant fighting men with their despicable foes. Another serialized book, Unfortunate *Englishmen,* was advertised in the *London Morning Post* for September 13,1740 as an account of how a number of English sailors, who had been captured at sea by the Spanish were put ashore at Porto-Cavalo in the West Indies, "naked and wounded."

Graphic news reports of Spanish atrocities appeared in the English press that highlighted the country's barbarous nature and cowardly behavior. For example, during a time of growing tensions between Spain and British America, it was reported in the *London Morning Post* of March 21,1740 that one night, in the colony of Georgia, two unarmed Highlanders who had gone out into the forest to get some firewood were captured by the Spanish, who had secretly landed in the vicinity. Later, search parties "Found the two Highlanders murder'd in the woods, their heads cut off and cruelly mangled." It was also noted that the Spaniards fled after they had "butchered the two unarmed men." On March 15, 1740, the same newspaper also reported that the Negroes in South Carolina had been encouraged to revolt against their masters "by the insinuations of the Spanish emissaries."

In addition to being cowardly, barbaric, and perfidious, the Spanish, in contrast to the British, were an indolent people who failed to take advantage of the benefits of a rich colonial empire. A writer in *Mist's Weekly Journal* of February 11,1727 notes: "England possesses no mines either of gold or silver, her wealth consists in the industry of her inhabitants." Spain, he believes "has very properly been compared to a sieve thro which all the silver which is dug out of the mines of New Spain does but pass, and those who sell cheapest, and mind their business best will always get most of it."

For one writer, in *The British Journal* for May 9,1724, even the weather is a factor in England's superiority over Spain and Italy. The cool temperatures of the British Isles, which calms people's tempers and encourages toleration stands in contrast to the heat of these Papist nations "where the power of the sun and of priests and ignorance prevails so abundantly and godly savageness of all kinds prevails in proportion."

A typical statement in the contemporary press that summarizes the English attitudes towards foreign powers, and the threat that these nations represent to the status quo, appears on the front page of *Mist's Weekly Journal* of July 8,1727. In a criticism of the practice of sending young men to the Continent to complete their education, the writer notes:

> Some of our greatest men have laid
> the foundation of their fame in a domestick
> education only....Let us not unbalance the
> whole solidarity of the British genius, and
> lose the critereon of its characters in the
> affection of foreign accomplishments. We
> are the greatest and richest and freest of all
> nations; let us also be the wisest.

Thus, the Jews of eighteenth century England were but one of the many religious, ethnic, racial, and national groups who made up the fabric of a complex, diverse, and often violent society. They were also only one of the many "others," at home or abroad, who were considered to be a real or potential threat to the physical safety and to the alleged religious and moral superiority of the majority culture. Only in this broader context of shifting prejudices and fears, can their own history and the anti-Semitism of the times be understood.

7

The Jewish Experience

....as nothing is useless but because it is in
improper hands, what is thrown away by one is
gathered up by another; and the refuse of part of
mankind furnishes a subordinate class with the
materials necessary to their support.[1]

Crossing the way again into Cornhill, if the
stranger has a curiosity to behold a modern
copy of old Jerusalem, let him turn into the
Rainbow, and the twelve tribes of Israel,
strikingly epitomized, will present themselves! –
dark beards and dirty faces in abundance![2]

To the God of Israel our prayers were directed,
He has been graciously pleased to answer us
propitiously, And the recovery of your Majesty's
health has restored happiness to your people.
As much impressed by our religious principles
as by the full sense of the many benefits we enjoy
under the protection of your Majesty's government,
the equity of the laws, & the liberal spirit of the
British Nation, Our duty and inclination unite in
devoting our prayers to the Almighty disposer of
events, for the long continuation of your Majesty's
health & government, & the glory & increasing
felicity of your kingdoms[3]

---

[1]John Hawkesworth, "On the Trades of London" *The Adventurer* 57 (June 26,
1753): 399.
[2]*London Pocket Pilot, or Stranger's Guide Through the Metropolis* (London: J. Roach,
1793),p. 54.
[3]Letter sent to George III in 1789 by the Bevis Marks congregation expressing
their good wishes on his recovery from illness. Cited in David S. Katz, *The Jews in
the History of England 1485-1850* (Oxford: Clarendon Press, 1994), p. 284-85.

The first organized Jewish community in England can be traced back to the reign of William the Conqueror, who, soon after his victory in 1066, brought over a small number of Jews to serve as royal tax collectors. In a land that had virtually no middle class, their financial skills were sought after by the Crown; in return they enjoyed the special protection extended to the "King's Men." Nevertheless, England was the first country in medieval Europe where the charge of ritual murder was leveled against the Jewish people; it was here that the Legend of the Wandering Jew was first introduced into Western Europe. For the most part, the populace viewed them with scorn. Encouraged by the teachings of the Church, they considered this tiny, but visible minority in their midst to be not only strangers and infidels, but agents of the Devil as well. Money lending, one of the few occupations that was open to the Jews, aroused the hostility of the people. The York massacre of 1190 was one example of how the fury of the mob could be directed against them for both their financial and religious practices. On a higher ecclesiastical level, Stephen Langton (d.1228), the Archbishop of Canterbury, held a synod at Oxford in 1222 where it was declared, among other things, that Jews were forbidden to build new synagogues; that they could not have Christian women servants or wet nurses; that they were to wear a badge on their outer garments to separate them from Christian society. Other local synods added further restrictions on Jewish money lenders and the use of churches for the safekeeping of their valuables.

By the end of the thirteenth-century, after suffering systematic impoverishment and having been replaced by Italian bankers who could meet the needs of the growing national economy, the Jews were no longer of any significant value to the Crown. Edward I (1239-1307), with the blessing of his lords, knights, townsmen, and clergy, banished them from his realm. Thus, it was England that set a pattern for the rest of Europe with the first nation-wide and total expulsion of the Jewish population of a country.[4] James Shapiro believes that this "first and only story of mass deportation of people from England.... has meant that Englishness has in part defined itself by the wholesale rejection of that which is Jewish."[5]

The expulsion of 1290 may have removed virtually all of the Jewish people from England, but stereotypes built up over the span of more than two centuries persisted in both religious and secular literature. The

---

[4]Zefira Entin Rokeah, "The State, the Church, and the Jews in Medieval England." in *Antisemitism Through the Ages*. ed. Shmuel Almog (Oxford: Peragamon Press, 1988), p. 116.
[5]James Shapiro, Shakespeare *and the Jews* (New York: Columbia University Press, 1996), p. 4.

hooked nosed, red bearded, despised money lender and contemptuous crucifier of innocent Christian children, remained a very real figure in popular imagination.[6] Throughout the medieval period, the Jews served as foils for Christians to demonstrate the superior qualities of the daughter religion. Thus, alleged Jewish greed and Pharisaic legalism stood in contrast to Christian charity, mercy, and compassion. Though the physical Jew was expelled from the land, old memories could be conjured up by the clergy and by religious dramatists to meet this need. With the passage of time, this stereotype was transformed to meet the demands of a more worldly age. The Christ killer image was secularized so that the theological outsider now became the Jewish alien; the perfect foil for the native born and bred Englishman. Another carry over from the medieval world was the use of the term "the Jew" in sermons, ballads, plays, and religious tracts. This abstraction functioned primarily as a symbol of menace and referred only secondarily to real human beings. One Jew was identical to all others, and any and all individual character traits were suppressed.[7]

Throughout what has been called the "Middle Period" of Anglo-Jewish history (1290-1609), Sephardic Jews from the Iberian Peninsula trickled into the country. Their numbers were bolstered by handfuls of their Ashkenazic co-religionists from Central and Western Europe. However, it was not until the time of Oliver Cromwell that there was any serious attempt to formally readmit the Jews to England. The Whitehall Conference of 1655 that was called to look into this matter generated so much anti-Jewish sentiment on the part of the clergy and the merchants that nothing official was done to change the status quo. Any Jews who decided to settle in the country came in through the back door, and they were obliged to maintain a semi-clandestine community.

In spite of English Jewry's unofficial status, they enjoyed greater religious and economic freedom than their co-religionists on the Continent. Unlike the Jews of Holland, for example, they were not required to secure the right of residence from the individual locality where they wished to settle. In addition, in contrast to English Jewry, even those Jews who were born in Holland were considered to be aliens who could be legally expelled. For French Jewry, the medieval edict of expulsion had never been repealed. Although this was overlooked in the case of Sephardic Jews, it had not been revoked for Ashkenazic Jewry.

---

[6]For a study of just how deeply ingrained this negative image of the Jew was in a country that was virtually *Judenrein*, see Bernard Glassman, *Anti-Semitic Stereotypes Without Jews : Images of the Jews in England 1290-1700* (Detroit: Wayne State University Press, 1975).

[7]Gavin Langmuir, *Toward a Definition of Anti-Semitism* (Berkeley and Los Angeles: University of California Press, 1990), p. 109.

Permission for them to reside in various localities was based on the good will of local authorities. Many towns in France were closed to Jews while in others they could only be allowed to reside if they paid extra taxes and agreed not to enter into certain occupations. In Germany, Jews were subjected to special taxes in order to inherit property or to cross frontiers. In 1777 Moses Mendelssohn(1729-1786) tried to avert the expulsion of the Jews from Dresden for failure to pay their specified poll tax. Although he pleaded for mercy, he never challenged the basic assumption that the Jewish people were a peculiar source of revenue to the state.[8] At this time, the Jews of England were not subject to special codes of law or taxation. They were not shut up in ghettos nor were they, like Alsacian Jewry, a unique and isolated class of creditors who were viewed as oppressors by a peasant population.[9]

Free from many of the restrictions found on the Continent, a Jewish community slowly evolved in London; the first one in Jewish history to be established on a voluntary basis without its own legal and fiscal authority.[10] In December of 1656, a house was rented in Creechurch Lane which became the first official synagogue since the Expulsion. By 1663, the Sephardic Jews who established this place of worship were able to draw up a body of Ascamot or regulations that were to officially govern their religious life. Rules were established not only to control the forms of worship and to maintain synagogue decorum, but also to shield the members from any conflict with the Christian world around them. The need for the community to maintain a low profile is evident in the following statutes found in the record book, *El Libro de los Acuerdos*, of the Spanish and Portuguese Synagogue of London.

> No Jew may hold dispute or argument on matters
> of religion with Guim, nor urge them to follow
> our holy law, nor may offensive words be spoken
> against their profession, because to do otherwise
> is to disturb the liberty which we enjoy and to make
> us disliked....(31st)

> No person who is not of our nation, Portuguese and
> Spaniards, may be circumcised, and no Mohel shall
> be allowed to circumcise them under pain of Herem...(32nd)[11]

---

[8]Jacob Katz, *Out of the Ghetto; the Social Background of Jewish Emancipation, 1770-1870* (Cambridge, Massachusetts: Harvard University Press, 1973),p. 17.
[9]Henriques, *Religious Toleration in England*, p. 179.
[10]Todd Endelman, *Radical Assimilation in English Jewish History, 1656-1945* (Bloomington and Indianapolis: Indiana University Press, 1990),p. 57.
[11]Lionel D. Barnett, trans. *El Libro de los Acuerdos, Being the records and Accompts of the Spanish and Portuguese Synagogue of London From 1663 to 1681* (Oxford: Oxford University Press, 1931).

The fears of the emerging Jewish community were not unfounded. In 1670 the House of Commons appointed a committee to search into the spread of Catholicism and "to inquire touching the number of Jews and their Synagogues and upon what terms they are permitted to have their residence here." Although the committee ignored this task, English Jewry was concerned about a potential governmental inquiry into their religious life.[12] In the final decade of the seventeenth-century the Jewish community provided the same tempting target that had existed prior to the Expulsion. Once again they were viewed as a rich source of revenue to be tapped by the Crown. In order to extract from them as much money as possible, William III subjected them to a special tax of £100,000, a forced loan, the payment of alien duties, and a special poll tax. Though these acts of fiscal discrimination ended with the success of the Glorious Revolution, they indicate the precarious position of the Jews in English society. Fortunately, the upheaval that was taking place in the country spared them from being the target of further attacks. As David Katz points out:

> The invasion of the Dutch ruler seemed to change
> all that, for it subsumed the entire subject of dual
> loyalties in the much larger and more significant
> question of the role which William and his Dutch
> followers might play in England. At a stroke the
> Glorious Revolution transformed an issue in which
> the Jews were worryingly conspicuous into one in
> in which they were only a sideshow.[13]

By being, for the most part, "only a side show" to the momentous events of the period, the Jewish community avoided much, but not all, of the animosity that was directed to other more significant or visible groups. In 1715 the general population of England and Wales was approximately five and a half million, and by the last decade of the century it reached about nine million. On the other hand, the Jewish population in 1700, concentrated mostly in the London area, numbered about 1000. By 1800 there were between 15,000-20,000 Jews in London and an additional 5000-6000 in the provinces.[14] Although percentage-wise this was a dramatic increase in the Jewish population that came about through natural increase and immigration, Jews were clearly a tiny minority throughout this entire period. Between 1689 and 1700 some

---

[12]Albert M. Hyamson, *The Sephardim of England: A History of the Spanish and Portuguese Jewish community 1492-1951* (London: Methuen & Co., 1951), pp. 45-6.
[13]David Katz. "The Jews of England and 1688" in *Persecution and Toleration* (Oxford: Blackwell, 1984), p. 249.
[14]Aubrey Newman *Anglo-Jewry in the Eighteenth Century. T. J. H. S. E.* 27(1978-80) : 1.

2,418 buildings were registered for public worship by Congregationalists, Baptists, and Presbyterians.[15] Clearly, the first very modest synagogue erected by the Jewish community was lost in the shuffle of this large number of dissenting churches. For those who were even aware of its presence, it could not have appeared to be a very serious threat to the Anglican faith. Bigots, however, have the ability to alter the facts to suit their own needs and to exaggerate the power and the influence of the "other" in society. Beneath the surface, covered by a thin veneer of reason, moderation, and candor – the hallmarks of the age – there were medieval memories that proved to be fertile grounds for those who attacked the Jewish people.

For example, in 1702, an act was passed in Parliament which obliged Jewish parents to maintain and provide education for their children who converted to Protestantism. The Act (I Anne, st. I, c.30) further states that if the Jewish parents refuse to do so in order to persuade their Protestant child to return to Judaism, then "it shall be lawful for the Lord Chancellor, Lord Keeper or Commissioners to make such order therein for the maintenance of such Protestant child, as he or they shall think fit." Henriques notes that in the early days of its existence "vigorous attempts had been made to enforce it, and there had even been a disposition on the part of zealous Chancellors to give the words of the enactment the most extensive interpretation."[16] In the case of *Vincent v. Fernandez,* the Protestant "child" was a forty-four year old married woman. Yet, Lord Chancellor Parker gave some strong reasons why she should receive support from her father's estate.[17]

In *The Jews Charter*, the most virulent anti-Semitic work published at the beginning of the century, the author lists all the classical and modern reasons for keeping the Jews out of England. He begins by appealing to the religious and patriotic sentiments of his countrymen; he urges them not to allow "the enemies of the Cross of Christ and his scorners" to live among good Christians and thereby taint their nation's special relationship with God"(p. A2).There are some who claim that if the Jews would be expelled from England, the woolen industry might suffer. However, many honest Christians would be involved in this enterprise had they not been discouraged by the "several artifices the Jews use to undermine others, and engross the trade to themselves" (p. A3). Not

---

[15]Horton Davies, *Worship and Theology in England From Watts and Wesley to Maurice, 1690-1850* (Princeton: Princeton University Press, 1961), p. 35.
[16]H.S.Q. Henriques, *The Jews and the English Law* (Oxford: Oxford University Press, 1908), p. 4.
[17]Ibid.

only are Jews no significant help in foreign trade, but in time of war they can insure their ships and goods for much less than the native English and thereby undercut their prices (p. A4). To strengthen his arguments against a Jewish presence in the country, the author then chronicles the history of the Jews in England from the time of William the Conqueror. He comes to the conclusion that "the real privileges of the Hebrew alias the Jewish nation among us are blank, and they have taken advantage of their position to amass wealth for themselves at the expense of true Englishmen"(p. 5). In keeping with the stock approach of the bigot to overestimate the power of the "other", the author exaggerates the number of the Jews in the country, the size of their synagogue, and their control of the West India trade. Though he admits that it is possible to find some good moral people among this despised group, he believes that "a disaffected Jew is the worst of spies" – a reference to popular suspicions concerning Jewish patriotism to their adopted country (pp. 6-7). The author suggests that the only solution to the problem is to expel them from England and to allow them to carry off only the wealth that they acquired by honest means. The rest of their funds should be turned over to the parishes adjacent to their present neighborhoods to be used for charitable purposes (p. 7).

Though nothing came of such a proposal, the Jewish community and its leadership were well aware of the tenuous place that they had in English society. When, in 1701, David Nieto (1654-1728) arrived in England to assume the position of the Sephardic Chief Rabbi, his task was not only to care for the spiritual needs of his people, but to serve as the Jewish spokesman to the general community as well. He soon learned that if Jews and Judaism were to become a respectable part of English society, it was necessary during his tenure to demonstrate the political loyalty of the newly arrived immigrants, and to stress the common principles that Judaism shared with the Church of England. By constructing his own public image of Judaism that was, in many ways, similar to that of the Anglican social and intellectual elite, Nieto hoped to present a positive image of the Jewish faith which would insure the civic welfare of the fledgling community.[18] To some degree he succeeded in both of these areas.

During the next decades, Sephardic Jews from Portugal, Spain, the Canary Islands, Amsterdam, Leghorn, and Hamburg continued to emigrate to England. Several who came from the Iberian Peninsula managed to bring their considerable wealth with them. Thus, "as the

---

[18]David Ruderman, "The Career and Writings of David Nieto," *Proceedings of the American Academy for Jewish Research* 58 (1992): 218.

refugees escaped from Portugal so did the bullion."[19] In addition, connections to their former domiciles were an important source of the precious metals needed for the minting of coins in their new country. Sephardic Jews were proud of their mercantile heritage, and they continued to serve as agents of Iberian firms as well as wholesale traders of precious stones and coral. They were financiers, discounters of bills of exchange, and stock jobbers. A list of some 350 Jewish investors in the Bank of England between 1694-1725 shows that, without exception, they were all of Sephardic origin. At the turn of the eighteenth century one-ninth of the 107 proprietors who held at least £4000 of stock in the Bank were Sephardic Jews with such names as Da Costas, Fonseca, Henriquez, Mendez, Nunes, Rodriguez, Salvador, Teixera, de Mattos, and Medina.[20] In 1726, Francis Pereira had the largest single holding in the Bank which amounted to almost £105,000.[21] Though there were any number of Sephardic Jews who were dependent upon charitable contributions from their co-religionists, there were many who, in a few decades, acquired substantial fortunes. As former Marronos or their descendants, they were quite accustomed to living in a Christian world. Their opulent estates equaled and often exceeded those of the English gentry, and they dressed, entertained, and educated their children in the style of their new station. Although the revival of the dreaded Inquisition in the Iberian Peninsula increased their numbers, the Sephardic Jews gradually lost their numerical superiority in the Anglo-Jewish community. Conversion to Christianity, emigration overseas, and marriage to Ashkenazic Jews, diminished their numbers.

During the seventeenth and eighteenth centuries, large numbers of Eastern European Jews migrated westward towards lands of comparative security. Limited economic opportunities, political strife, and religious persecution in Poland as well as the emergence of Western Europe as an important center of finance, trade, and culture, encouraged this population shift. The gradual emergence of a viable Jewish community in England as well as the low cost of passage, encouraged even the poorest Eastern European Jews to cross the Channel. The threatened expulsion of the Jews of Bohemia and Moravia swelled their numbers, and this began to alter the make-up of the Anglo-Jewish community.

---

[19]Richard D. Barnett, "Diplomatic Aspects of the Sephardic Influx from Portugal in the Early Eighteenth Century," *T.J.H.S.E.*, 25 (1973-75): 210.
[20]John Clapham, *The Bank of England: A History 1694 -1797* Vol I (Cambridge: Cambridge University Press, 1945), p. 279.
[21]Ibid., p..282.

The Sephardic and Ashkenazic communities were hostile to each other in most social and religious matters that affected their internal workings. However, common problems that stemmed from the Christian world around them did foster some degree of cooperation among the two groups. For example, in December of 1751, the *Mahamad* (governing body) of the Spanish and Portuguese Synagogue sent the following letter to the Ashkenazic community:

> Gentlemen:
> Being persuaded that you will join with us in all things that tend to preserve the present happy toleration, we take this opportunity to acquaint you as worthy representatives of your congregation, of a growing evil among us, viz., that of permitting proselytes, for which end we have heard that two or three Christians have come hither from Norway with that intention, and lest these practices should extend to English proselytes, which is contrary to the express condition annexed to our first establishment here, we have thought proper to forbid in our Synagogue any from aiding and assisting them therein in any manner whatsoever, under the penalties as we send you enclosed.[22]

The penalties that were included in the letter consisted of expulsion from the synagogue, being forbidden to be buried in the Jewish cemetery, and the denial of all religious privileges to the guilty party and to his family as well.[23]

The regulations that were drafted in 1772 to govern the newly formed Ashkenazic synagogue in Duke's Place reflect some of the animosities, fears, and "growing pains" of this immigrant group. Thus, any disputes between members of the synagogue were not to be brought to the secular courts. Instead, they were to be submitted to Jewish communal officers for arbitration. Only after the defendant had failed to appear on three occasions were the civil authorities to become involved in the litigation. However, the strong sense of communal control and solidarity that had been so prevalent in Jewish communities on the Continent never took root in the country. English Jews were not a corporate group that was subject to state regulation. As a result, they had the option of either accepting or rejecting the dictates of their communal leaders. This led to greater freedom and quite often, defection as well.

By the middle of the eighteenth century, several Ashkenazic Jews became as influential and as wealthy as the most prominent members of the Sephardic community. In the years that followed, their power

---

[22]Cecil Roth, *Anglo-Jewish Letters* (London: Socino Press, 1938), pp. 126-27.
[23]Ibid.,

continued to increase, and by the end of the century Sephardic preeminence had come to an end. This change in the balance of power was the cause of additional friction between the two groups that occasionally erupted into outright antagonism. Yet, when Christian merchants drew unfavorable conclusions about the Jews as a whole from the misdeeds or the bankruptcy of a particular Jewish firm, no distinction was made between the two groups. In the literature and the prints of the period, stereotypical Ashkenazic speech patterns were associated with individuals with Sephardic surnames or appearance. For the satirist and the bigot, all Jews sounded alike.

It can be argued that prejudice diminishes through personal contact and that negative stereotypes of minority groups weaken through daily shared experiences. However, a survey conducted in 1992 by Marttila and Kiley for the Anti-Defamation League refutes the conventional wisdom that the more contact an individual has with Jews, the less likely he or she will be anti-Semitic.[24] Allport believes that the lessening of animosity depends upon the nature of the interaction, the kind of association that occurs, and the make-up of the people involved.[25] Robert Wuthnow feels that when contact is between equals it reduces prejudice, but when it takes place among people of different socioeconomic standings it can actually increase. In addition, the interaction has to be relatively close if it is to be of any real value. It is not enough to simply be in the same context with Jews. In fact, such a situation may reinforce stereotypes. Since no ethnic or religious group is free from negative qualities, casual acquaintances are more likely to be aware of them than anyone else. Thus, those who are only aware of a Jewish presence are likely to have their perceptions remain at the level of generalizations and criticisms.

Some good examples of this can be found in accounts of synagogue visits made by curious Christians. One such individual, John Greenhalgh, who was obviously unprepared for his encounter with a traditional Jewish prayer service, writes in a letter to a friend dated April 22,1667, how dismayed he is with the "barbarous sight" of "hooded, guized, veiled Jews" participating in worship that lacked any semblance of decorum or reverence. Though Greenhalgh was moved by the sight of the "banished sons of Israel" praying in a strange land and confessing their sins and those of their ancestors, his curiosity had been satisfied,

---

[24]Jerome A. Chanes, "Antisemitism and Jewish Security in America Today: Interpreting the Data. Why Can't Jews Take 'Yes' for an Answer?" *Antisemitism in America Today ; Outspoken Experts Explode the Myths,* ed. Jerome R. Chanes (New York: Birch Lane Press, 1995),pp. 10-11.
[25]Allport, p. 251.

and he was reluctant to return for another visit. [26] Other superficial contacts with the Jewish community by inquisitive Christians would produce similar results.

The Jews were, for the most part, a visible, but little understood or appreciated minority. Various restrictions imposed upon them in regard to retail commerce pushed them into dealing in second-hand goods and becoming part of the precious metal and jewelry related trades. Nearly 16% of those Jews who took apprentices were in some way involved in jewelry or diamond processing occupations; while another 12% were watchmakers.[27] Apprenticeship registers show a surprising variety of other trades open to Jews that primarily reflect the London scene. They include: glass cutting, shoemaking, book selling, collar making, pencil making, engraving, and peruke making.[28] However, it was the Jewish peddler, particularly of old clothes, who became a familiar figure in London's streets and alleys and who was most closely identified with his people.

By focusing attention upon these dealers in old clothes and including their stereotypical images in their works, Anglo-Jewish historians imply that this occupation was virtually a Jewish monopoly. This was far from being the case. The secondhand clothes trade was an established part of English life that had existed for centuries before the Jews entered into it. It was a huge, complex, industry, a means for millions of people from all strata of society to satisfy their needs and wants in preindustrial and early industrial England. As Beverly Lemire notes, "But, from top to bottom on the social scale, used clothing would be purchased when a bargain was available and when the items flattered the buyer, either physically or financially." [29] Advertisements in the newspapers and periodicals of the time show how the buying and selling of this important commodity was in the hands of many English firms outside of London's Jewish neighborhoods. As colorful as they were, the Jewish peddlers of secondhand clothes were not always subjected to special attention or prejudice. The streets of London were full of people selling their wares and hawking their services. With their foreign mannerisms and accents, the Jews were only a small part of the ebb and flow of the

---

[26]Cohen, *Scrapbook*. pp. 260-67.

[27]Aubrey Newman, *Anglo-Jewry in the 18th Century: A Presidential Address*, *T.J.H.S.E.* 27 (1978-80): 4.

[28]Arthur P. Arnold, "Apprentices of Great Britain 1710-1773," *Misc. J. H.S.E.* 7 (1970): 145-6.

[29]Beverly Lemire, "Consumerism in Preindustrial and Early Industrial England: The Trade in Secondhand Clothes." *Journal of British Studies* 27 (1988): 3.

metropolis; aliens among a mixed multitude of other immigrant and native peddlers, street musicians, chair-menders, and chimney sweeps.[30]

As in the case of other ethnic groups, newly arrived unskilled immigrants who could not pay the fees for apprenticeship found peddling to be a way to get started in their adopted country. The Jewish community provided them with a small sum of money to purchase used clothing and discarded harnesses, saddles, and cloth. Their limited capital often forced them to sell in the afternoon what they had purchased or bartered in the morning. Usually, they took what they acquired to Rag Fair where dealers were waiting to purchase their goods. Some of the hawkers were involved in petty crime for, even if they were honest in their dealings, their line of work brought them into contact with criminals who had established a center for buying and selling both second hand and stolen goods in London's East End. This real and imagined association with criminal elements in society was to plague the Jewish community throughout the century; it became deeply ingrained in contemporary literature and in popular imagination as well.

Unlike conditions on the Continent, an official Jewish Ghetto never developed in England, and there was complete freedom of movement for Jewish peddlers. When the local market for their goods was saturated, they would leave London and head for the flourishing seaports of the southern and western parts of the country where these areas became the new base for their operations. They carried in their packs an assortment of buckles, brushes, clothing, cutlery, watches, eye glasses, quill pens, cheap jewelry, and any portable items that were in demand. The Jewish peddlers either bought their goods or they served as agents for provincial or London dealers. Some of them roamed the countryside as traveling entertainers, pawn brokers, and medical quacks. They appear in any number of contemporary prints where, with their straggly beards, shapeless hats, long coats and packs on their backs, they are easily recognizable as a distinct part of the contemporary scene.

From about 1740, Jewish peddlers were attracted to the cities of Portsmouth, Plymouth, and Chatham, where for the next eighty years they sold jewelry, clothes, fresh fruit, and other wares to the sailors of the Royal Navy. After a long voyage, only a few trusted seamen were allowed on shore. Fearing mass desertion, the authorities kept most of the men on board where they were a captive audience to the hawkers and peddlers who rowed out to the ships to display their wares. These small businessmen also made loans to the sailors and they discounted their wage tickets. Contemporary

---

[30]Betty Haggar, *Jewish Pedlars and Hawkers: 1740-90.* (Surrey: Porphyrogenitus, 1992), p. 54.

naval prints depict unflattering bearded figures trading with the men, and at times being subjected to practical jokes. In popular imagination, the actual number of Jews engaged in this lucrative business was exaggerated since anyone who lent money was nicknamed, "Jew", by the sailors.[31]

During the period of the Resettlement, Jews were considered to be aliens who could not engage in retail trade. As a result, some of them became broker's agents who acted as wholesale middlemen for merchants on a commission basis. These transactions went through the Royal Exchange where stocks and bonds were also traded. It was only a matter of time before Jews gravitated to this lucrative endeavor as well. Although a broker in securities was required to be a freeman, a status that was denied to the Jews, individual members of the Jewish community were licensed to perform these services by the Lord Mayor and the Court of Alderman. By 1697, the number of brokers on the Royal Exchange was set at one hundred. Some twelve places were put aside for members of the Jewish faith.

Stock Jobbing, an occupation that was despised by the English public, became another conspicuous Jewish occupation. Susannah Centlivre (1667?-1723),in her play, *A Bold Stroke for a Wife*, depicts a scene on the Exchange during a Jewish holiday where one of the characters asks about the whereabouts of the Jews (3. 1). Obviously, their absence on festivals was as noteworthy as their presence on workdays. Unfortunately for the Jewish brokers, in the popular imagination, stock jobbing was compared to the "itch of Gaming," and it was considered equally difficult to overcome. According to Daniel Defoe(1659?-1731), what began as an occasional transfer of interest and shares from one party to another, became a trade that was "managed with the greatest intrigue, artifice and trick." [32] He was convinced that stock jobbing was nothing more than a "compleat system of knavery," an occupation that was "founded in fraud, born of deceit, and nourished by trick, cheat, wheedle, falsehoods and all sorts of delusions."[33]

During this period, the less affluent members of society were encouraged to speculate in the shares of Joint Stock Companies by requiring them to make only a small down payment of between five and ten percent of the price of these securities. The remainder was to be paid

---

[31]Geoffrey Green, "Anglo-Jewish trading connections with officers and seamen of the Royal Navy, 1740-1862," T.J.H.S.E. 29 (1982-86): 97-8.

[32]Daniel Defoe, *An Essay on Projects* (1697), p,29-30. Cited in P.G.M. Dickson, The *Financial Revolution in England: A Study in the Development of Public Credit 1688-1756* (New York: Macmillan, 1967), P.33.

[33]Daniel Defoe, *The Anatomy of Exchange-Alley: or A System of Stock-Jobbing* (London: Printed for E. Smith, 1719), p. 3-4.

out in successive calls over an extended period of time. This practice, which resembles the modern technique of buying on margin, was very risky, and it resulted in any number of personal bankruptcies among the different classes. Stock jobbers, who dealt with both the shares of private companies and government securities, were often accused of not only manipulating stocks for personal gain at the expense of both the rich and the poor, but also of endangering national security.[34]

Christian stock jobbers and money lenders were, as a sign of reproach, nicknamed "Jews" by their contemporaries. They were considered to be their "brother usurers" since they too grew rich without honest labor.[35] In William Chetwood's (d.1766) play, South-*Sea or the Bitter Bit.*, Alderman Scrapeall, who is obviously not Jewish, is called an "extortioning Jew" when he charges 50 percent interest to a country bumpkin who wants to buy stock at "Change Alley" (I: 1). Later, when the farmer asks about the religion of the people he sees milling about, he is told: "Religion! why they don't mind religion in Change Alley. But Turks, Jews, Atheists, and Infidels, mingle there as if they were a kin to one another" (I :1).

Members of the Jewish community who were on the Exchange were very visible even to casual observers, and their misdeeds were fully noted. For example, when Nathan Solomon, a leading Jewish financier, went bankrupt and caused a financial crisis, the *Gentleman's Magazine* of September, 1783 refers to him as "the great Jew broker" (p. 803). Soon after, in the *Rambler Magazine* for November of that year, a caricature of him appears leading four lame ducks who are followed by another Jew.[36] The physical presence of Jews on the Exchange was highlighted in a contemporary ballad which contains the verses:

> In London stands a famous pile
>   And near the pile an alley
> Where merry crowds for riches toil
>   And Wisdom stoops to folly,
> Here stars and garters do appear
>   Among our lords the rabble,
> To buy and sell, to see and hear
>   The Jews and Gentiles squabble [37]

In the pages of the *Craftsman* for December 23, 1727 there is a description of a visit to Exchange Alley, "a mysterious Emporium,"

---

[34]Dickson, pp. 487-88.

[35]*Craftsman* 47 Saturday, May 27, 1727.

[36]*Rambler Magazine* November, 1783 cited in Rubens *T.J.H.S.E.* 23 (1969-70),p. 99.

[37]Tout, *History of England* Part III(1910) cited in A.S. Diamond, "Problems of the London Sephardi Community, 1720-1733-Philip Carteret Webb's Notebooks" *T.J.H.S.E.* 21 (1968): 39.

which proved to be a babble of noise, hurry and confusion. The writer describes traders who are "mad with success" as well as others who are "frantic with despair." He claims that they are fearful of any prospect of peace which would "put an end to their game." Instead, the Jews would prefer a state of war or national uncertainty to promote their nefarious schemes(pp. 237-8). Thus, he creates the illusion that, in some way, European affairs are manipulated by a small group of Jewish brokers in Exchange Alley.

The speculative fever was so intense among the Jews of London that the physician, Meyer Schonberg (1690-1761), a dignitary of the Jewish community, castigated those co-religionists who, after attending Sabbath worship services, would walk by the Exchange to inquire about the price of India bonds and South Sea notes. He lamented that a good part of their sacred day of rest was spent discussing securities and bills of exchange[38]

Although Jews were closely associated with "Change Alley" and often linked to the manipulation of the prices of securities, when the most serious stock crash of the century occurred they were not blamed for the financial debacle. The bursting of the famous "South Sea Bubble," which affected the purses of all strata of the population, had the potential for a wave of anti-Semitic outbursts. Yet, even with a perfect scapegoat in place, the Jewish community was left virtually unscathed. To appreciate why nothing of significance happened to jeopardize the safety of either the Jewish stock jobbers or their co-religionists, both the events leading up to this financial crisis as well as its aftermath should be studied.

In 1711 the South Sea Company, with the enthusiastic support of prominent Tories, and a group of leading merchants, was established to restore public credit. In exchange for assuming the public debt of some ten million pounds, these government and business leaders were granted a monopoly of trade to the South Seas. They expected to make a substantial profit trading English manufactured goods for South American gold and silver. Unfortunately for them, Philip V of Spain (1683-1746) had other ideas. He limited the trade to but one ship a year, and he also demanded one quarter of the profits of the venture. Though the disruption of relations with Spain ended all trade between the two countries, the need to reduce the national debt kept the South Sea Company in the public eye. As a result of this public exposure, stock in the company continued to be in demand. Men like Sir John Blunt, chairman of the company, did everything possible to raise the price of the stock by circulating rumors of free trade treaties with the Spanish

---

[38]Sheet 7 of *Emunat Omen* cited in *T.J. H. S. E.* 20 (1959-61) : 112.

colonies that had the potential to yield enormous profits for astute investors.

With visions of instant wealth, crowds descended upon "Change Alley." They were anxious to buy stock not only in the South Sea Company, but in any number of other hastily formed joint stock ventures, nicknamed bubbles, that were created to satisfy this need for financial gambling. The public did not know nor did it care about the projects in which they were investing. These varied from plans to build perpetual motion machines, to transmutating quicksilver into a malleable fine metal. One of them was actually labeled, "A company for carrying on an undertaking of great advantage, but nobody to know what it is."[39] Although some projects were more practical, the speculative madness doomed them as well.

Through various stock offerings, the directors of the South Sea Company amassed enormous wealth which was accompanied by equally huge amounts of arrogance. When the bubble finally burst and fortunes were lost, these men and their Tory supporters became scapegoats for the madness that had swept through the country. There was a public outcry to confiscate their wealth to compensate the victims of this financial disaster.[40] Ultimately, stripped of their fortunes and labeled as frauds and cheats, they became the butt of jokes and a stimulus to the art of political satire. In one of Hogarth's prints, the artist pictures a whirling device that is being worked by the South Sea Company Directors. On it are a number of investors who are literally "being taken for a ride." A figure, "Self-Interest," is breaking "Honesty" upon the wheel while a villainous personage is flogging "Honor". No stereotypical image of the "Jew Broker" appears in the print.[41]

Though there is a brief mention in *The Whitehall Evening Post* for March 24-26, 1720 of a Jewish stock jobber who allegedly lost £100,000 in some nefarious schemes, contemporary publications did not report any direct Jewish participation in the affair. In addition to the directors of the South Sea Company, blame was placed upon those in government who were the patrons of "projectors and bubble mongers."[42] These individuals were much more tempting targets than the "Jew Brokers" of the exchange. In assessing the mood of the people, one writer notes that it was really of little value to pursue the lesser cheats since they acted entirely in character. The true "authors of villainy" are those in

---

[39]Charles Mackay, *Extraordinary Popular Delusions and the Madness of Crowds* (1932; rpt. New York: Harmony Books, 1980),p. 55.
[40]Ibid., p. 72.
[41]Paston. Social *Caricature in the Eighteenth Century.* p. 95.
[42]*Craftsman* Saturday, January 8, 1732.

prominent places who hired these underlings to do their bidding. They are the ones who deserve a Parliamentary enquiry.[43] An anonymous poet echoed these sentiments with the words:

> As fishes on each others prey,
> The great Ones swallowing up the Small;
> So fares it in the Southern Sea:
> But Whale Directors eat up all.

> When stock is high, they come between,
> Making by second-hand their Offers;
> Then cunningly retire unseen,
> With each a Million in his Coffers.[44]

In addition to those who blamed men in high places for the debacle, there others who considered it to be a problem that went beyond the dealings in "Change Alley". In the play, The *Broken Stock-Jobbers or Work for the Bailiffs*, a victim of the bursting of the bubble, Sir Frippery, laments his losses with the words:

> Well, this is a most implacable Thing. My broker, I
> believe, is the greatest Rogue in the Alley....and that
> Son of a Whore....that Jew, Damn his Circumcision,
> a dog, he has bit me fairly, by Jupiter (p. 6).

Although blame is heaped upon the "Jew broker" by the character in the play, the anonymous author of the work makes it quite clear that it is greed and stupidity that led to Sir Frippery's downfall. For Hogarth, religion as an institution is also to blame; in another one of his etchings on the subject he depicts Catholic, Protestant, and Jewish clergy casting coins for Jesus' robe.[45]

For the Jewish community, the repercussions of the bursting of the South Sea Bubble were more in the realm of stereotypical remarks than in actual physical violence. Yet, they convey all of the pent up fears and hatreds of the majority culture that are based on a sense of mistrust that had been nurtured for centuries. The following verses which appear in *The Weekly Journal or British Gazeteer* of December 31,1720 may seem to have been written in jest. However, they contain several negative images of the Jews that were obviously well known to the reading public.

> A crafty Jew pretending to retail
> Stock at low price, when he had none to sell
> The angry brokers merrily chastiz'd him

---

[43]*The Sense of the People Concerning the Present State of Affairs* (London: J. Peele, 1721),pp. 6-7.
[44]*The Bubble: A Poem* (London : 1721), p. 6.
[45]Jack Lindsey, *Hogarth: His Art and His World* (New York: Taplinger Publishing Co., 1979), p. 18.

And in a horse pond twice or thrice baptiz'd him....
Says a rich Jew to a young buxom lady
I'll give you so much stock to let me bed ye;
Quoth she, you lewd, old, circumcised Tom Coney,
I've stock enough, I deal for ready money....
A Jew to buy up South Sea Stock employ'd,
Swears that it cost him more than it did;
His principal replies fie, Moses fie
I Doubt you never swear, but when you lie.

In the years following the debacle, the press continued to report the painful aftershocks of this financial disaster. For example, the *British Journal* of July 24, 1724 notes that a "Mr. Burray, a Chichester gentleman, said to be a sufferer by the South Sea scheme, lodging in the Old Exchange, near Cheapside, threw himself out of a window, two pair of stairs high, and instantly died". Prejudice against the denizens of Change Alley, both Jew and Christian, continued to be part of the British psyche, and these villains' deeds, which are considered to be a danger to the nation, are often condemned in the press. The *Penny London Post* of February 7, 1726 expresses in a rather vulgar way these sentiments.

We hear that there is a rod in piss for some of
the brokers and stock jobbers in Exchange Alley,
Jews as well as others, for endeavouring to
wound publick credit without any reason for so
doing, and at the very time when our vigilent ministry
are taking the necessary precautions for our greater security.

Not only were the dealings of the stock jobbers on the Exchange mistrusted, but it was believed that these nefarious creatures also manipulated the news for financial gain. The *London Penny Post* of June 8, 1726 mentions a certain Mr. Perry, of Exchange Alley, who was charged with committing a high misdemeanor "in attempting to publish a false scandalous paragraph in the newspapers intending thereby to depreciate public credit ". His actions were obviously fairly common. For example, when it was noted in the *London Morning Post* of April 19, 1740 "that several persons positively asserted that Spanish men of war sailed out of Cales bay with land forces on board," an action which, if true, would certainly would affect the price of stock, the reporter cynically added that "this is thought to smell of Change Alley."

The bursting of the South Sea Bubble was not the only major financial crisis that involved stock jobbers. The period following the end of the Seven Years War in 1763 was one of credit crises, bankruptcies, and a sharp rise in the national debt. In May of 1769, in the midst of this economic turmoil, stock in the famed East India Company crashed. Once again stock jobbers became the focus of the wrath of those who had lost their fortunes in speculative investments. However, as in the case of the

South Sea Bubble, it soon became obvious that the problem went beyond "Change Alley". First of all, it was members of the press who had deliberately distorted the news concerning a French attack on the Company's holdings which had caused the stock to drop from 272 to 230 in a seven day period. Secondly, the directors of the East India Company had shown fiscal irresponsibility both in maintaining an inflated market price for the stock and in continuing the 12.5% dividend. These actions, which they claimed were in the public interest, were clearly for their own financial gain.[46]

Another factor which drew public attention away from the Jewish stock jobbers was the presence of "Nabobs", former officers of the Company who had "shaken the Pagoda tree" and returned home to England where they ostentatiously displayed the treasure that they had amassed. Those who had lost their fortunes speculating in the stock of the East India Company bitterly resented these newcomers who bought a position for themselves in English society with the money they had acquired from a company which exploited the natives and had bankrupted so many at home. The "Nabobs'" ravenous appetite for country estates and the trappings of nobility threatened to overturn England's social culture, and it made them the objects of anger and scorn. Edmund Burke noted with alarm how they succeeded in marrying into the best families, raised the value of landed property, bought control of eight seats in the House of Commons, and bribed government officials.[47] Clearly, they eclipsed the place that some of the more affluent Jewish stock jobbers had in the public eye.

A similar situation affected the public perception of the Jewish money lender. For many years after money lending was no longer a major Jewish occupation, the myth of the Shylock type, hard-hearted, unscrupulous usurer persisted in the popular imagination. Often, a direct link was made between the attitudes and the ethical code of the "Jew money lender" and the Jewish stock jobber and businessman. Endelman believes that this negative stereotype was not only the result of centuries of myth making, but that it was due to Jewish involvement in the personal loan trade where money lenders supplied capital to those upper class Englishmen who could not pay their gambling debts. Thus, in the popular mind, Jews were the corrupters of the young and inexperienced gentlemen who came to them after they had suffered loses at the gaming tables. By supplying these irresponsible gentry with funds

---

[46]H.V. Bowen " The Pests of Human Society: Stockbrokers, Jobbers and Speculators in Mid-eighteenth-century Britain." *History* 78 (February, 1993): 44.
[47]Leo Damrosch *Fictrions Of Reality in the Age of Hume and Johnson* (Madison: University of Wisconsin Press, 1989),pp. 196-98.

many believed that the Jewish money lenders encouraged their bad habits.[48]

It was also quite evident that Jews were not the only ones who took advantage of young Christians – particularly in the handling of their inheritances. When Parliament decided to take action, and a bill was drawn up to end, these abuses, The *London Evening Post* for May 1-3, 1777 notes:

> The Annuity Bill hangs like a sword over the
> heads of the many vultures who have for too
> long a time fed on the vitals of the distressed.
> The Jewish tribe (whether Heathenish or Christian,
> are equally unconscionable and rapacious)....
> are afraid of entering into fresh negotiations with
> beardless school boys and brainless gamblers.

In Sheridan's, *School for Scandal*, a play about a good-natured man who is reckless with his money and who falls into the hands of usurers, there is Moses, "a friendly Jew" who is a money lender. However, there is a more sinister principal usurer in the background who is a Christian.

Although members of the Jewish community tried to escape from public attention, two individuals, Daniel Mendoza (1764-1836), a boxing champion, and Samson Gideon (1699-1762), a wealthy Sephardic financier, made their mark on English society. In very different ways, both of them perpetuated and, perhaps to some minor degree, modified the old stereotypes of the Jew.

Daniel Mendoza, born in Algate, London, became attracted to professional boxing after he collected fourteen pounds from bystanders who watched him defend himself on the streets of the metropolis.[49] In January, 1788, he fought the first of three fights with Richard Humphries, and he was soundly beaten. In a contemporary account of the match, a sportswriter describes how Humphries "planted a dreadful blow on the neck or near the Jaw of the Jew, which sickened and almost disabled him." As a result of Mendoza's defeat in the ring, the writer claims that "upwards of £20,000 sterling of bets will be transfer'd from the Jews to the Christians." [50] In "The Odiad," an epic poem that was inspired by the match, much stronger anti-Semitic sentiments appear.

> Now Bets urge Bets, at Synagogue and 'Change
> And all the Rev'rend Rabbis (sic) round him range
> With grinning joy, their puny David bless

---

[48]Todd M. Endelman, "The Checkered Career of ' Jew 'King," *Association for Jewish Social Studies* 7- 8 (1982-3) : 74-5.
[49]For a colorful sketch of his life see: Daniel Mendoza, *The Memoirs of the Life of Daniel Mendoza*. ed. by Paul Magriel (New York: Arno Press, 1975).
[50]*European Magazine and London Review* 13 (February, 1788): 139.

And like their pristine prophets, bode success.
Thus plum'd thus trained the second Shylock stood,
But lost his gold, nor shed the expected blood.[51]

In addition to this work, with its reference to the odious stereotype of the Jew created in *The Merchant of Venice*, a number of unflattering prints of the fight were circulated that poked fun at both Mendoza and the deluded Jews who backed him. In a rematch that took place in May of the following year, Mendoza beat his opponent and he became the champion of England. The two fought one more time, and again, Mendoza was declared the winner. For a few years he was one of the most popular men in the country. Unfortunately, his fame was short-lived. Within about three years he had squandered his money, and he found himself in debtor's prison. For the rest of his life, Mendoza struggled to support his family; at the time of his death he was penniless.

In his prime, Mendoza was called "The Light of Israel" by the Jewish community-testimony that his victories in the ring were a deep source of pride to many of them. Mendoza has been praised as a man who "demonstrated to a not too friendly world, not always prompt to believe it that Judaism and courage often go together,"[52] No doubt, to some degree, he showed a skeptical Christian society that Jews could hit back, and that they do, in a larger sense, have the courage to fight for king and country. It is doubtful, however, if his successes had any significant long-term positive effect upon Christian-Jewish relations or if, as Frank Felsenstein claims, his sporting prowess "did much to assuage traditional antipathies."[53] Like Moses Mendesohn in Germany, Mendoza was viewed as the exception that proved the rule. The German people could not accept other Jews as enlightened philosophers, and Britons felt the same way about the Jewish boxer's physical strength and courage.

Sampson Gideon's place in the public eye was far different from the one that Mendoza had occupied for such a short time. For decades, he was considered to be the most prominent Jew of his time; one of England's leading financiers. Gideon, a natural born Englishman, came from a Sephardic family who had escaped the Portuguese Inquisition and had settled in London. He began his career as a dealer in lottery tickets, and by the age of thirty he was one of the twelve Jewish brokers on the Exchange. As Gideon's fortunes grew, he attracted the attention of those in power. Through the years, he served as financial advisor to successive administrations where he earned their respect as well as the enmity of those who were jealous of his growing power in governmental

---

[51]Lewis Edwards, "Daniel Mendoza," *T.J.H.S.E.* 15 (1939-45): 79.
[52]Ibid., p. 92.
[53]Felsenstein, p. 230.

circles. In the 1740's the term "Gideonites" was applied to all loan contractors and stock jobbers as a class.[54]

During the War of the Austrian Succession (1742-48) and the Jacobite Rebellion of 1745, Sampson Gideon and other Jewish brokers extended credit to the government which helped to stabilize the Bank of England. In addition, he imported bullion to shore it up during a time of severe crisis. Until his death, he continued to raise the funds that were so necessary for England's wars, and as a reward for his services to the Crown, a private act of Parliament was passed which enabled him to officially own land. His subsequent purchase of magnificent estates was the source of additional animosity for those who resented Jewish encroachment upon the landed gentry's domain. Gideon's personal ambitions grew with his wealth. With the help of a dowry of £40,000, he arranged for his daughter, Elizabeth, to be married to Viscount Gage. Although Gideon never received a title, his son, born of his non-Jewish wife and who was raised as a Christian, became a Baronet and later a Peer. As Lucy Sutherland notes : "For on one side stood the anti-Semitism of English society and of George III, but on the other the desire of the ministry to serve a useful man."[55]

Samson Gideon's special relationship with the Pelham ministry was the object of considerable jealousy and contempt. In the play, The *Temple of Laverna*, written by Arthur Murphy (1730-1805) and published in 1752, the main character, who is clearly intended to represent Gideon, is named Caiaphas, the High Priest of the Temple in Jerusalem and Roman collaborator who was involved in the Crucifixion. He is portrayed as a wealthy "Jew Broker" who, though unable or unwilling to run for Parliament, has aspirations for his son to enter royalty.[56] Having been born in England, Samson Gideon was not a champion of Jewish naturalization for his newly arrived co-religionists. However, his prominent place in Anglo-Jewish affairs drew him into public view when, in 1753, this subject became the center of bitter controversy. Gideon was harassed by the mob, and he became the butt of numerous jokes and satirical prints that depicted him as a mock messiah who paved the passage of the "Jew Bill" with gold. He was angered by the Jewish communal leaders who used his name without permission, and he formally removed himself from the synagogue rolls. This did not end the slander that was heaped upon him by those who viewed him as a Jew who had mastered the sinister craft of stock jobbing and who had

---

[54]Dickson, p. 224.
[55]Lucy Stuart Sutherland. "Sampson Gideon and the Reduction of Interest 1749-50," *Economic History Review* 16 (1946): 15.
[56]Endelman, The *Jews of Georgian England*, pp. 28-9.

used his nefarious skills to profit from his country's need to finance two wars.[57] Gideon was the symbol not only of the upstart Jew who uses his wealth to buy respectability, but of the corruption of English society by members of the financial world who increased their fortune at the expense of others.

When Gideon died in 1762, it was discovered that during the years of his estrangement from the Jewish community he had anonymously paid dues to the synagogue. In his will he bequeathed £1000 to the congregation and to other Jewish charities, and he requested that he be buried in the Jewish cemetery. In addition, his name was to be read on each Day of Atonement along with the other major supporters of the synagogue. Gideon's final requests, like so much that he did in his lifetime, did not go unnoticed by the press. In an obituary that appears in the *Gentleman's Magazine* for October 1762, specific mention is made of his bequest to the synagogue. It is also noted that Gideon had been taken to the "Jews burying-ground where he was interred agreeable to the rites of the Jewish religion" (p. 503).

In addition to whatever personal contact the English people may have had with members of the Jewish community, contemporary newspapers and periodicals contained stories about both local and foreign Jews that captured the attention of an ever growing literate population. Although the actual size of the reading public is difficult to determine, it is estimated that by the end of the century approximately 80,000 out of a population of 6,000,000 had mastered the written word.[58] The impact of journalism went beyond the number of works that were actually printed. Newspapers, tracts, broadsides, and pamphlets, were regularly read aloud and discussed in the coffee houses. It is estimated, that in this way each copy of a periodical, like the Spectator, would reach no less than ten people.[59]

Several of the articles about individual Jews or special events in the Jewish community were not related to either love or hatred, but simply to satisfy the curiosity of the reading public. The following wedding announcement, found in the *British Journal* of August 10, 1723 was typical of those that were written for Christians, and it contains the kind of information (usually exaggerated) that was of interest to the curious of all faiths.

---

[57]Lucy Stuart Sutherland, "Sampson Gideon: Eighteenth Century Financier," *T.J.H.S.E.* 17 (1951- 52): 79.

[58]Ian Watt, *The Rise of the Novel: Studies in Defoe, Richardson and Fielding* (Berkeley: University of California Press, 1971), p. 35.

[59]John Carswell, *From Revolution to Revolution* (New York: Charles Scribner's Sons, 1973),pp. 29-30.

A treaty of marriage we hear is concluded
between Mr. Elisha Levi, a young Jew, just
come to a considerable estate, and a daughter
of Mr. Moses Hart, whose fortune is said to be £ 12,000.

In another wedding announcement, that appears in the *British Journal* for December 21,1723, the groom is described as "a son of Mr. Marcus Moses the rich Jew, who lately brought with him from India, a fine green diamond drop of very great value." In 1720 the "very famous Jew Wedding" of Aaron de Moseh Senior Coronel to his cousin, Rebecca de Salomah Senior Coronel, attracted considerable attention in the press. The details of the ceremony, to which the Prince and Princess of Wales and numerous dignitaries were invited, as well as the general description of the synagogue, was read with interest throughout the country.[60] In the next decades, news about the weddings of other prominent members of the Jewish community continues to reflect the growing acceptance of at least certain Jews by Christian society. For example, in Hooker's *Weekly Miscellany* for September 22,1738 it is reported that :

On Sunday last M Gedalia Viginima, an
eminent Jew merchant in Seething-Lane,
was married to Miss. Machado, daughter of
Mr. Moses Machado, a young lady of great merit;
there were present at the ceremony the French,
Spanish, and Portuguese Ministers (p. 3).

Other curiosity pieces written about contemporary Jews also contain some of the anti-Semitic prejudices of the age. For example, The *Weekly Journal or British Gazeteer* for October 8,1720 describes in detail how the Jews of London set up some 400 or 500 booths, covered with all sorts of greens, to observe the Feast of Tabernacles. The writer then concludes the piece with the words:

Thus those deluded people mimick that
great festival that was kept in the month
Tizri among the Jews, and which was
ordained for a memorial of the Children
of Israel living in tents when they were in
the wilderness.

Often, the implication of the religious "otherness" of the Jewish people does not require any special comments : it is present even in the more positive news articles that are written about them. For example, in Hooker's Weekly *Miscellany* for January 12, 1739 there is an account of a general fast that was proclaimed as the country prepared for war with Spain. After it is noted that the fast was "universally observ'd with the

---

[60]Aubrey Newman, p. 5.

utmost decency and solemnity" and that the people who had it in their power practiced acts of benevolence and charity, in the next paragraph the writer mentions that" the Jews kept the same at the several synagogues in the most solemn manner."

Some of the deeper fears about Jews often appear in articles based on the author's observation of contemporary Jewry. For example, in a critique of Abbe Gregoire's *Essay on the Physical, Moral, and Political Reformation of the Jews,* found in the *European Magazine and the London Review* for October, 1790, the reviewer comments about "the prodigious multiplication of the Jewish people" which he believes is due to their emphasis on early marriage and on having large families. In addition, their laws concerning sexual intercourse are also "most favorable to propagation." Since Jews consider sterility a disgrace, abhor celibacy, are exempted from taking up arms, never expose themselves to the dangers of the sea and live a moderate life, he feels that they tend to multiply faster than the general population"(p. 273-74). The possibility of this minority ultimately taking control of the country is left to the reader's imagination.

Jewish converts to Christianity were of such interest to contemporary readers that brief statements about them often appear along with the news of the day. Two examples of these conversion announcements read as follows:

> A Jew, very skillful in the Hebrew and Caldee was, after proper confession of his faith, publickly baptiz'd at the meeting-house in Paul's Alley Barbican.[61]

> Mr. Solomon Avola, a Bohemian Jew, embraced the Christian faith, and was publickly baptized at the Savoy Chapel.[62]

On the other hand, stories of how the Jewish community mistreated those who left their ancestral faith also appear in contemporary publications. In the *British Journal* of February 2, 1723 it is reported that the eldest son of Marcus-Moses Livy petitioned the court "that it not be in the power of his father to deprive him of a proper maintenance by reason of his conversion to the Christian faith." The court directed the father to be obligated for £5000 for the support of his son until the full value of the estate could be determined. In a more sensational story that appears in the *Gentleman's Magazine* of September, 1732, a young Jew in Bomberg was seized by his co-religionists when he expressed his desire to convert to Christianity. Though the Prince and the Bishop of the city

---

[61]*Gentleman's Magazine* 17 (February, 1748): 90.
[62]*Gentleman's Magazine* 19 (October, 1749): 474.

withdrew their protection of the Jewish community until he would be released, he was never heard from again (p. 983).

Stories of Jews involved in scandals of a less serious nature are also featured in popular publications. One particularly juicy piece of gossip, found in the *Gentleman's Magazine* for April, 1783 centered around Rachel Hagar de Behus, the daughter of a wealthy "Jew merchant" of Frankfurt. She is described as a woman with an "uncommonly elegant figure" who, while visiting Vienna attracted the attention of the local prince. Ultimately, he made her his mistress, and he indulged her in a world of royal luxury. After two years, he lost interest in her and "the little Israelite" became attracted to another member of the court who "in his hours of recreation would let her into such secrets as no woman should have been instructed with." The enraged prince banished them both from his realm, and the writer notes that the two have since married and now live in "utmost harmony"(p. 323). Abraham Payba, a London Jew, achieved a certain amount of notoriety in the press that was a source of delight to the general public. After his father had died, Payba inherited a considerable fortune which he increased through his successful insurance business. Unfortunately, he had a weakness for gambling, particularly betting on the horses. After several losses at the track, and the bankruptcy of his business, he found a female companion who went with him to France. There, he changed his name and continued to get into trouble. No less than four tracts were written about his adventures, and he is always referred to as "Abraham Payba, the Jew."[63]

As previously mentioned in Chapter II, when the Jewish people are mentioned in the foreign news columns of the press, such stories occasionally deal with their persecutions in countries that were England's traditional enemies. Invariably, these articles are motivated more by the hatred and fear of old foes as well as a desire to attack the tenets and practices of Catholicism, than by any real concern for the Jewish people. A particularly vivid description of an auto de fe' in Valencia and the means used by the Inquisition to extort confessions from its Jewish victims that appears in the *British Journal* of May 11, 1723, is followed by a warning that such horrors could easily come to England at the hands of those "who strive for Popery or a Popish Ruler." On July 25, 1724, in the same newspaper, there is a detailed account of the conclusion of a session of the Spanish Inquisition's tribunal where five persons convicted of Judaism were executed and sixteen who had died in prison were burned in effigy. In addition, nineteen other prisoners

---

[63]See, for example, *The Memorial Presented to the High Court of La Tornelle at Paris in Favour of Abraham Payba, the Jew, a Native of London Against Edward Wortley Montagu Esq. and Theobold Taaffe Esq.* (London: 1752).

received 200 lashes. Then, after their property had been confiscated by the state, these unfortunates were sent to the galleys. The article concludes with the words: "This view of the blessings of Popery, where it flourishes in its perfection, may serve to endear to us the possession of our happy freedom here, to awaken in a nation of Protestants, a just horror of such execrable religion." In the *European Magazine* for March, 1792, there is an English translation of a German lecture delivered by Moses Mendelsohn that describes the tortures inflicted upon a Spanish Jew by the Inquisition. After the victim is brutalized by the Church, he is condemned to death "for not making an article his creed that a piece of thin paste and a glass of stale wine is the very body and blood of his Creator." The author notes that although his religious sentiments may vary from those of the Jewish people, their complaints against the Church are worthy of the attention of good Christians (p. 174).

England's own financial interests were also a definite factor in bringing reports of Jewish persecutions to the public's attention. For example, in the *London Morning Post* of February 27, 1740, it is reported that the King of Naples had issued an edict permitting the Jews to settle in the city for trading purposes. In the edition that appears on March 6, 1740 it is noted that:

> The clergy there are out of humour with
> the introduction of the Jews....However,
> though the clergy's discontent in this case
> is the result of bigotry and self interest,
> Britain may nevertheless turn it to good
> account at a proper opportunity – but she must
> strike the iron while it is hot, if she intends to
> make anything of it.

The story continues for a few more weeks with comments made concerning Jewish wealth and economic power. They are clearly an important economic asset to any country – a people who possesses considerable liquid assets. In the edition of March 8,1740 it is noted:

> As no where the Jews are permitted
> to purchase land or houses many of
> them are bankers, and their estates
> consist wholly in specie, jewels, and
> other valuable commodities; the retreat
> of but one or two rich Jews, might prove
> very detrimental to the publick.

The association of Jews with wealth and special privileges appears in any number of articles in the popular press. Though not necessarily anti-Semitic, these brief pieces add to the stereotype of the influential "rich Jew." For example, the *British Journal* of July 18, 1724 notes that: "On

Tuesday, Baron Suasso, and several others of the richest Jews of this city, took oaths according to the late act of Parliament, which allows them to swear upon the Old Testament instead of the New."

There is also a sinister side to the Jews who often appear in the foreign news sections of the periodicals and newspapers of the time. Dispatches from abroad often provide fresh material for the reader's already distorted image of the Jewish people. In Hooker's *Weekly Miscellany* of January 12, 1739, there is a story of an uprising in Russia where a certain Mr. Lierman, the Jew, was attacked by the mob for being a favorite of the Prince of Couland who supposedly did nothing without consulting with him. The foreign correspondent, who wants his readers to be aware of the real power behind the throne, reports that this Jew banker "may be said in some degree to govern all of Russia." The following dispatch, which appears in *The Weekly Journal or British Gazeteer* of April 12,1720, is a reminder of the alleged involvement of the Jewish people in the Crucifixion and their subsequent mocking of Christianity.

> They write from Hamburg, that twenty Jews
> have been apprehended there, being accused
> of having dress'd up several figures representing
> the Passion of our Saviour, to be made use of in
> ridicule, in a masquerade acted among themselves.
> Our magistrates have fin'd the whole body of
> the Jews in this city at 20,000 Rixdollars for this
> affront to the Christian religion, and threaten to
> expel them from the city, if it is not complied with.

Other dispatches from foreign countries that appear in the press enhance the negative image of unethical Jewish business practices. For example, *The Penny London Post* of March 9, 1726 reports that the corporation of the city of Lublin has resolved to send a deputy to the King to complain about the Jews "who very much obstruct their commerce in defiance of the laws of the kingdom."

During the eighteenth century, the growth of newspapers and periodicals, with their lurid tales of brutal murders, vicious beatings, and sensational court trials, provided an expanding form of popular amusement. Native Jews, particularly those from the lower classes, appear both as victims and as criminals in contemporary publications and prints. Stories of bloody incidents involving Jewish peddlers are fairly common. In one such news article, which appears in the *Gentleman's Magazine* for September, 1783, Isaac Levy, a peddler, was struck over the head with a hedge-stake and robbed of his goods by a criminal named Fox. Few of the gory details of the crime were left to the reader's imagination, and it was clearly stated that the innocent victim was a "Jew lad"(p. 800). On the other hand, in the accounts of a murder trial held at the Old Baily, the Jews are portrayed as a rowdy group who are a threat to innocent Christians. In this instance, Joseph Redout was tried for the murder of Moses Lazarus, a thirteen year old boy, whom he shot and killed in what he claimed was an act of self-defense. According to the *Gentleman's Magazine* for October, 1784, the defendant told the court that at the time when the Jewish community was celebrating "the anniversary of the promulgation of their law" a mob of them assembled and began to throw "serpents, squibbs, and crackers," at him. Though Redout sought help from the civil magistrate and the constable of the parish, none was forthcoming. The Jews, he claimed, surrounded him, beat him, and then dragged him to the ground. Although he managed to escape from their clutches, they pursued him with "groans and hisses." Then, they followed him into his house where they threatened to kill him. When the Jews refused to disperse, he fired into the crowd and killed the youngster. The writer of the piece notes that after the laws of self-defense were explained to the jury, they acquitted the defendant "without a minute's hesitation"(p. 793).

Lurid stories of alleged atrocities committed against innocent Christians by Jewish mobs that appeared in the foreign affairs section of contemporary periodicals, added to the prejudice that the English had against their Jewish neighbors. A news article from Vienna that appears in the Gentleman's *Magazine* for September, 1732, describes how five Jews were imprisoned for the murder of a young beggar. They had paid a peasant 300 crowns to lure him into a forest where "They hung him on a tree by the feet, cut his belly in the form of a Cross, and then scourg'd him in that posture to death" (p. 983). Although this is obviously a fabrication based upon medieval tales of Jews crucifying innocent Christians for nefarious purposes, it is reported in a very matter-of-fact way as an actual event. Some of the stories that appear in the foreign news columns were damaging to British Jewry by singling them out and stressing their "otherness" in various countries. For example, Hooker's *Weekly Miscellany* of July 22, 1737 notes that when the Great Duke of Tuscany became ill, his subjects displayed their concern for his welfare. As proof of every one's love, the writer notes "that the very Jews in particular observed a solemn day of prayer and fasting."

The Jewish community had its share of criminals who appeared in the newspapers and periodicals of the period. The hand-to-mouth existence of many of the immigrants was a key factor in attracting them to a life of crime. In addition, their skill in seal cutting, calligraphy, engraving, and watch making, was easily transferred to forgery, lock picking, and counterfeiting. Jewish involvement in pawnbroking and in dealing with second hand goods, which went back to the medieval church's policies of restricting their employment to degrading work unfit for Christians, provided them with a ready means of disposing of stolen goods. Patrick Coloquhoun (1745-1820), in his work, *A Treatise on the Police of London*, which was cited in popular contemporary periodicals,[64] makes several references to Jews "of the lower order" who are involved in criminal activity, especially the selling of counterfeit coins, or dealing in stolen goods. He mentions, for example, "Itinerant Jews wandering from street to street, holding out temptations to pilfer and steal, and Jew boys crying Bad Shillings, who purchase articles stolen by servants, stable boys, etc."(p. vii). Coloquhoun claims that "Jew dealers" have extensive connections in England and throughout the Continent to handle stolen goods and to enable them to make immense profits from their illegal labors (p. 136).

In one of the popular Chap Books of the time, *The Trials of all the Felon Prisoners, Tried, Cast, and Condemned, this Session at the Old baily....to which is added An Account of the closing of the Sessions and a correct List of all the Prisoners tried, and the Sentences passed on them*, it was mentioned that "Isaac Solomons was convicted of selling counterfeit halfpence, for less value than they purported to be – he was sentenced to one year's imprisonment, and a fine of £100" (p. 7).The fact that Solomons' ties to the Jewish community are not mentioned is a rare exception to the rule. Invariably, if Jews committed a crime, if they were brought to trial or if they faced execution, their religion was mentioned in the press. In Hooker's *Weekly Miscellany* of March 10, 1738 there is a brief mention of a certain Dutch Jew who, during the worship services conducted by the Society for Reformation of Manners, "was taken up at the door of the church for exposing to sale little boxes with obscene figures. "For this act he was brought before Sir John Salter who committed him to hard labor at Bridewell (p. 3). The *British Journal* of March 30, 1723 notes that, "A Jew who fraudulently transfer'd £250 of bank stock belonging to Mrs. Stanley, and fled to Germany is (at the instance of His Majesty's Secretaries) seiz'd by the order of the Emperor, and imprisoned at Frankfurt, in order to be prosecuted with the utmost rigour." The same newspaper reports in its November 7, 1724 edition that :" 'Tis said a petition will be presented to His Majesty on behalf of Moses Ouseman the Jew, now under sentence of death, sign'd by a great number of the most eminent merchants of this city." The *Penny London Post* of February 11, 1726 reports that "On Tuesday last, a large seizure of foreign snuff was brought into the Exchequer, amounting to 40,000 pounds weight; being imported by some Dutch Jews as British manufactured, to the great

---

[64]See, for example, The *Edinburgh Magazine or Literary Miscellany* 9 (January, 1797): 17-22.

prejudice of the revenue and fair traders. "The following appears in the *London Morning Post* of February 9, 1740: "An eminent Jew Broker has been detected forging bills of exchange, and negotiating the same, and has since made his escape." In this same spirit of specifically labeling Jewish criminals, *Mist's Weekly Journal* of August 10, 1728 reports that: "Joseph Hyans, a Jew, is committed to Surry Gaol for filling and cutting Broad Pieces." When the "Jews synagogue" in Duke's Place was burglarized, it is noted in the *Gentleman's Magazine* for March 1748, that "Jeremiah Levi, a Jew," had stolen silver plate and vestments that were valued at £300 (p. 137). Jewish prisoners, particularly those who observed their traditions behind bars, also received the attention of contemporary newspapers. *Mist's Weekly Journal* of August 12, 1727 notes that:

> Several Jews, who are prisoners in the Fleet,
> have erected there a little hut in the corner of
> the place, calling it a tabernacle, and have cover'd
> the same with green boughs and fruit, in order to
> celebrate the Jewish Feast of Tabernacles according to
> their mock manner.

When a group of criminals was taken from Newgate to Tyburn for execution, special mention is made in the Gentleman's *Magazine* for September, 1783 that three of them were Jewish, and that they "were attended by a priest of their own religion" (p. 802).

Jewish women who were involved in criminal activities also had their religion mentioned in the press. For example, the following appears in the *Penny London Post* of April 29, 1726 :

> At the same time and place, one Vincent, a Newgate
> solicitor, and Rachel David, and her mother, Jew women
> were convicted of conspiring to charge one Mr. Nunes, a
> Jew, with rape on the body of said Rachel, and were
> sentenc'd all three to stand in the pillory at the Royal
> Exchange, and suffer six months imprisonment in
> Newgate. And Vincent also fined 20 Marks.

The most infamous act of violence committed by Jewish criminals occurred in the Fall of 1771 in Chelsea when four Jews, in the course of a burglary, killed a servant. Ultimately, they were caught and given a speedy trial. Prior to their receiving the death penalty, the *Gentleman's Magazine* for December, 1771 reports the following:

> The Recorder prefaced the sentence with a
> judicious and just compliment to the principal
> Jews, for their very laudable conduct in the
> course of this prosecution, and hoped no
> person would ignorantly stigmatize a whole nation

for the villanies of a few, whom they had done
everything they consistently could to bring to punishment (p. 566).

Nevertheless, the Jewish community, as a whole, was subjected to a barrage of slurs, threats, and public denunciations. In order to convince the general public that the individuals who had committed the crime were also condemned by their own people, the leaders of the Jewish community placed an advertisement in the newspapers stating that those "Foreign Miscreants" who had been involved in criminal activities or who dealt in stolen goods would not be granted "Burials or other Religious Indulgence" by the synagogue and that they would be excommunicated from the Jewish faith.[65]

During the course of the trial, the *Gentleman's Magazine* for November of 1771 noted that Jewish gangs were recruiting "fresh miscreants" from abroad to participate in their "many daring and mischievous plans" (p. 518). This prompted the Wardens of the Great Synagogue to urge the authorities to limit the immigration of poor Jews who did not have any means of livelihood. As a result of their pleas, the Secretary of State issued instructions to the Postmaster-General that only those Jews who had the ability to pay their passages in full and who had passports from an ambassador or minister abroad would be permitted to enter the country. Free passes were offered by the Lord Mayor to poor Jews who wanted to leave and return to their native lands.[66]

In addition to publicizing the violent acts of Jewish criminals, the press also called special attention to cases of fraud committed by Jews against Christian businessmen. For example, in the listing of bankrupts found in the *Gentleman's Magazine* of March, 1731, the names of Richard and Thomas Woodward appear. It is also mentioned that "The cause of their failure is charged on the Jews. who borrowed large sums of them, which belonged to English merchants, with which they traded, but took no care to reimburse according to their engagements." No comments are made concerning other bankruptcies on the list, and no one else is blamed for other cases of financial ruin (p. 129). Later, in the October issue of the same journal, there is an article entitled, "Of Lying, Swearing, and Blasphemy." The author discusses how different cultures in the ancient world viewed perjury. He notes that during the period of Philo Judaeus, it was a capital crime. However, since that time, the Jewish people has been poisoned by the Talmud, a work which he claims allows them to nullify their vows, promises, and oaths. Modern Jews, "use the same artifice, thinking that they may then lawfully deceive

---

[65]Nathan Elkan Adler, *London* (Philadelphia: Jewish Publication Society of America, 1930), p. 152.
[66]Roth, *History of the Jews in England*, p. 235-36.

Christians" (pp. 414-15). These assertions are reinforced, in the public's imagination, by a number of real and imagined accounts of trickery where the perpetrator's Jewishness is clearly labeled. For example, *Hooker's Weekly Miscellany* for May 13, 1738 reports that in the Quarter sessions for the County of Surrey "several prisoners, some for very large sums were clear'd by the late act of insolvency." However, a "noted Jew, charged with the best part of £100,000 was remanded back not being thought by the Court to have a just title to the benefit of the Act."

Most stories about Jewish fraud center around Change Alley. Along with Christian cohorts, Jews periodically appear in the press not only to highlight their manipulation of stock values, but the prices of lottery tickets as well. In the September 1,1739 Issue of *Hooker's Weekly Miscellany*, the writer notes:

> By the tricks and cunning of the Jews,
> Stock Jobbers and their several understrappers,
> we see that lottery tickets are now sold at 5L. 8s. 6d.
> though t's certain the real value of a ticket is no
> more than £4.3s. These worthy set of gentleman
> sharpers take it for granted, that by the
> number of fools coming to Exchange Alley,
> they can bubble the people out of no less
> a sum then £20,000.

The word "cunning" was used by the same newspaper in its issue of September 1, 1739 to describe a certain Gypsy who "bewitched" the money of a gentleman through a fanciful tale of hidden treasure. Obviously, the press saw a connection between the activities of these two groups.

Biased travelers' accounts of Jews in other countries also contributed to negative stereotypes. In one of these that appeared in the *London Magazine* of June 1760 a visitor to Morocco notes that the Jews in the country are "the most fraudulent people under the sun, who, however, have engrossed the chief trade, and are, in fact, the brokers, coiners, and bankers of the realm" (p. 335).

The growth of the cotton spinning industry in Manchester created new anti-Semitic criminal stereotypes that caught the public's eye. Jews are accused of being "traveling plagiarists" – industrial spies who reveal the secrets of the emerging textile factories to foreign competitors. In the media, "Jews and other foreigners" threaten the destruction of the country's trade. Although not a single Jew was ever convicted of this crime, these fears continued for over a half a century.[67]

---

[67]Williams, *The Making of Manchester Jewry*, pp. 9-10.

In addition to these very negative statements, there were some positive articles written about Jews as well. From time to time, favorable images appear in the obituary columns of the leading periodicals. The following stylized selection found in the *Gentleman's Magazine* of February, 1796, which could have been written about any prominent merchant, reflects this other side of Jewish character that appears in the media.

> At his house in Bevis Marks, aged 89, Levi Cohen
> esq. merchant, respected for his upright conduct
> religious precepts, honourable dealings, charitable
> practices, amiable condescensions, rendering general
> services, a loving husband, a good father, and a loyal
> subject; thus his life ended in the most exalted virtues
> and in domestic happiness(p. 168).

In many instances praise for them is utilized to either bolster Christian theological beliefs or to convert them. In the main article in the Spectator for September 27, 1712, the author claims that he admires the Jewish people whom he has met during his travels. He believes that, as international traders, they serve the vital purpose of keeping channels of communication open between nations all over the globe. "They are like the pegs and nails of a great building, which, though they are little valued in themselves are absolutely necessary to keep the whole frame together." The author is impressed with the number of Jews in the world who, in spite of centuries of persecution, have maintained their faith throughout the lands of their dispersion. He attributes this steadfastness to the workings of Providence; for by their actions, the Jews are witnesses to the truth of the Hebrew Scriptures which contain the prophesies of the coming of Jesus as the Messiah. Their continued existence provides the strongest arguments for the Christian faith. In an almost medieval fashion he notes:

> Had the whole body of the Jews been converted
> to Christianity, we should certainly have thought
> all the prophecies of the Old Testament that relate
> to the coming and the history of our blessed Saviour
> forged by Christians.

The Jewish peddler, stock jobber, boxer, merchant, criminal, and victim, became recognizable figures to many of the English people through limited personal contact and through the numerous publications that included them in the domestic and foreign news of the day. However, in many instances, the theological stereotypes of past centuries still lingered in the popular imagination. John Toland (1670-1722), well aware of the dark side of the Age of Reason notes:

> So strong is the force of prejudice that I
> know a person, no fool in other instances,
> who laboured to persuade me, contrary to the
> evidence of his own eye and my eyes (to mine
> I am sure) that every Jew in the world had one eye
> remarkably less than the other, which silly notion
> he took from the mob. Others will gravely tell you,
> that they may be distinguished by a peculiar sort
> of smell, that they have a mark of blood on one
> shoulder, and they cannot spit to any distance.[68]

The force of prejudice that came from past memories was rooted in many different sources. Perhaps the most vile of these portrayals of the Jewish people was tied to the medieval *Judensau*, the image of the Jews sucking the teats of a sow. This visual obscenity is a strong statement that they belong to an abominable and despicable category of beings who must turn to their mother, the pig, for nourishment. It is a repulsive way to perpetuate the idea that Jews are not truly human – a popular conception particularly found in both the secular and religious literature of the medieval German states and which, to some degree, continues into the modern world as well.

The *Judensau* motif, as such, does not appear in eighteenth century England, but the Jewish prohibition against eating pork products does emerge as a source of popular fascination and humour. Felsentein points out that Hanoverian England was not immune to the obscenities that were long associated with the *Judensau*. He believes that it was an accepted part of the folklore of the period that Jews had a special secret appetite for pork products.[69] In the caricatures, cartoons, and satirical prints, there is the association of the Jews with pigs. Only now, the Jew is portrayed as the buffoon rather than the subhuman. During the clamor over the "Jew Bill "of 1753, cartoons appear that depict Jews riding on pigs. Later in the century, they are portrayed as pig keepers and pig thieves, but the more sinister overtones of a less "enlightened" past still remain in the popular imagination.

As the Jews assimilated into English society, they took on the trappings of their neighbors' way of life. Among other things, they emerged as a distinct and very visible group of pleasure-seekers in the various brothels of London. In one popular street ballad, *The long Vocation*, (c. 1700) which refers to the period in the summer when the Court and courtiers depart from the Metropolis for cooler places, there is the stanza:

> When the Season was too hot for the Goggle-Ey'd Jews

---

[68]Cohen, Scrapbook, p. 324.
[69]Felsenstein, p. 128.

To exercise their Faculties in Drury Lane Stews....[70]

It is noted in the chap book, *A Trip Through the Town*, (c.1730) that young Jews frequented the Convent Garden bawdy houses where they were lavish spenders – equals to their Gentile friends' elaborate dress and low moral standards. Jewish attraction for prostitutes is also mentioned in various contemporary newspapers.

The *British Journal* of August 24, 1723 reports that: "On Monday last one Susannah Newport, formerly a fruitress in Stocks-Market, much admir'd by the Jews on account of her youth and beauty, but by her great commerce with those gentlemen, was lately reduced to the degree of walking shopkeeper" stole a silver tankard and was committed to Newgate. References to Jewish sexual appetites appear in some of the popular expressions of the period. For example, one observer of the contemporary scene describes those who would benefit from the death of the wealthy with the words:

> "These low heel'd gentlemen shall watch as impatiently for the last gasp of a person of quality as a Jew for an opportunity to debauch his maid."[71]

Exaggerated sexual desires have been attributed to any number of "others". But for Jewish males, circumcision adds new dimensions to the common stereotype. For centuries this rite has been viewed by many Christians as a barbaric practice. It has also maintained a prominent place in anti-Semitic literature as a deep source of unconscious fear that is tied to castration and a threat to manhood.[72] In eighteenth-century England, circumcision now becomes a source of humor that is often related to other negative Jewish traits. However, its sinister side, though not always visible, still lingers in the background.

One brief selection which pokes fun at circumcision in the context of other popular prejudices against the Jews is Alexander Pope's (1688-1744) satire, *A Strange But True Relation How Mr. Edmund Curll, of Fleet Street, Stationer, Out of an Extraordinary Desire of Lucre, Went Into "Change Alley," and was Converted From the Christian Religion by Certain Eminent Jews; and How he was Circumcised, and Initiated Into Their Mysteries*. The publisher, Edmund Curll (1675-1747), was a bitter enemy, and Pope ridiculed him in his three part work.

The last section is a satire, in sermonic form, that targets Curll, the Church, and also the Jews. Pope describes how Curll becomes interested

---

[70]E.J. Burford, *Wits, Wenchers and Wantons: London's Low Life: Covent Garden in the Eighteenth Century* (London: Robert Hale, 1986), p. 35.

[71]*A View of London and Westminster: or the Town Spy* (London: Printed for T. Warmer, 1725), p. 23.

[72]Allport, p. 240.

in converting to Judaism when he first learns about the immense sums of money they make in their various "bubbles." Hoping to make his fortune, he leaves his shop and seeks out the Jews in "Change Alley." He is assured by them that upon his conversion he will become "as rich as a Jew." In addition, if he would be willing to poison his wife, he could marry the daughter of one of the richest Jews of London. The money-hungry Jews recognize a person with their own weaknesses, and in what Pope believes is a good Jewish tradition, they bargain with Curll to renounce his Christian beliefs for financial gain. Finally, after Curll has agreed to their terms, the Jews prepare to circumcise him. Pope uses various Sephardic names like Gideon Lopez, Joshua Pereira, and John Mendez to add a touch of authenticity to his story. He also draws upon typical stereotypes when he describes one of them as a "meagre man with a sallow countenance, a black forky beard, and long vestments" who holds a large pair of shears in his left hand and a red hot searing iron in his right. When Curll changes his mind and is unwilling to go through with his conversion, the Jews seize hold of him, unbutton his breeches and throw him on the table. They threaten to declare all contracts made with him to be null and void if he will refuse to accept this outward sign of Judaism. Curll then reconsiders their proposal. However, "by an unfortunate jerk upward of the impatient victim" he "lost five times as much as ever a Jew did before." The Jews then go back on their word, cast him out of the synagogue and nullify all of their promises. It appears that Curll "was too much circumcised" and this is worse than not being circumcised at all." To add insult to injury, the Jews preserve in their coffee house the "memorial of Curll's indignity." Pope concludes his satire with a mock prayer that summarizes the hypocrisy, cruelty, greed, and thirst for blood that he believes characterizes the Jews whom he lumps together with Papists, Stock Jobbers, and Satan.

There are, of course, more serious discussions of circumcision by those Christians who believe that God demands the circumcision of the heart and not of the flesh or by those who want to discourage conversion to Judaism. Some of these attacks are based upon what they consider to be the life-threatening nature of such an operation. Often, distortions of Jewish sources are used to buttress these criticism. In the face of overwhelming scorn, mockery, and fear of the ritual, a few brave souls dared to refute the misinformation that was being circulated. In one such pamphlet, the anonymous writer, who was probably a member of the Jewish community, shows how the words of the medieval sage, Maimonides, had been misquoted regarding the medical dangers of this operation. In addition, he points out that "many have come from Spain and Portugal and have been circumcised at the age of sixty, or seventy, and have never died of it."[73] It is doubtful, however, if such a work had any significant impact upon public opinion.

In spite of ethnic and religious slurs and the reappearance of old stereotypes, various members of the Jewish community, as well as those who chose to leave it, found a niche for themselves in their adopted country. As they began to move up in society, they socialized with their Christian neighbors in the coffee houses, at various civic and charity dinners, and in the ballrooms and salons of the landed gentry. The social structure of eighteenth century England was based on "the grand principle of subordination" where everyone was expected to know his or her place in the scheme of things. Only a select group, on the top rung of the ladder could enjoy a comfortable, secure existence, and live in what might be termed a "gentleman's utopia."[74] Yet, as Humphreys points out, society was "not so rigid that the energetic poor man might not rise far in almost any walk of life."[75] It was possible to climb the economic and social ladder, and the Jewish immigrant community enjoyed an upward mobility that, at the time, was not found in most other countries where their co-religionists had settled. Free from governmental harassment and arbitrary restrictions on where they might live, those Jews who had the means sought out the lifestyle of the upper classes. For example, after Moses Hart (1675-1756) won the lottery, he proceeded to build a substantial estate at Isleworth and to take on the trappings of a country gentleman. He was soon followed by several other members of his family who settled close by. Later, when he moved to Richmond, he was accepted into some of the social circles of the Christian community. Daniel Defoe, in his work, *A Tour Thro' the whole Island of Great Britain* (1722), reports that wealthy Jews had already country retreats in High-gate and in Hamstead where they have "butchers of their own to supply them with provisions kill'd their own way" and a private synagogue as well (pp. 382-83). No doubt, the presence of Kosher butchers, and private synagogues on these estates were novelties worth mentioning. But, by this time, the pressures of assimilation were mounting. The prosperity that was enjoyed by a select few was, in various degrees, spreading, and, as a result, the glue that had held the Jewish community together was also weakening. [76]

---

[73]*An Answer to the Letter to Dr. Waterland. In Relation to the Point of Cicumcision* (London: J. Crownfield, 1731), p. 31.
[74]James L. Clifford, ed. Man *Versus Society in Eighteenth-Century Britain* (Cambridge: Cambridge University Press, 1968),pp. 133-34.
[75]Humphreys, *Augustan World*, p. 2.
[76]For a comprehensive study of the effects of this new world on Anglo-Jewry see Todd Endelman, *Radical Assimilation in English History, 1656-1945* (Bloomington and Indianapolis: Indiana University Press, 1990).

During the first half of the eighteenth century, Jews who had fled from the Iberian Peninsula or who had left the ghettos of Central and Eastern Europe for a better life, looked at England as a safe haven from oppression and a land of economic opportunity. Compared to the various "others" in England, the Jewish minority was in an enviable position. Unfortunately, this period of relative calm was shattered in the middle of the century. It was not ended by a pogrom or by an edict of expulsion, but by an innocuous act of Parliament that was intended to ease the naturalization process of a small number of foreign Jews. Although the turmoil in England was limited mostly to words and not to violent deeds, the "Jew Bill," as it was often called, demonstrated some of the deeper irrational feelings towards the Jewish people that, for any number of reasons, would now come to the surface.

8

The "Jew Bill" of 1753 and Its Aftermath

IV

But Lord, how surpriz'd when they heard of the News,
That we were to be Servants to circumcis'd Jews,
To be Negroes and Slaves instead of *True Blues,*
    Which Nobody can deny,....

XIII

Then cheer up your spirits, let *Jacobites* swing.
And *Jews* in our Bell-Ropes hang when they ring,
To our Sovereign Lord Great *George* our King,
    Which Nobody can deny, deny,
    Which Nobody can deny.[1]

A Call to the Jews

Come, Abram's sons, from ev'ry quarter come,
Britain now bids you call her land your home,
Here you may live secure from future harms,
A fairer Can'an courts you to her arms.
If you have gold, you nothing have to fear;
Bring with you gold, for that does all things here;
A New Jerusalem you soon may raise,
And give to golden calves again your praise:
Revenge (your fav'rite passion) you may hoist,
And once more trample on the cross of Christ.[2]

---

[1]"The Jews' Triumph: a Ballad To be Said or Sung to the Children of Israel on all popular occasions by all Christian People. London: Printed for Issac Ben-Haddi. Cited in Albert M. Hyamson. "The Jew Bill of 1753" *T.J.H.S.E.* 6 (1908): 167.
[2]*The Scots Magazine* 15 (May, 1753): 247. cited from *The London Evening Post* June 5, 1753.

No doubt, it was both the persistence of Joseph Salvador (1716-1786), a leader of the Sephardic synagogue, and the desire for the Pelham administration to repay the Jewish community for its financial support of the Hanoverians, that encouraged legislation in Parliament to expedite the naturalization of foreign Jews. The acceptance of certain Jewish financiers by their Christian neighbors as well as the hope that wealthy Jews from abroad would enrich the country, gave additional support to this act of Parliament. Up to this point, Jewish immigrants, like other aliens, could not own land or real property. In addition, they suffered certain disabilities if they wanted to be renters. As aliens, foreign Jews could not own a British vessel nor could they participate in the colonial trade. In those areas of commerce which foreign Jews were permitted to enter, they were subjected to special "alien duties" that put them at a competitive disadvantage with native merchants. True, foreigners who had resided in the American colonies for seven years could become naturalized citizens, but less than two hundred Jews, most of whom had been residents of Jamaica, took advantage of this process. Foreign Jews could also purchase royal lettres-patent and become "free denizens." However, the colonial trade would still be closed to them. If their children had been born abroad before this privilege was purchased, in the eyes of the law they would be aliens, and they could not inherit their father's real property.

The "Jew Bill" of 1753 provided that in the future Parliament could, if it so desired, naturalize foreign Jews and end their disabilities. However, all interested parties would still have to go through the very costly proceedings of obtaining the passage of a private act of Parliament. Obviously, only a small number of wealthy individuals would be affected by such legislation, and its overall effect upon immigration would be minimal.

The Bill was before the House of Lords for a period of five weeks so that its provisions would be thoroughly understood. It received unanimous support without a debate; it was then sent on to the Commons. By this time political opposition motivated by an upcoming general election was mounting. Clearly, the naturalization of foreign Jews appeared to be an issue that could easily stir passions and embarrass the administration. The slurs against the Jewish people that were uttered in Parliament would later be heard throughout the country. Tory political figures like William Northey denounced the Bill on the grounds that it was an attempt to rob the Britons of their Christian birthright. Using a familiar biblical story he notes:

> We know what a curse Esau brought upon himself
> and his posterity, by selling his birthright to
> to his brother Jacob for a mess of potage, when he

was faint and at the point of dying for hunger: his
posterity were to serve the posterity of Jacob: ought
we not to fear, that this may be the fate of our posterity,
as we are now about to sell our birthright to the posterity
of that same Jacob?[3]

After mentioning the alleged bribe of £200,000 that the Jews offered to Cromwell for naturalization, and an even greater one during the reigns of William and Anne, he suspects that now that they are more numerous and wealthy than ever before, they would be willing to offer even more money for this privilege. Northey, harping on the dangers of Jewish wealth, warns of hordes of Jews coming from abroad and buying up choice estates. He compares them to the ancient Israelites who divided up the Land of Canaan among the tribes without concern for the native inhabitants. In addition, the wealthy Jews would attract great numbers of their poor co-religionists. "For we know," he claims, "that they can make use of none but Jew butchers, bakers, poulterers and the like trades, which, of course, must make them soon become very numerous in this country."[4] He also wonders what would happen if a naturalized Jew would return to a country like Portugal from which he had been banished and would be arrested by the Inquisition. What protection could England offer him?[5] In essence, Northey argues that a "foreign incident" is too high a price to pay for Jewish naturalization.

Sir Edmund Isham, another Tory opponent of the Bill, objected to naturalizing foreign Jews without demanding that they convert to Christianity. He echoes the exaggerated fear that the Bill would naturalize multitudes of foreign Jews – the poor following in the footsteps of their rich brethren. Unlike the Huguenots and the Palatines, he believes that the Jews coming from abroad would not assimilate into English society. He notes:

....the unconverted Jews can never incorporate
with us: they must for ever remain Jews, and will
always deem themselves to be of the Hebrew
not the English nation.[6]

Instead, they would resemble their ancestors in Egypt who grew from one family into a nation of 600, 000 fighting men as well as women, children, and servants. To dramatize his fears of a growing Jewish presence in the country and to emphasize their otherness, in the midst of his speech he pauses and he tells his colleagues:

---

[3]*Parliamentary History* vol. xiv, 1366.
[4]Ibid., 1372.
[5]Ibid., 1373.
[6]Ibid., 1380.

> I hope I am speaking to a Christian assembly:
> how long I may indulge myself in this pleasing
> hope, I do not know; but I do not yet see a Jew
> among us – unless he is in the gallery.[7]

Isham supports his arguments against the Bill by pointing out that if it would pass, it would invalidate the Christian doctrine based on the prophesies found in Christian Scripture, that the Jews are to remain dispersed until they accept Jesus to be the Messiah. Only then would they be gathered from the four corners of the earth and be restored to their native land. Clearly, the Bill would give them a permanent place of settlement without the required acknowledgment of Jesus being the Messiah.

Isham's opposition to the Bill goes much deeper than many of his contemporaries. Not only is he opposed to the naturalization of foreign Jews, but he also questions the right of those who are already living in England to practice their faith. He feels that Parliament should appoint a secret committee to determine whether the Jewish people are allowed to maintain a synagogue or any place of public worship in the country. If they have this right, he wants to know by what authority was it given to them. He is of the opinion that there are several specific laws against it ; the Act of Toleration excludes any group that does not accept the Trinity. Though no secret committee was formed, the debate went deeper than embarrassing the government over the naturalization of foreigners. Old animosities were unleashed that could threaten the status of the existing Jewish community.

The head of the opposition to the Bill was Sir John Barnard (1685-1764), the leading M.P. for the City of London, a bitter enemy of Samson Gideon and those who were involved with Change Alley. His deep hatred of the Jewish people is evident in his opening remarks when he claims that giving a particular invitation to the Jewish people to settle in the country is tantamount to abandoning Christianity.

> The Jews Sir, are, and always have been,
> the most professed enemies of Christianity,
> and the greatest revilers of Christ himself: they
> are the offspring of those that crucified our
> Saviour, and to this day labour under the curse
> pronounced against them.[8]

Though supporters of the Bill contend that it will bring the Jews into the Christian fold, Barnard questions the possibility of Jewish conversion. He is convinced that if a Jew comes to take the sacrament, it would probably

---

[7]Ibid., 1381.
[8]Ibid., 1388.

be an artifice to achieve some financial gain. No clergyman, he believes, should "administer it to a reputed Jew without a sufficient testimony of his having regularly embraced the Christian faith, not privately, but according to custom, before a multitude of witnesses."[9]

Following his arguments that are based upon religion, Barnard then enters the realm of finance, and he appeals to the pragmatic sentiments of his colleagues. He points out, for example, that Jewish immigration would cause English merchants to suffer since significant portions of their business would fall into Jewish hands. The Jews would ultimately become the nation's only merchants and shop-keepers thereby reducing Christians to the performance of menial tasks for their Jewish masters. Not only would the English mercantile classes become impoverished, but the landed gentry would also suffer and, as a result, they would be forced to sell their estates to the Jews.

Barnard concludes his speech with religious sentiments that are almost medieval in tone and content. He warns his colleagues of the curse that "attends the(Jewish) nation in general, and will attend them until they acknowledge Christ to be the Messiah." He believes that by indulging those Jews who will not honestly convert to Christianity, the English people will bring their nation "into the same contempt which they are held by all nations under the sun." Barnard hopes that if foreign Jews would be allowed to settle in Britain, they would "not bring along with them the curse that has pursued them through all countries and for so many ages."[10]

Other speakers, like the Tory politician, Nicholas Fazakerley, compare the Jews to the Irish Papists who never converted to Protestantism. Instead, they engaged themselves in several "plots and conspiracies" to force the Protestants to embrace Catholicism. Since he believes that the Jews are as obstinate as the Papists, he fears for the safety of his countrymen. Basing his arguments on the Book of Esther, he warns of the dangers of allowing Jews to get too much power into their hands. In biblical times, in the city of Shushan, they put to death some 76,000 of their enemies. Who knows what they would do in England if the same situation would present itself to them once again?[11]

Those in favor of the Bill, like Lord Dupplin, offer familiar arguments that would be repeated in the pamphlets issued in the ensuing months. In essence, Jews would bring capital into the country, and they would stem the drain of gold that was sent abroad to pay

---

[9]Ibid., 1390.
[10]Ibid., 1395.
[11]Ibid. 1403.

dividends on government loans.[12] In addition, by encouraging Jews to settle in the land, they would become prime candidates for conversion to the Anglican faith. Since it is unfashionable to be of a religion different from that of the established national church, Jewish immigrants or their children or grandchildren would one day convert. On the other hand, the Jewish people did not proselytize Christians. Therefore, the English people would be safe from their corrupting influence.[13] Other speakers in favor of the Bill also point out the commercial advantages of naturalizing foreign Jews. Special emphasis is placed on their custom to provide for their own poor as well as their loyalty to the Crown during the crisis of 1745.[14]

Pelham concludes the debate with a refutation of the charges that the foreign Jews pose a threat to Christianity. They are, he believes, less dangerous than the Dissenters because they never attempt to seek converts. Since they do not, as a rule, intermarry there is little danger that they would convert English women to their faith. Pelham challenges the notion that the passage of the Bill would prevent the fulfillment of biblical prophesy, and he emphasizes the commercial benefits that they would confer upon the country.[15]

On May 7, after Pelham had finished speaking, a vote was taken: in spite of opposition by Tories and dissident Whigs, the Bill passed by 95 to 16. Instead of ending the matter, the final passage of the bill by 96 votes to 55, following its third reading on May 22, opened the floodgates of emotions. They, like the bacilli of Camus' novel, *The Plague*, appeared to come out of their hiding places to tap the fears and emotions of all strata of society. Once again, the cry of "The Church in Danger" was heard as the religious passions and the bigotry of prior centuries, manipulated to some degree by political agitators, broke through the thin veneer of restraint and moderation which had kept them fairly well in check during the first half of the century. Those who had been unsuccessful in defeating the Bill in Parliament, now turned to the people for support. Their sentiments were echoed in a plethora of widely circulated pamphlets, newspaper articles, songs, and political prints. At the same time, mobs paraded through the streets of London chanting: "No Jews, no Naturalization Bill, Old England and Christianity for ever." Even seasoned politicians were stunned by the ferocity of the Bill's opponents. Horace Walpole described it as "a Christian zeal which was thought happily extinguished with the ashes of Queen Anne and

---

[12]Ibid. 1376.
[13]Ibid. 1383-1385.
[14]Ibid. 1402.
[15]Ibid. 1412-1417.

Sacheverell."[16] Six months after its passage, the bill was repealed. Then, overnight, anti-Semitic agitation virtually disappeared, and at least on the surface, things returned to normal.

The incident raises some serious questions concerning the real target of the emotional outbursts. Was it the Jewish people or the party in power? Was it an expression of latent anti-Semitism or simply part of the political scene? If it did reflect hatred of the Jewish people, why was virtually no Jewish property damaged and no pogroms initiated against the Jews.? (Certainly, violence was a common way for the people of the time to deal with their grievances.)

Thomas Perry believes that once the passage of this insignificant bill caught the public's attention, it became an election issue between Whigs and Tories with the standard attack and defense that had been used in debates over prior naturalization legislation for other minority groups. He feels that the arguments used by both sides followed familiar patterns with "incidental pro and anti-Jewish variations which unquestionably added to the controversy but did not alter its essential nature as a dispute over immigration and naturalization."[17] It was, he believes, party politics and not bigotry that was the driving force behind most of the anti-Semitic propaganda that was part of the uproar against the bill. The heat that was generated during the controversy was that of political partisanship and not anti-Jewish hysteria. It was typical, he believes, of the low level of eighteenth-century politics where the real targets were the Whigs and not the Jewish people. What some moderns might find as evidence of anti-Semitism, Perry believes are often "clichés of partisan abuse."[18] John Carswell echoes Perry's sentiments, and he believes that the main thrust of the opposition to the "Jew Bill" is a "demonstration of exclusiveness and insularity" rather than any feeling against the Jews as such."[19] Perry's and Carswell's emphasis on politics and not on anti-Jewish prejudice, is supported in one of Hogarth's election pictures where the candidate, flanked by banners filled with slogans against the "Jew Bill," quietly buys trinkets from a Jewish peddler to seduce his female friends.

Jacob Katz, a scholar interested in the development of Western anti-Semitism, accepts the fact that the outcry against the Naturalization bill was not spontaneous and that it took place during Parliamentary

---

[16]Cited in A.S. Tuberville, *The House of Lords in the XVIII th Century* (Oxford: Clarendon Press, 1923), p. 277.

[17]Thomas W. Perry, *Public Opinion, Propaganda, and Politics in Eighteenth-Century England* (Cambridge, Massachusetts: Harvard University Press, 1962), p. 178.

[18]Ibid., 196.

[19]John Carswell, *From Revolution to Revolution: England 1688-1776* (New York: Charles Scribner's Sons, 1973), p. 117.

elections when the Tories were doing everything possible to bring the government down. Yet, he sees in the propaganda of 1753 allusions to classic anti-Semitic themes and stereotypes that were nourished for centuries by Christian tradition. He argues that they would not have been used so extensively by the Tories to frighten the populace with the threat of a Jewish takeover if they were not widely known and believed by the people of the time.[20] Todd Endelman believes that the religious protestations that were raised by London merchants concerning the passage of the Bill should not be discounted as simply a smokescreen for their very real economic interests. "Authentic religious bigotry and economic self-interest," he believes, "are often complementary."[21] Mel Scult is of the opinion that although the election may be of key importance in the conflict, it was theological considerations that explain the vehemence of the opposition to the bill and the tendency to exaggerate its contents.[22] Frank Felsenstein notes that at no other time during this period "did the social, political, and economic position of the Jews in England excite so much unbridled passion and arouse so much raw publicity."[23]

A survey of the press accounts of the events, real and imaginary, leading up to the ultimate repeal of this naturalization bill and the periodical literature, sermons, pamphlets, and political prints that were circulated both for and against it, can provide an excellent insight into the content and the depth of the anti-Semitic sentiments of the period. True, the great bulk of these works were originally motivated by political considerations, but their content was shaped by a very definite hostility towards the Jewish people which Endelman believes was originally engendered by medieval anti-Semitism and became part of England's cultural heritage.[24] The basic issues that were raised in the Parliamentary debates are repeated in them *ad nauseam*. However, the added embellishments to these basic arguments; the use of certain "buzz words" and stereotypical images designed to trigger latent hostility, make them text book cases of group prejudice.

The fears of the effects of the passage of the Jew Bill upon English life were exacerbated by articles in the media that described alleged Jewish crimes against Christianity. Some of them reinforced tales of Jewish perfidy that had been circulated in the country since the Middle Ages. For example, the *Scots Magazine* for July, 1753 reported that the Jewish

---

[20]Jacob Katz, *From Prejudice to Destruction: Anti-Semitism, 1700-1933* (Cambridge, Massachusetts: Harvard University Press, 1980), pp. 31-2.
[21]Endelman, *Jews of Georgian England*, p. 26.
[22]Mel Scult, *Millennial Expectations and Jewish Liberties*, p. 58.
[23]Felsenstein, *Anti-Semitic Stereotypes*, p. 187.
[24]Endelman, Jews of Georgian England. p. 90.

Community of Copenhagen, "prompted by a zeal for their religion," was involved in the disappearance of a young man who went to a Lutheran Priest in order to be converted to Christianity. After being invited to dine in the Jewish section of the city, he disappeared. The writer claims that "it is positively asserted that he was trepanned and sent off." Furthermore, he notes that the King of Denmark has ordered the Jewish community to produce the young man within a certain time limit or pay a fine of 8000 German Crowns(p. 356).

It was the *London Evening Post* that played a leading role in stirring up the passions of the people against the Jews through the use of religious prejudice, economic fears, and sheer superstition. The "Big Lie" which achieved such notoriety in Nazi Germany in our own century, was skillfully used by its editor as he searched for real and imaginary examples of Jewish crimes and perfidity to fill its pages. His poison was doubly potent because throughout the length and breadth of the land provincial newspapers reproduced his venomous diatribes, fables, pithy verses, and jokes directed against the Jewish people.[25] In the issue for May 24,1753 he warns his readers of the dire consequences of the passage of a bill that would make the English people slaves of the Jews, a people who "have seventeen hundred years punishment to revenge upon that Christian kingdom that falls into their hands." Not only would the naturalization act be a sin against God, but the influx of foreign Jews and the power of their money would totally corrupt and destroy the English way of life. He literally calls his readers to arms to combat this menace with the words:

> Awake therefore, my fellow Britons, Christians
> and Protestants! it is not Hannibal at your gates,
> but the Jews, that are coming for the keys of
> your church-doors....who know no goodness
> but that which blasphemed and murdered the
> Lord from heaven; nor desire any glory, but that
> of putting an end to all Christian churches, kings
> and kingdoms.

The London Evening Post intensified the dispute over the Bill by making it a Jewish-Christian issue. On July 24, in the midst of the controversy it made it clear to its readers that :

> the denominations of Whigs and Tories,
> Churchmen and Dissenters, with the other
> useful appelations are now entirely under
> the two more important distinctions of Jews

---

[25]G. A. Cranfield, *The Development of the Provincial Newspaper 1700-1760* (Oxford: Clarendon Press, 1962), p. 137 and G.A. Cranfield, "The 'London Evening-Post' And The Jew Bill of 1753" *The Historical Journal* 8 (no. 1 1963): 17.

and Christians

Like our own modern tabloids that must continue to seek the most bizarre, humorous, and frightening material to hold the attention of their readers, the *London Evening Post* seems to have stopped at nothing to maintain its circulation or to promote its political purposes. The alleged Jewish involvement in ritual murder as well as supposed historical accounts of their practicing cannibalism all found their way into its pages. To relieve the monotony of its hate message, humorous pieces were dispersed among the regular news items. For example, in its issue for June 2, a mock advertisement that was copied by other periodicals, announced, with tongue in cheek, that Moses ben Amri, Surgeon, was available to perform circumcisions "In the Safest, Easiest, and most Expeditious Manner," The *Craftsman's* popular feature, "News From 100 Years Hence in the Hebrew Journal: in 1854," was also cited by several other contemporary publications. Thus, people all over the country could learn, for example, that in the future a statue to Sir John Barnard would be replaced by one of Pontius Pilate and that a bill for naturalizing Christians would be thrown out of the Sanhedrin. To stir the fears of the Christian reading public, spurious news items such as: "A Jew, A_ F_ Esq. has bought the Manor of P_ in the County of Leicester for £41,000" appear among genuine material.[26]

Arthur Murphy's *Gray's Inn Journal* made its contribution to fanning the flames of anti-Jewish sentiment by reprinting a scene from the play, the *Temple of Laverna* in its Issue of November 17,1753. The selection highlights the usual negative stereotypes associated with the Jews of Change Alley and with the Jewish people in general. This includes their unscrupulous pursuit of wealth and their secret passion for ham. Special emphasis is placed on the potential dangers awaiting the English people now that foreign Jews have been given the opportunity to become naturalized. In the play, a country gentleman, during his tour of Change Alley, is asked if he has ever seen so many Jews together in one place. He replies:

> No, never to be sure – but we shall soon have
> them swarm in all Parts of the Kingdom,
> now that they are naturalized....But
> prithee, Friend *Worthy*, is the Report we
> have in the Country true? Why, they say,
> Mon, that there will shortly be laid a Fine
> upon any one, who is convicted of going
> to Church. Woons! if this should be the
> Case, notwithstanding the Love I have for

---

[26]R.J. Robson, *The Oxfordshire Election of 1754: A Study in the Interplay of City, County and University Politics* (London: Oxford University Press, 1949), pp. 88-90.

> *Old England,* I am determined to sell my
> Acres, and retire to some *Christian Protestant*
> Country, for I would not become a Jew,
> no, not to be a Minister of State (p. 28).

In several of the pamphlets that condemn the naturalization bill, the Jews are viewed as the age old bogey man of Christian society. The writers portray the Anglican Church as an institution under siege, threatened by this infamous "other" who is plotting to destroy the very fabric of English life, and who is set to impose its own religion on the hapless populace. These intense emotions are more than political propaganda. They reflect the fears and insecurities of those who see a world where, as previously noted, a wide range of religious, ethnic, racial, and social groups are threatening the status quo. Now it is the Jews' turn to be put in the spotlight. Sometimes they appear alone; on other occasions they are joined with the hated Catholics or the French. Every attempt is made to dredge up the most vicious medieval and pre-modern stereotypes to stress their "otherness." Exaggerated claims about the "Jewish Menace" abound in the pamphlets in order to exploit the pathological fears that have been part of the popular mentality for centuries. Some politically motivated writers may not have realized the depths of emotions that their hastily written pamphlets would tap. Others, capitalizing on the hubbub created over an insignificant piece of legislation, now had an avenue for hate literature that could be justified by a patriotism amply supported by Christian teachings.

The pamphlet that contains the vilest tirades against the Jews, *Admonitions From Scripture and History, From Religion and Common Prudence, Relating to the Jews,* is a bridge between medieval and modern anti-Semitism both in tone and content. In the opening paragraph, the author, the pseudonymous Archaicus, refers to the Jews as "that people which crucified the Lord of life, and with a curse of vengeance on their heads for the same, cried out – His blood be on us and our children"(p. 5). He believes that this "irreversible sentence and decree of God" should shape Christian conduct towards the Jewish people until their ultimate conversion to Christianity. They are "betrayers and murderers of the Lord of Life" as well as the cruel persecutors of Jesus' followers. The author refers to them as people who are "stiff-necked and uncircumcised in heart." They are "seducers and vipers" who are "cast off from God and forsaken of all men"(p. 6-8).

In keeping with classic Christian theology, the author views the destruction of the Temple in Jerusalem and the subsequent exile of the Jewish people as punishment for their role in the Crucifixion. He believes that because of their crime God has decreed that they are to be captives among the nations – wanderers like Cain who have no right to a homeland or naturalization in any country. Because the Jewish people continue to hate Christians, curse them in their synagogues, crucify their innocent children, and cheat them in business, they must be segregated from society and viewed as aliens, outlaws, and outcasts (p. 14).

Following this stinging condemnation of the Jewish people that is a reminder of the medieval calumnies directed against the Jews, the author then returns to the issues of his own time, and he enumerates the potential dangers to English life if the naturalization act would be passed. The Deists, he believes, would want the same rights and privileges that the Jews are currently seeking. Jewish wealth would be used to purchase land and to control the Parliamentary elections; synagogues would ultimately become as numerous as Dissenter meeting houses, and Great Britain would be called "Little Jewry" (p. 25). Rekindling theological hatreds of past centuries, he points out that naturalizing infidel Jews would open the door to the "Great Antichrist" who would reveal himself "with all the fury and outrage of the infernal legions" (p. 27). The country would also be flooded with a host of hucksters, peddlers, and usurers who would not only cheat the people, but who, in times of war, would be a dangerous subversive group in their midst. Thus, the naturalization of foreign Jews must be avoided at all costs since it would lead to both the spiritual and physical destruction of England – the end of everything that natural born Englishmen hold dear (p. 28).

A Full Answer to a Fallacious Apology, written by the pseudonymous author, "A Christian," and addressed to the Lord Mayor, Alderman, and Common Council of London, is another pamphlet which is a bridge between medieval and modern anti-Semitism. In this case, legal arguments are also used to support prejudice. For example, the author believes that the uneasiness felt by Christians concerning legislation to naturalize foreign Jews is justified. He rejects the argument that the act of Parliament passed in 1610 which requires the taking of the Sacrament for those seeking to be naturalized did not apply to the Jews since they were not in the country at that time. It may be true, he believes, that it was intended to keep out foreign Catholics in order to maintain the purity of the Church of England. However, if it would serve the same purpose against the Jewish people, so much the better. The Jews who are the professed enemies of the Christians and who still justify "the horrid act of crucifying our beloved Saviour," should be excluded from entering England. They are actually worse than the Catholics since they openly declare their hatred and aversion to Christianity, and they do everything in their power to oppose it. Catholics, though they err in "the manner of profession," are still Christians(pp. 5-6).For a brief moment, the author, finding a more challenging object of prejudice, allows the Jews to draw away the venom that he normally reserves for the hated Catholics.

Following this, he lists various medieval statutes to prove that Jews are not entitled to purchase estates. He further blackens their image by presenting evidence of Jewish cruelty to those of their faith who convert to Christianity (p. 15). In the last section of the pamphlet, the author rebuts the stock arguments in favor of the naturalization bill. He argues that there is no advantage in having rich Jews settle in England since they might be influenced by financial gain to become a modern day Judas and betray their new country. He is not impressed with the argument that they will be loyal to England since they have no homeland of their own for refuge. Their homelessness, he believes, is a curse from God and not a reason for special privileges.

> Why have they no place to go to?
> Is it not by the Decree of Providence,
> as a curse for their Obstinacy, which,
> while they persist in, I cannot help thinking
> every one who countenances them a
> partaker of their evil Deeds? And though
> our Saviour prayed for their Forgiveness
> (because they knew not what they did) I
> cannot find he gave any command to put a
> Sword into their Hands to turn against our
> own Breast (p. 18).

Finally, after he has spewed his venom, the author urges his readers to be informed where their representatives stand on the naturalization of foreign Jews so that they, as voters, can make the right choices in future elections (p. 19).

Those writers who begin their works with rational arguments against the Jew Bill, invariably turn to religious prejudice to support their claims, and they often make it the key part of their pamphlets. Critics who, for example, deal with the legal and economic aspects of Jewish naturalization also utilize classic anti-Semitic stereotypes to buttress their arguments.

In the pamphlet, *A Reply to the Jewish Question,* the author states that from his examination of the statutes, Jews never had the right to purchase freeholds, farms or manors; they could only own houses for their own use or to be leased to other Jews (p. 38). After tracing this legal history, he then cites arguments used by the clergy at the time of Cromwell to deny to the Jews the right to reside in England. They include: the danger of their seducing the English people in matters of religion, the scandalous nature of their worship, their unlawful customs of marriage and divorce, and their inability to honor sacred oaths(p. 67).

The author believes that because the Jews maintain laws and customs as well as a manner of living that is so different from that of the English people, there isn't even the remotest possibility of "engrafting them into the mainstream of English life"(p. 80). Periodically, he puts aside legal arguments to stress his own religious conviction that if the Jews stubbornly refuse to accept Christianity, they should not be naturalized either in England or America. Their present state, he believes, "can be ascribed to nothing but the just judgment of God still hiding the things of peace from their eyes and giving them up to the same kind of fatal hardness and blindness which about 1700 years ago was the cause of their destruction" (p. 80).

In *A Review of the Proposed Naturalization of the Jews*, the author begins his arguments against the Jew Bill from an economic perspective. He believes that there is considerable unemployment in England; the country needs new trades and manufacturers rather than having foreigners compete for jobs in existing industries. Instead of bringing in labor from abroad, he believes that it would be better to improve the quality of native workers. He argues that since "none of the Jews are husbandmen, manufacturers, mechanics, soldiers or sailors, they of all mankind have the least title to naturalization" (p. 23).

The religious roots of the author's anti-Semitism become evident when he leaves the realm of the role of the Jewish people in modern society and begins to dredge up prejudices based upon interpretations of Christian Scriptures. He notes, for example, that the crucifixion of Jesus was a national crime for which the Jewish people have been rightfully punished (p. 28). As long as they continue to follow the faith of their fathers, It is the will of Providence that they be preserved as a distinct people who can never be incorporated into other nations. Only, he believes, through their conversion to Christianity, will their national punishment cease (p. 32). The author states quite emphatically that : "The Jews, I conceive, are not entitled to naturalization for two plain reasons; the first is, because they are Jews; the next is, because they are not Christians" (p. 33). However, he argues against using naturalization as a means of converting Jews to the true faith since Christianity should not be prostituted for the sake of making converts (p. 39). If the gentle treatment that they have already received in England has not changed them, then it is doubtful that naturalization will have any effect upon such a stubborn people. Furthermore, the Jewish dispersion is proof of the truth of the Christian faith. Any attempt to naturalize these scattered people would actually "wound" Christianity (p. 39).

Looking at the scope of Anglo-Jewish history, the author doubts that the Jews were actually guilty of crucifying Christian children. However, he believes that these stories show that they were truly wicked people who were never really part of English society (p. 49).Putting religious issues aside, the author comes to the conclusion that, at the present time, it is in the best interests of the Jews themselves not to be naturalized. They are, after all, treated very well, and they should know their place. Seeking special privileges will only bring on persecution; the Jews of England should be grateful for what they have and not push for any additional rights (p. 60). The inconsistency of the author's bigotry is quite evident in his approach to the alleged wealth of the Jewish people. On one hand, he notes that there are no more than twenty truly affluent families in the upper strata of Anglo-Jewish society. On the next level, there are no more than forty brokers. Beneath them, there is a multitude of hawkers, peddlers, and traffickers in second-hand goods. Finally, at the bottom, there are a great number of poor Jews who scorn honest labor and who are involved in begging and in criminal activities. Naturalization of foreign Jews will attract the riffraff from abroad who will join the ranks of the lowest group in the Jewish community; the author questions if Jews of any substance will want to settle in the country (pp. 67-71). Following this, he contradicts himself by raising fears that the Jews, who will be naturalized, will buy land and influence the common people of England to give up their Christian faith (p. 75). Obviously, he can not decide whether to attack Jews for their poverty and the trouble it causes English society or for their wealth and its potential dangers to Christianity. He is certain, however, that although some individual Jews are seeing the error of their ways, morally "they are not inspired by the same principles as the Christians"(p. 84). It is their misguided sense of superiority that makes it impossible for them to be part of the world around them. The author notes:

> We are apt to consider the Jews as vagabonds
> and wanderers, but they boast themselves of
> being a *separate people, the chosen of God;*
> and I will be bold to say, that for this very reason,
> every good man among the Jews must either
> disapprove of this attempt, or be distressed how to
> reconcile it. The notion they suck with their milk
> is, that they are a *great nation,* and all mankind
> usurpers of their sovereignty. This consideration
> reconciles their pertinacious adherence to the
> religion of their forefathers; and invalidates their
> claim to mix with any other nation....(p. 85)

Clearly, to be considered truly English, one must follow the tenets of Christianity. All arguments in favor of naturalizing foreign Jews are contrary to this point of view. They are "dishonorable to liberty and inconsistent with the dignity of an English subject" (p. 106).

In William Romaine's (1714-1795) work, *An Answer to a Pamphlet Entitled Considerations on the Bill to Permit Persons Professing the Jewish Religion to be Naturalized; Wherein the Free Reasoning, Gross Misrepresentation of Facts, and Perversion of Scripture, are Fully Laid Open and Detected*....there is also an appeal to history that is heavily tainted with both classic Christian anti-Semitism and modern jealousies. In the preface, the author notes that he is disturbed by the defense of the Naturalization Act ; he believes that the Jews have done their cause a great deal of harm by their "impudent actions." They are, in his opinion, a people who do not know their place in English society and who have gone against their best interests by displaying bad manners. He notes that "they cannot pretend that we have given them any precedent for their ill treatment of us." His pamphlet, therefore, is a necessary response to unfair charges leveled against the good citizens and merchants of England whose fine reputations have been slandered. Here is a classic case of the victim being blamed for the deeds of the attacker.

Romaine begins his arguments against Jewish naturalization by refuting the notion that Jews born in the king's dominions are natural born subjects who are entitled to the rights and privileges of Englishmen (p. 2). He claims that throughout British history they were always considered to be foreigners and aliens. It was Jewish gold that brought them into England at the time of William the Conqueror and during the rule of Oliver Cromwell. On both occasions, it was through bribery that "blaspheming" Jews came from abroad to settle in the country (p. 5).

Viewing their history in England, he believes that members of the Jewish faith were never welcomed by the masses. During the medieval period, they were considered to be "wretched usurers" who plundered the public and who were justly punished for their "ill gotten wealth" by being expelled from the country. From the time of Edward the Confessor until 1290, they were vassals, the property of the king; later, after their readmission they were simply aliens. He believes that it is impossible to view them as freeborn subjects since they deny the truth of Christianity which is the very basis of English law and government. They are "subjects to the devil" who are in "perpetual hostility to Christ." Therefore, there can be no peace between them and the English people (p. 10). Citing the verse in First Corinthians 16:22, "If any Man love not the Lord Jesus Christ, let him be Anathema Maranatha," he believes that Jews who do not accept Jesus are an anathema, and they should be cast out of Christian society (pp. 14-15). Furthermore, the modern Jews follow the examples set by their forefathers' infidelity and their hatred of Christians. If ever they would be given the opportunity to gain power, just as their ancestors murdered Jesus, they would murder innocent Christians (p. 21). The author refers to the Jews as "Synagogue of Satan."

and he accepts, as fact, the centuries' old charge that Jews frequently crucified Christian children on Good Friday (p. 23). Jews are malefactors and impostors, and thus:

> ....the attempt to naturalize the Jews
> is an attempt to naturalize disgrace upon
> Christ, and every Jew naturalized,
> naturalizes fresh dishonour upon the Christian
> religion, because every one of them is a
> Blasphemer of Christ and his religion, and to
> admit them, as such into our Christian community,
> is giving to Blasphemers the honours of that community....(p. 24).

The author, like so many of those who opposed the Bill, rejects the popular argument that by bringing foreign Jews to England they would be converted to the true faith. He notes that little headway has been made in the conversion of the native Jews. What success, then, can the English hope to achieve with their foreign co-religionists (p. 30)?In the next chapters of his pamphlet, the author challenges the notion that naturalizing foreign Jews will hasten the coming of the Messiah or that it will produce additional loyal subjects who will enrich the country. On the contrary, contemporary Jews who copy the actions and attitudes of the ancient Pharisees will actually be a threat to the nation (p. 62). In addition, they could not possibly benefit foreign trade because, as a people who reject Jesus, their money is tainted and God will not allow them to prosper (pp. 76-78).

For the author, the whole issue of Jewish naturalization is not one between political factions, but it is actually a Jewish-Christian conflict which, in spite of Jewish attempts to do so, should not divide the nation (p. 92). Again, in the spirit of blaming the victim for his or her oppression, he condemns the Jews of England for defending the Naturalization Bill with "hard words." Though it was in their interest to treat the English people better, they refused to do so (p. 95). He concludes his pamphlet with the words:

> Who is the best friend to the government
> – the Christian – or the Jew? The Christian
> who is a natural-born subject, and who
> serves his God, his King and his Country out
> of principle: Or the foreign outlawed Jew, who
> has no God, no King, and no Country, and
> who never acts upon any higher principle
> than self-interest (p. 96).

Another pamphlet that brings both Christian theology and religious bigotry into the arguments against the Bill is *The Rejection and Restoration of the Jews According to Scripture Declar'd* by the pseudonymous author,

Archaicus. In this work, a number of verses from both Jewish and Christian Scriptures are used to demonstrate the Jewish people's sins and the causes of their exile and dispersion all over the globe. This, the author believes, is God's punishment that will only be altered when they accept Christianity. Therefore, the granting of "new and unheard temporal privileges" is contrary to the divine will (p. 29). Naturalization would "harden and fix the Jews themselves more and more in their inveterate unbelief and rebellion against God" (p. 31). The author repeats the stock anti-Semitic accusations that have been leveled against the Jews for centuries which include the poisoning of wells and their "insatiable thirst for the blood of Christians, especially, of Christian children which they often steal and solemnly crucify" (p. 35). He admits that, on the surface, the modern Jews have lost "much of the old Jewish venom" and that they have become more humane and civil than their ancestors. Yet, he reminds his readers that when a serpent that is numbed by the cold is brought inside and warmed by the fireside, it soon recovers its serpentine qualities and it can ultimately drive a person from his house. This, he believes, is the potential danger of the passage of the Jew Bill, and he urges that it be repealed (p. 36).

Similar sentiments appear in *A Modest Apology for the Citizens and Merchants of London,* a pamphlet which stresses the effect that the naturalizing of foreign Jews will have upon religious liberty. The author views the Jews who lived at the time of Jesus as traitors and rebels against God. The present day descendants of these nefarious creatures follow in their footsteps. They are, in his opinion, guilty of this same treason; had they the opportunity, they would crucify Jesus again (p. vi).The Bill is "entirely of a religious nature" and, he notes that "it strikes at the root of our present establishment and affects the very being of Christianity. Trade is not an issue." Furthermore, England's civil and religious establishments are based on the doctrines of Jesus. Therefore, Jewish beliefs and practices contradict the very foundations of the British system of government and of the Christian faith as well (p. 7). Modern Jews, he believes, "live in continual uneasiness, tormented and haunted like murderers." Their crimes can be sensed in their distinguishing features, particularly in their eyes which reflect a "malignant blackness." Their very looks are enough to convict them of being crucifiers (pp. 8-9).After introducing this racial element into the problem of Jewish naturalization, he returns to the classic argument that God has punished the Jewish people for their crimes. Therefore, to welcome them into the country before He removes this anathema would be in opposition to the decrees of providence. In medieval fashion, the author refers to the Jews as murderers and betrayers who are "children of the Devil" and whose synagogue is "Satan's meeting house" (p. 13).They are identified with the Antichrist, and he argues that "if we naturalize such persons, how can we avoid involving ourselves in their guilt?" England has already been punished for its disobedience of God's will with a terrible civil war. Further acts that are contrary to divine plans can only result in further catastrophes (p. 15).

Arguments against the naturalization of foreign Jews reached a wide audience through their insertion in the popular Chap Books of the time. For example, in a work entitled, *The True Life of Eleanor Gwinn A Celebrated Courtezan in the Reign of King Charles II and Mistress to that Monarch*, two articles concerning the Jew Bill appear. The first, "The 1753d Chapter of the Jews," written in a mock biblical style, describes how the Jews, who had been scattered after the destruction of Jerusalem, came to settle in England where they "trafficked greatly, and supply'd the wants of the extravagant and the proud, and (those) increased in riches and power."(p. 39) Their leader, Shylock, "who was well known to the greatest men of the land," encouraged their co-religionists to join them in this "promising land."(p. 40) The second selection, "The Humble Petition of the Turks, in behalf of themselves and other Musslmen, praying that a Clause may be added to the Jew Bill, to enable them also to be naturalized..." argues that since the Muslims, like the Jews, are circumcised and reject, blaspheme, and deny Christ's mission, they too should be naturalized. This would induce the richest of them along with their Christian slaves and numerous wives and concubines to settle in the land. It would also put "Mohametans, and other Infidels on an equal footing with the Jews." (p. 40)

As if the numerous pamphlets and Chap Books written in 1753 which condemned the Jewish people were not enough, earlier hate literature was also pressed into service to stir up popular resentment. One such work, *An historical treatise concerning the Jews and Judaism in England; giving an account of the particular crimes and impieties that have brought upon them the heavy punishments they have sustained in this kingdom, from the reign of Edward I,* was first published in 1720 at the time of the building of the synagogue in Duke's Place. The author collected a long list of massacres, persecutions, and banishments over a period of several centuries in various countries to support his notion that if any people suffered so much they certainly must have deserved such treatment at the hands of Christian nations. The *Monthly Review* of August, 1753, which briefly summarizes the work, calls the author an "outrageous bigot of most unchristian and persecuting spirit", and it sees through his scheme of blaming the victim for the deeds of the oppressor (p. 157). Whether those who read this pamphlet concurred with the editors of the "Monthly Review" is difficult to determine.

Supporters of the naturalization of foreign Jews were a diverse group who included party hacks, pragmatic economists, liberal thinkers (who showed streaks of religious bigotry to other groups like the Catholics), Christian missionaries, and millenniumists. They were outnumbered by those who attacked the Bill by about three or four to one; approximately fifteen pamphlets, sermons, and leaflets were distributed in favor of naturalizing foreign Jews.

In a pamphlet, *The Jew's Advocate*, the author is dismayed over the uproar raised by the opponents to the Bill. He scoffs at the allegations that, as a consequence of the passage of the act for naturalizing foreign Jews, the English people "will become incorporated with a race of vagabonds and the professed enemies of the Christian religion" who, when they get powerful enough, will pull down the churches and erect synagogues in their place. Such fears, he believes, are totally groundless. Though, in the past, the Jewish people were persecuted, they never posed a threat to the either the State or to the Church. Their oppression was simply a pretense "to fleece them of their money" (p. 101).[27]

The author notes that "great pains have been taken of late to blacken and asperse the Jews, as if they were a people mark'd out, by the decrees of Heaven and the voice of all mankind for utter detestation and abhorrence." However, he believes that this is nothing more than a reflection of party politics (p. 103). He quotes from both Paul and John Locke to show that even though the Jews have stumbled, they are not without hope of recovery. He argues that if Abraham, Isaac, and Jacob – the roots of their faith – were holy, then the modern day branches are as well. If some of these branches were broken off and rejected, thereby allowing the Gentiles to enjoy the blessings of Abraham and his descendants in their place, no disrespect should be shown to the Jews who deserve to be treated with "tenderness and affection." Even though "blindness overstates their understanding," the Jews are still God's people. If Jesus prayed during his last moments on earth that they should be forgiven, can modern Christians do any less (p. 107)?

The author then leaves the realm of theology to view the Jews through the eyes of history. He finds that they are a good, industrious people who have nothing in their religious teachings that is at all subversive to a civil society. The oppression that they have experienced through the centuries stems from their ability to amass wealth and not from religious differences. He stresses their loyalty to the Crown during the last rebellion as well as their willingness to lend money to the

---

[27]The page citations for *The Jews Advocate* are from a reprint in Paul Radin, ed. *Sutro Branch California State Library Occasional Papers Eng. Series No. # 3.* (San Francisco: California State Library, 1939).

government to support public credit (p. 140). The author concludes his pamphlet with a scathing criticism of those who believe that if the Jew Bill will not be repealed, the country will be over-run with infidels and blasphemers (p. 141).

Much of what appears in *The Jew's Advocate* can also be found in the pamphlet, *Considerations on the Bill to Permit Persons Professing the Jewish Religion to be Naturalized by Parliament etc.*, by the pseudonymous author, Philo Patriae.[28] He too shows that throughout history, with the exception of periods of extreme persecution, the Jewish people found a place for themselves in Christian society. Any number of Christian countries, he believes, have granted them liberties, and they have even allowed the Jews to achieve positions of honor and profit with no apparent ill effect (p. 71). It is clear that Philo Patraie, like so many other supporters of the Jew Bill, also views this legislation as a means of hastening their conversion. He notes that there are already many Jewish converts to Christianity in the country. By allowing foreign Jews to come to England by degrees, a few at a time, they will more readily enter the ranks of those who have joined the Christian fold (p. 72).

The author also believes that the Jews pose no danger to the State. They only number about eight thousand people which, he points out, is only one thousandth part of the inhabitants of the country. In addition, they are loyal to the government since they follow the rabbinic dictum that, "the laws of any state are as binding on them as their own." He too believes that the coming of foreign Jews will be a definite asset to the country since their wealth "must increase trade of the nation; and the more that is increased the more beneficial it must be to the nation" (p. 79).

Like the other supporters of the Bill, Philo Patrie also mentions the Jews' role in defending the country during the rebellion of 1746 as well as their work in restoring confidence when the government's credit was sinking and specie was scarce (p. 91). In the concluding pages of his pamphlet, the author observes that, "many who approved the measure, disapproved it publicly, not from the sense of conviction, but merely from party" (p. 96). The opposition stems from envy, greed and "a view to future elections; and not from Christianity, as the pretense is" (p. 98).

Josiah Tucker (1712-1799), who was at the time of the Jew Bill controversy Rector of St. Stephen's in Bristol, bases his arguments for the support of the Jew Bill primarily on economics. As Leslie Stephen notes, "Nature had designed for him a shrewd tradesman; fate had converted him into a clergyman."[29] Far ahead of his time, he believes that the true

---

[28]Ibid.
[29]Stephen, p. 301.

wealth of a nation is dependent on a growing population. He was, in spite of considerable opposition, an advocate of increased immigration. In his work, *A Second Letter to a Friend Concerning Naturalization,* Tucker condemns the use of such slogans as "No Jews ! No Naturalization! Christianity and Old England for ever!" for being invented purely to inflame the unthinking people for political gain (p. 2). But he is not simply concerned about the economic benefits that foreign Jews would bring to the country. As an Anglican cleric, he believes that the passage of the Jew Bill would also aid in the conversion of the Jewish people by allowing them to experience a superior form of benevolent Christianity. He notes:

> Indeed this much is certain, that kind usage is
> the only reasonable and justifiable way of making
> converts.... Besides, since the general conversion
> of the Jewish Nation must begin somewhere, and
> none can tell how soon, why should we endeavour
> to prevent its beginning here (p. 42)?

He believes that Paul, who brought so many people into the Christian fold, would have approved of the passage of the Jew Bill had he been a member of Parliament (p. 44).

The author (Thomas Dicey?) of the work, *A Sixth and Last Letter, or Address to the Parliament, As well as to the People of Great Britain,* looks back at the events of 1753 and comes to the conclusion that it is absolutely ludicrous to believe that a handful of Jewish families "of character and fortune" who would have settled in London could have threatened the property and the religious liberties of seven million Protestants. He blames the press for their "shameful, licentious, impolitic, and unjust insinuations" which poisoned and inflamed the people against an act that would have brought additional wealth to the country (pp. 23-4).

Those who defended the Jewish community during this tumultuous time, also managed to combine some lofty enlightenment sentiments with crude attacks upon other more hateful groups in English society. Edward Aveling, in the introduction to his pamphlet, *A Looking Glass For The Jews: Or The Credulous Unbelievers,* notes that Jews should be laughed at rather than feared by the populace; their "superstitious gambols" should entertain and not be a cause for alarm. After proclaiming that the Jews are "common brethren derived from one common stock with the rest of mankind," Aveling then proceeds to buttress his arguments by shifting prejudice to others who are more deserving of serious concern. He asks:

> Can Jews be so bad subjects as Papists,
> or Protestant Jacobites, who if possible,
> are worse than Papists? Are they more

> prone to rebel and subvert the government
> they live under; of which we have frequent
> instances, and which we are daily threatened,
> by the Papists (p. iv)?

Jews, unlike the Catholics, are not obligated by their ecclesiastical laws and councils, "under pain of damnation," to use their power to persecute Protestants. They have not been involved in holy wars and massacres nor are they guilty of creating an Inquisition to hunt heretics. The Jews detest the Papists for their idolatries, and they would never join with them against the Protestants. Though they do not accept the tenets of Christianity, they are still more Christian than the Catholics. Although Aveling notes that he hates Popery, not Papists, this does not exclude Catholic priests, "the source of all the bloodshed and cruelty against Protestants and others," from his tirades (p. v).

Returning to the Jews, he claims that hating them is anti-Christian. He urges the reader to be patient in the hope that if they "find not a Messiah of their own, they must take up with yours at last" (p. vii).They should be protected so that the completion of the prophesies concerning the Second Coming will take place. Though Aveling sees the need, from a theological perspective, not to persecute the Jewish people, he is not completely devoid of prejudices towards them. He warns the reader to be on guard "for otherwise, by their industry and frugality, two good qualities, which they have in greater perfection than you, they may in time get the advantage of you" (p. vii).

Partisan politics may have been the catalyst that brought feelings about the Jewish people to the surface, but these sentiments, both pro and con, then began to assume a life of their own beyond the issues of the day. The controversy over the Jew Bill created an increased interest in the Jewish people as well as a strong desire to convert them to Christianity. In the pamphlet, *The Jewish Ritual or the Religious Customs and Ceremonies of the Jews,* the anonymous Christian author presents a remarkably thorough survey of Jewish religious practices. After a brief introduction where he notes that "no people in the world are so jealously tenacious of the precepts of the Jews," and that even the omission of a minute detail which would be of no real consequence to a Christian is of great importance to them (p. 1). He does a credible job of dispassionately covering a wide range of Judaic topics which include life cycle events, the dietary laws, the Jewish calendar, and a host of superstitions. Considerable folklore concerning evil spirits appears alongside his descriptions of traditional practices. Although he does question the rationality of the Jewish worship services, the material is presented in a scholarly manner that is in the spirit of scientific inquiry. On the other hand, the pamphlet, *A persuasion and exhortation to the Jews,* was simply a plea to the Jewish people to consider the scriptural evidence and to accept Jesus as the Christ who has already appeared in history.

Although it would be unfair to project modern expectations of social concern for the "others" in society upon eighteenth century clerics, they present, with few exceptions, a picture of individuals motivated more by political forces than by genuine concern for the rights of the Jewish people. It was as ministerial supporters that they were castigated by the press for their position on the Jew Bill. The *London Evening-Post* was particularly vicious in its attacks upon the Anglican clergy. The following, found in the issue for September 1, 1753, is a sample of the slanders, often filled with anti-Semitic stereotypes, that were heaped upon them for their support of the administration.

> Sell Christ and the Church! And Bishops to sell' em?
> Is Herod still living? Was Herod a P(elham)?
> Hail B(ishop)s Apostate! Hail King of the Jews!
> – Beware! Oh, beware, of old Judas's Noose!

The bishops, following "the party line", supported both the passing and the eventual repeal of the Jew Bill. What is most revealing, however, are the occasional glimpses of their personal attitudes towards the Jewish people.

Thomas Herring, Archbishop of Canterbury (1693-1757), in a letter to Newcastle dated March 5, 1751, notes that in regard to the admission of foreign Jews he is "constitutionally prone to indulgences," nevertheless, certain questions come to his mind concerning the wisdom of such an act of Parliament. "In the first place," he notes, "they are a peculiar people and no one knows of their turn at home, the spirit of their economy, the true influential Principles of their religion, the nature of their connections and private engagements, the degree of their reverence for any Laws of government but of their own cast, their sentiments of Christians and their obligations to live well with them." He is very cautious about committing himself to extending to them any additional privileges, and he believes that before this could take place it would be a good idea to "know more of them." He notes that in America Locke had required a belief in the tenets of Christianity as being essential for naturalization. Certainly, He argues, if Jews would receive this privilege why shouldn't it also be extended to Mohammedans?[30]

When the clamor against the Jew Bill reached its peak in the autumn of 1753, Herring cared little for either the maintenance of the Act or its repeal. He was ashamed for the bitter, widespread prejudice that was generated against it. However, he is careful to note that the bill is utterly

---

[30] Aldred W. Rowden, *The Primates Of The Four Georges* (London: John Murray, 1916), p. 205.

unconnected to the Anglican faith and to the Church itself. "However faction, working upon the good old spirit of the High Church has made wild work with the nation. As the obtaining the Bill was really worth no hazard, so the repealing it seems hardly worth a debate." Herring's only concern is that there may be a danger if the government is seen giving in to public clamor.[31]

Thomas Secker, Bishop of Oxford (1693-1768), was a friend of the Ministry and a supporter of its policies which included the naturalization of foreign Jews. He was primarily concerned with one provision of the Bill which might give ecclesiastical patronage to those Jews who purchased landed estates. In a letter to Harwicke he notes : "We have laws against Popish patronages: and though the danger from Jewish may not be so great, yet the shame of them is much greater."[32] Secker tried to quiet the clergy, but he admitted that they had sincere questions about Jewish legal rights that he could not answer. When the public clamor grew, the members of Parliament were in the embarrassing situation of passing a law in one session and then repealing it on the first day of the next. It was Secker who came to the Government's help. Motivated more by politics than by religious convictions, he delivered a successful speech for its repeal. In it, he recognizes his former support for the Bill. However, he notes that "because it has given offense to so many of our Christian brethren," he feels that it is only right that he "sacrifice his opinion" for the greater good of the majority faith.[33]

On the other hand, from the start, the parish clergy in the provinces who had High Church and Tory sympathies enthusiastically joined in the outcry against the passage of the Bill. These important molders of public opinion repeated the stock warnings that the Church was in danger from the pulpit, and they embellished them with tales of Jewish wickedness taken from both Jewish and Christian Scriptures. The Book of Esther, with its graphic examples of the vengeance taken by the Jewish people against their enemies, was a particular favorite.

The sermons that condemn the passage of the Jew Bill use classic Christian teachings, political lies, and half-truths to convince the listeners of the dangers of such legislation. The pamphlet, *Some Queries Relative to the Jews*, was written as a reaction to one such sermon that the author felt was filled with "misguided zeal" (p. iv). For the sake of both religious liberty and Christian charity, he challenges the attacks made against the Jewish people. He scoffs at the notion that granting a few Jewish families certain advantages that are, in reality, less than those that the native Jews

---

[31]Ibid.
[32]Secker to Harwicke, Nov. 12, 1753. cited in Perry, p. 47.
[33]*Parliamentary History* Vol. XV. 115.

enjoy will be contrary to biblical prophesies and Christian theology concerning their despised status in the world (p. 13). The author questions if Christians have any right to "distress, persecute or afflict others merely for being Jews." He wonders if it is not hypocritical for the followers of Jesus' teaching to display those same qualities which they see in the Jewish people (p. 14). In addition, in spite of the fears of those who believe that once granted naturalization the Jews will seek the power to send members to Parliament, the author doubts if such a tiny minority actually poses a real threat to Christianity. If, as some claim, God has declared that the Jews are an accursed people, this does not, he believes, authorize good Christians to reproach them (p. 36).

There were some clerics who did express their concern for the welfare of the Jewish people from their pulpits. Unfortunately, their sympathies stemmed from a desire convert them and not from any real social concern. Their arguments for naturalizing foreign Jews are similar to those offered in the previous century by those who favored the readmission of Jews to England.

Thomas Winstanley, in a sermon delivered during the heated Jew Bill controversy, makes it clear that he is not anxious to get involved in the bitter debates that were raging all over England. He simply wants to show the advantage of this legislation to both Jews and Christians. If the Jews would be given greater opportunities for naturalization, he believes that they would become a more civilized people. Furthermore, they would gradually develop a more favorable opinion of Christianity which would lead to their ultimate conversion to the true faith.[34] He concludes his sermon with a prayer that is in keeping with traditional Christian attitudes towards Jews and all the "others" in society.

> Have mercy upon all Jews, Turks, Infidels, and
> Hereticks and take from them all ignorance
> hardness of heart and contempt of thy word;
> and so fetch them home, blessed Lord to Thy
> flock, that they may be saved among the remnant
> of the true Israelites.[35]

Another cleric, Peter Peckard (1718?-1797), echoes these same sentiments in a sermon that he delivered on that same Sunday in October of 1753. He, too, is unhappy over the clamor raised by the opponents of the naturalization of foreign Jews. He believes that any one who "presumes to make use of force in religion or justifies any degree of persecution for difference of opinion" is acting "contrary to the whole

---

[34]Thomas Winstanley, *A Sermon Preached at Parish – Church of St. George, Hanover – Square Sunday October 28, 1753.* (London: 1753), pp. 13-14.
[35]Ibid.

tenor and genius of the Gospel of Christ."[36] Like Winstanley, he asks, "Why do we drive from our fold those who at fair opportunity might be willing to enter among us?"[37] Here, too, conversion is the motivating factor behind the preacher's humanitarian sentiments.

The immediate reaction of the general populace to the news of the repeal of the Jew Bill was joy mingled with a sense of relief. Bonfires were lit and church bells were rung throughout the land to mark this great day of deliverance from the threat of the Jewish subversion of Christianity and the English way of life. It appeared as if Parliament had heeded the wishes of the people, and now all was right with the world.

In a remarkably short time the normal chaotic pace of eighteenth century life was restored, and the tirades against the Jews that had filled the air came to an end. This abrupt halt to public expressions of fear and hatred of the Jewish people seems to support the opinions of those scholars, like Allan Peskin, who believe that the whole episode should not be blown out of its true proportions and turned into a major issue; nor should it be cited as evidence of British anti-Semitism. It was, in his opinion, nothing more than a temporary aberration.[38] Yet, he does admit that the excitement of 1753, that "was built on the solid foundation of the fears and the prejudices of the English people," was more than a hoax dreamed up for the forthcoming election.[39]

In reality, the powerful negative feelings that had been focused upon the Jewish community could not, and did not, disappear. In some cases, they were shifted to other more visible and threatening targets like the Gypsy villains of the Canning Trial. They also lay dormant and waited for new opportunities to arise. The spirit of bigotry behind the outbursts of 1753 was so strong and its effect on Anglo-Jewry was so profound, that it took almost a century for the Jews to achieve full emancipation. Latent anti-Semitism forced them to return to the general policy of maintaining a low profile and not making any political demands upon the majority culture. They found consolation in the economic opportunities and in the rights and privileges they enjoyed that were denied to a good number of their co-religionists on the Continent. Unfortunately, continued fears of conspiracy and of Popery at home, as well as the growing revolutionary fervor across the Channel, created situations which were beyond their control and which occasionally thrust them, as an alien minority, into the limelight. Their reactions to

---

[36]Peter Peckard, *The Popular Clamour Against the Jews Indefensible: A Sermon Preached at Huntington October 28, 1753* (Cambridge: 1753), p. 21.
[37]Ibid., p. 22.
[38]Allan Peskin, "England's Jewish Naturalization Bill of 1753" *Historia Judaica* 19 (April, 1957): 28.
[39]Ibid., p. 27.

these new problems resembled the approach of past generations to combat popular feelings of distrust. The need to constantly prove their loyalty to the Crown also shows something about their own insecurities.

In July of 1779, for example, when a French invasion was expected, the following resolutions were passed and recorded in the Minute Book of the Bevis Marks Synagogue:

1.   That it be recommended to the Yehidim or Members of our Community in Case of Publick Subscriptions for the Defense of the Kingdom to enter Liberally in such subscriptions.

2.   That in Case of an Actual Invasion in any part of Great Britain it is recommended that our Yehidim & Others of our Community should enter Cheerfully, Personally or otherwise into such Loyal Associations which may be formed.[40]

The final major crisis that Anglo-Jewry had to face in the eighteenth century was the French Revolution. No doubt, the emancipation of French Jewry was welcomed by them as a harbinger of better things to come on both sides of the Channel. But, as Alfred Rubens suggests, most of the Jews of England were too occupied in the daily struggle for subsistence to have the time for political activities.[41] When public opinion in England turned against the revolution, and England was threatened with a French invasion, the Jews, as members of an immigrant community, were particularly sensitive to accusations of disloyalty. The Alien Act of 1793 resulted in sporadic raids on Jewish peddlers and petty merchants and the deportation of a number of them. In addition, synagogues were required to register Jews who had been born abroad; it was also mandatory for innkeepers to check the credentials of all alien lodgers. Jewish communal leaders demonstrated their patriotism by contributing to the national defense, participating in days of public humiliation, and reciting prayers for the well being of the royal family. Periodically they publicly expressed their gratitude to God for being blessed with a just government which protected both their persons and their property.[42]

As an immigrant community, the Jews were particularly sensitive to accusations of disloyalty to the Crown. Many of their fears were not unfounded. For example, when the French army occupied Venice in

---

[40]Lionel D. Barnett, *Bevis Marks Records Part I* (Oxford: Oxford University Press, 1940), p. 47.

[41]Alfred Rubens, "Anglo-Jewish Caricature 1780-1850" *T.J.H.S.E.* 23 (1969-70): 96.

[42]*Manchester Mercury* March 18, 1800. Cited in Williams, *The Making of Manchester Jewry* p. 17.

1797, the British Consul, John Watson, made several negative references to Jews in his dispatches. In one of them he notes:

> The French here avow publicly their intention
> of invading Great Britain with their armies,
> which I hope with the help of God will be
> punished; however, I must signify to your
> Lordships that they reckon very much on the
> Emigrants and on the Jews. By the connivance
> of the Jews here, which came to my knowledge,
> I have reason to think that they hold a regular
> correspondence with their brethren in England
> to this purpose.[43]

The rise of Napoleon increased the pressures on English Jewry by arousing new suspicions of their loyalty. Prior to his middle eastern campaign, a letter appeared from an anonymous Italian Jewish source that was directed to world Jewry. It urged them to seize this special moment and to support Bonapart's efforts to conquer what was once the ancient Land of Israel. The writer urged that an elected council be established by the Jews in the Diaspora to negotiate with the French Directory for the restoration of a Jewish commonwealth. This would allow world Jewry to live under their own laws and to end their oppression.[44]

This "Letter" was viewed with particular interest in England where it was reproduced in various contemporary journals. In one of them, the *St. James Chronicle*, there was a significant change in its text. Instead of the words, "O my brethren, let us rebuild the temple of Jerusalem," the passage now read: "let us reestablish the Empire of Jerusalem." If this was not enough to raise the question of English Jewry's dual loyalty, Napoleon's famous proclamation that he issued in April 1799 while he was besieging Acre exacerbated the problem. At that time, he urged the Jews of the Diaspora, "the rightful heirs of Palestine," to enlist under his flag and to join his expeditionary army to regain their ancient homeland. Napoleon directed his proclamation to those Jews whom he hoped would use their financial and commercial power to support France's cause not only in the Middle East, but throughout Europe as well.[45]

British Jewry showed little interest or public support for Napoleon's grandiose schemes. The Alien Act of 1793 held the threat of deportation over their heads, and they were kept in check by the concern that any Jacobin sympathies on their part would not go unpunished. Their fears were heightened by some of the popular caricatures of the period which

---

[43]*Miscellanies, J.H.S.E.* Part III (1937): 98.
[44]Franz Kobler, *Napoleon and the Jews* (New York: Schocken Books, 1976), pp. 30-31.
[45]Ibid., pp. 31-32.

portrayed them as supporting Napoleon's military exploits. In one of them, Cruikshank's "Easier to Say than to Do," there is the image of A Dutchman, a Spaniard, and a Jew assisting Napoleon in scraping England off the map. [46] Yet, they were in no real danger of governmental persecution: the Seditious meeting bill of 1795 was actually modified in such a way as not to penalize them.[47]

In reality, the Jewish community was once again only a side show to England's struggle with France and her sympathizers at home. Though at the time, Anglo-Jewry may not have realized it, assimilation and the ultimate loss of Jewish identity was a far greater threat to group survival than the discrimination, polite and otherwise, that they experienced in their daily lives. For the most part, economic concerns and not political rights occupied the attention of the growing Jewish community. It appeared to be both a safe and a very practical path to follow. But the price that the Jews paid for keeping such a low profile was a long delay until they, the last remaining politically disadvantaged religious minority, would finally achieve emancipation. It would come after the Dissenters and the Catholics, two very prominent "others," had, through their own struggles, paved the way. Once again, but in a different context, the fortunes of the Jewish people would be tied to those of the minority groups around them.

---

[46]Alfred Rubins, "Portrait of Anglo-Jewry 1656-1836," *T.J.H.S.E.* 19 (1955-59): 44.
[47]Roth, *History of the Jews in England*, p. 238.

Conclusions

It would be naive to assume that, like some quantum theory in physics, there is a set amount of hatred in society that expands or contracts as new situations arise. Yet, considering the events of the past century, the manipulative use of scapegoats can subject certain groups to some severe forms of persecution and discrimination while various "others" are given respite. For this reason, anti-Semitism must be studied in the broader context of the other "isms" of society that are, in some cases, just as virulent though not as universal nor so long lived. Perhaps like the mythological Proteus who could assume various forms that ranged from a wild boar and a scaly dragon to a ferocious lion, the hatreds that plague society can also change their shape and tone to meet the needs of new situations. Just as Proteus had to be held fast before he would reveal his secrets, it is often necessary for students of anti-Semitism to isolate one locality in a particular time frame – probe its depths and then carefully analyze the interaction of its constituent groups.

Compared to the cataclysmic events that shaped the Jewish experience both before and after the eighteenth century, what transpired during the relatively uneventful period of England's Age of Reason scarcely seems worth noting. Yet, in the "quiet" moments of the Jewish experience when the legacy of medieval memories is covered with a thin veneer of reason and enlightenment, there is a good opportunity to see how anti-Semitism can be placed in the broader context of the prejudices that affected more conspicuous groups.

From a Jewish historical perspective, all the buttons were in place for the destruction of property and the loss of life. Yet no individual or group in eighteenth century English society was willing to press them and thereby initiate serious actions that resembled either the Gordon or the Priestly Riots. Medieval memories of an accursed, deicidal people, in league with the devil and doomed to wander over the face of the Earth, were modified to some degree. However, the debate over the Jew Bill both in Parliament and in the media shows that the cynical political agitators of the period had in their arsenals a host of well known stereotypical images and "buzz words" to use in their verbal and written attacks against the Jewish community. On the other hand, many of those who defended the Jews appear to have been motivated either by party loyalty or by a strong desire to bring them into the Christian fold through kindness rather than other means of persuasion. The often praised philo-Semitism of the period was, in most instances, tied to a hope for the ultimate conversion of the Jewish people. The absence of pogroms or any significant physical threats to Anglo-Jewry does not necessarily imply that anti-Semitism was declining. It may mean that during this particular time and in this place factors outside of the realm of the Jewish community were present which limited or diffused this age old scourge and, in various ways, prevented it from being transformed into acts of physical violence.

Even in a limited spatial and temporal setting, no one theory can explain the dynamics of such a multifaceted phenomenon as anti-Semitism. This cancerous growth is, by far, too complex to be viewed in simplistic terms. The study of the protean nature of prejudice, with all of its limitations, is but one dimension of a fuller understanding of this form of bigotry and the other "isms" in society as well. Certainly, in the modern world, it deserves our serious consideration.

Bibliography

Primary Sources

An Account of the Late Insurrection in Ireland. London: Printed by J. Evans, n.d.

An Account of the Societies for Reformation of Manners in England and Ireland. London: 1700.

African Merchant. *A Treatice Upon the Trade From Great Britain to Africa: Humbly Recommended to the Attention of Government.* London: Printed for R. Baldwin, 1782.

Africanus. *Remarks on the Slave Trade and the Slavery of the Negroes.* London: Printed by J. Phillips, 1788.

The Anatomy of Exchange Alley: or a System of Stock-Jobbing 1719 reprinted in John Francis. *Chronicles and Characters of the Stock Exchange.* Boston: Cosby and Nichols, 1850. pp. 135-52.

Archaicus. *Admonitions from Scripture and History, from Religion and Common Prudence, Relating to the Jews.* London: Printed for R. Baldwin, 1753.

_____ *The Rejection, and Restoration of the Jews, According to Scripture, Declar'd.* London: Printed for R. Baldwin, 1753.

Arnall, William. *The Complaint of the Children of Israel Representing their Grievances under the Penal Laws.* London: 1736.

An Answer to the Letter to Dr. Waterland. in Relation to the Point of Circumcision. London: Printed for J. Crownfield, 1731.

An Answer to a Pamphlet, Entitled, Considerations on the Bill to Permit Persons Professing the Jewish Religion to be Naturalized. London: Printed for H. Cooke, 1753.

Aveling, Edward. *A Looking Glass For The Jews: Or, The Credulous Unbelievers.* London: Printed for B. Dickinson, 1753.

Barker, John. *Popery the Great Corruption of Christianity, a Sermon Preached at Salters-Hall, January 9, 1734.* London: Printed for Richard Hett, 1735.

Barnett, Lionel D. *Bevis Marks Records, Part I.* Oxford: Oxford UP, 1940.

_____ trans. *El Libro de los Acuerdos, Being the Records and Accounts of the Spanish and Portuguese Synagogue of London From 1663 to 1681.* Oxford: Oxford UP, 1931.

Baxter, Richard. *The Divine Appointment of the Lord's Day Proved.* London: Printed for Nevil Simmons, 1671.

Bennet, Benjamin. *Several Discourses Against Popery.* London: 1714.

Bentley, Richard. *A Sermon on Popery Preached Before the University of Cambridge November 5th 1715.* Cambridge: University Press, 1715.

_____ *Sermons Preached at Boyle's Lecture.* London: Francis McPherson, 1838.

Berriman, William. *The Gradual Revelation of the Gospel: From the Time of Man's Apostacy,* 2 vols. London: Printed for Ward and Wicksteed, 1733.

Bingley, William. *North Wales Including Its Scenery, Antiquities, Customs.* 2 vols. Longman and Rees, 1804.

The Blackamoor in the Wood. London: n.d.

The Black Prince, A True Story; Being An Account of the Life and Death of Naimbanna, An African King's Son. London: J. Evans, n.d.

Blackall, Ofspring. *The Excellency of Christian Revelation. as it Removes the Guilty Fears of Sinners and their Ignorance of God.* London: Printed by J. Leake, 1700.

Blunt, John Elijah. *A History of the Establishment and Residence of the Jews in England with an Enquiry into their Civil Disabilities.* London: Printed for Saunders and Benning, 1830.

The Broken Stock-Jobbers: or Work for the Bailiffs. London: Printed for T. Jauncy, 1720.

Brine, John. *The Baptists Vindicated.* London: Printed for John Ward, 1756.

Browne, Simon. *Jewish and Popish Zeal Describ'd and Compar'd.* London: 1715.

The Bubble: A Poem. London: 1721.

Bugg, Francis. *A Brief History of the Rise Growth and Progress of Quakerism.* London: 1697.

_____ *The Picture of Quakerism Drawn to Life.* London: Printed for W. Kettleby, 1697.

_____ *The Pilgrims Progress From Quakerism to Christianity.* London: Printed by R. Janeway, 1700.

Burke, Edmund. Reflections *on the Revolution in France.* London: J.M. Dent & Sons, 1910.

The Captivities of Jerusalem Lamented or a Plain Description of Jerusalem. Manchester: 1780.

The Case Stated Between the Church of Rome and the Church of England. London: 1713.

Cherbury, Edward, Lord Herbert of. *A Dialogue Between A Tutor and his Pupil.* London: Printed for W. Bathoe, 1768.

_____ *De Religione Laici.* Ed. Harold R. Hutcheson. New Haven: Yale UP, 1944.

_____ *De Veritate.* Ed. Meyrick H. Carre. Bristol: University of Bristol Press, 1937.

Chetwood, William. *South-Sea or the Bitter Bit.* London: J. Roberts, 1720.

Chubb, Thomas. *A Collection of Tracts on Various Subjects.* London: Printed for T. Cox, 1730.

_____ *Posthumous Works of Mr. Thomas Chubb.* Vol. 2, London: Printed for R. Baldwin, 1748.

Cibber, Theophilus. *The Harlot's Progress: or the Ridotto Al' Fresco.* London: 1733.

Cockson, Edward. *Quakerism Dissected and Laid Open.* London: 1708.

Colebrook, Sir George. *Six Letters on Intolerance.* London: 1791.

A Collection of Papers, Printed by Order of the Society for the Propagation of the Gospel in Foreign Parts. London: Printed by Joseph Downing, 1715.

Collins, Anthony. *A Discourse of Free-Thinking.* London: 1713.

_____ *A Discourse of the Grounds and Reasons of the Christian Religion.* London: 1734.

Colquhoun, Patrick. *A Treatise on the Police of London*. Philadelphia: Printed for Benjamin Davies, 1798.

*Considerations concerning the expediency of a general naturalization of foreign Protestants, and others......*London: Printed by E. Say, 1747.

Coombe, Thomas. *The Influence of Christianity on the condition of the world*. Printed for J. Robson, 1790.

Cooper, William. *The promised seed.. A sermon preached to God's ancient Israel the Jews, at Sion-chapel, Whitechapel, on Sunday afternoon, August 28, 1796*. Boston: Printed by Manning and Loring, 1796.

Cox, Daniel. *An Appeal to the Public on Behalf of Elizabeth Canning*. London: 1753.

Cumberland, Richard. *The Jew*. London: Longman, Hurst, Rees and Orme, n.d.

Defoe, Daniel. *The Anatomy of Exchange-Alley: or A System of Stock-Jobbing*. London: Printed for E. Smith, 1719.

_____ *A Brief history of the Poor Palatine Refugees*. Dublin: E. Waters, 1710.

_____ *An Essay at Removing National Prejudices Against a Union With Scotland*. Part I London: 1706.

_____ *The Fortunes and Misfortunes of the Famous Moll Flanders*. New York: Limited Editions Club, 1954.

_____ *Memoirs of an English Officer*. London: Victor Gollancz Ltd., 1970.

_____ *A Review of the State of the English Nation*. vol. 3. London: 1706.

_____ *Roxana: The Fortunate Mistress*. London: Oxford UP, 1964.

_____ *A Tour Thro' the whole Island of Great Britain*. 2 vols. London: Peter Davies, 1927.

Ellis,? *The Sense of the People Concerning the Present State of Affairs*. London: J. Peele, 1721.

An Entertaining History of the Jews; Part The First, Addressed to the Friends of Christianity. London: n.d.

An Exact Description of Scotland, With a True Character of the People and Their Manners. London: n.d.

The Expediency of a General Naturalization of Foreign Protestants, And Others. London: Printed for William Owen, 1751.

Fielding, Henry. *The Adventures of Joseph Andrews.* London: Blackfriers, n.d.

_____ *A Clear State of the Case of Elizabeth Canning.* London: 1753.

_____ *The History of Tom Jones.* London: Folio Society, 1959.

Francis, John. *Chronicles and Characters of the Stock Exchange.* Boston: William Crosby & H. P. Nichols, 1850.

Franklin, Andrew. *The Wandering Jew or Love's Masquerade.* London: 1797.

Free, John. *A Display of the Bad Principles of the Methodists in Certain Articles Proposed to the Serious Consideration of the Worshipful Company of Salters in London.* London: 1759.

_____ *Dr. Free's Edition of the Rev. Mr. John Wesley's Second Letter.* London: 1759.

_____ *A Sermon Preached at St. Mary's in Oxford Before the University on 5th of November 1745.* London: Printed by D. Browne, 1745.

_____ *A Sermon Preached Before the Whole University at St. Mary's in Oxford on Whitsunday 1758.* London: 1759.

_____ *The Whole Speech Which was Delivered to the Reverend Clergy of the Great City of London on Tuesday the 8th of May.* London: 1759.

A Genuine Intercepted Letter From Father Patrick Graham Almoner and Confessor to the Pretender's Son in Scotland to Father Benedick Yorke, Titular Bishop of St. David's at Bath. London: Printed for M. Cooper, 1745.

Gibson, Edward. *A Sermon Preached to the Societies For Reformation of Manners at St. Mary-le-Bow.* London: Printed for John Wyat, n. d.

Gilbert, Lord Bishop of Sarum. *Of the Propagation of the Gospel in Foreign Parts.* A Sermon Preach'd at St. Mary- le-Bow, Feb. 18, 1704.

Goldney, Edward. *A Friendly Epistle to the Deists, and a Rational Prayer Recommended to them, In order for their Conversion to the Christian Religion.* London: Printed for the Author, 1760.

_____ *A Friendly Epistle to the Jews, and a Rational Prayer, Recommended to them in order for their Conversion to the Christian Religion.* London: Printed for the Author, 1761.

A Good Husband for Five Shillings: or a Lottery for Ladies. London: n.d.

Grant, D. *Two Dissertations on Popish Persecution and Breach of Faith.* London: J. Murray, 1771.

Grigg, J. *A Sermon Preached at St. Albans and at Box-Lane, Chiefly With a View to the Apprehended Invasion.* London: Printed for J. Buckland, 1756.

The Gunpowder-Treason with a Discourse of the Manner of its Discovery. London: 1679.

Hancock, John. *Boyle Lectures 1691-1732* vol. 2. Ed. Sampson Letsome. London: 1739.

Hanway, Jonas. *A Review of the Proposed Naturalization of the Jews.* London: 1753.

Haslewood, Francis. *A Sermon Preach'd Before the Right Honourable the Lord-Mayor, the Aldermen and the Citizens of London, in the Cathedral Church of St. Paul on Nov 5th 1720.* London: Printed for Eham Mathews, 1721.

Heckford, William. *A Succinct Account of all the Religions and Various Sects in Religion....*London: William Lane, 1791.

Herbert, Edward, Lord Herbert of Cherbury, *A Dialogue Between a Tutor and his Pupil.* London: 1768.

The Highlander Delineated Or The Characters, Customs, and Manners of the Highlanders. London: 1745.

Hill, John. *The Story of Elizabeth Canning Considered.* London: 1753.

A Historical and Law Treatise Against the Jews and Judaism.... London: 1720.

Holcroft, Thomas. *A Plain and Succinct Narrative of the Gordon Riots.* London: 1780.

Hume, David. *The Natural History of religion.* Ed. H.E. Root. Stanford: Stanford UP. 1957.

Hutchinson, John. *Religion of Satan or Antichrist Delineated.* London: Printed by H. Woodfall, 1736.

Impartial Briton (Thomas Dicey?). *A Sixth and Last Letter, or, Address to the Parliament, As well as to the People of Great Britain.* London: Printed for the Author, n.d.

The Jewish Ritual: or the Religious Customs and Ceremonies of the Jews, Used in their Publick Worship and Private Devotions. London: Printed for M. Cooper, 1753.

The Jews Advocate. ed. Paul Radin. *Sutro Branch California State Library Occasional Papers English Series No. 3.* San Francisco: California State Library, 1939.

The Jews Charter, or An Historical Account of the Privileges Granted them by the several Kings and Parliaments of England.... London: Printed by A. Baldwin, 1702.

Junius. *Stat Nominis Umbra.* Vol. 1. London: Printed for Henry Sampson Woodfall, 1772; rpt. New York: Research Reprints Inc, 1990.

Keach, Benjamin. *The Jewish Sabbath Abrogated.* London: Printed for John Marshall, 1700.

Keith, George. *The Magick of Quakerism or the Chief Mysteries of Quakerism Laid Open.* London: 1707.

Leslie, Charles. *A Parallel Between the Faith and Doctrine of thee Present Quakers and that of the Chief Heretics in all ages of the Church and also A Parallel Between Quakerism and Popery.* London: Printed by John Hut, 1700.

_____ *Primitive Heresie Revived in the Faith and Practice of the People Called Quakers.* London: Printed for C. Brome, 1698.

_____ *A Short and Easie Method with the Deists.* London: Printed for George Strahan, 1711.

_____ *A Short and Easie Method with the Deists to which is added a Second Part to the Jews.* London: Printed for C. Brome, 1699.

_____ *A Short and Easie Method with the Jews.* London: Printed for George Strahan, 1737.

A Letter From a Catholic Gentleman to His Protestant Friend. London: 1745.

A Letter to the Right Reverend the Lord Bishop of London: Occasioned by Disputing with a Quaker. London: Printed for J. Roberts, 1737.

Locke, John. *The Reasonableness of Christianity in The Works of John Locke,* Vol. 7. 1823; rpt. London: Scientia Verlag Aalen, 1963.

_____ *A Second Vindication of the Reasonableness of Christianity in The Works of John Locke* Vol. 7. 1823; rpt. London: Scienta Verlag Aalen, 1963.

_____ *A Third Letter For Toleration in The Works of John Locke* Vol. 6. 1823; rpt. London: Scienta Verlag Aalen, 1963.

London Pocket Pilot, or Stranger's Guide through the metropolis. London: J. Roach, 1793.

M.W. *The History of Israel Jacobson, the Wandering Jew.* London: Printed for J. Nickolson, 1757.

Macready, William. *The Irishman in London: or, The Happy African.* London: Printed for W. Woodfall, 1793.

Mason, John. *A Letter to a Friend Upon his Entrance on the Ministerial Office.* London: Printed for J. Noon, 1753.

Mason, William. *Methodism Displayed and Enthusiasm Detected.* London: Printed for M. Lewis, 1761.

Mathew, Henry. *Popery a Spiritual Tyranny, Shew'd in a Sermon Preach'd on the Fifth of November 1712.* London: Printed for E. Mathews, 1712.

McLaren, Archibald. *Negro Slaves; or the Blackman and Blackbird.* London: A. McPherson, 1799.

The Memorial Presented to the High Court of La Tornelle at Paris in Favour of Abraham Payba, the Jew, a Native of London Against Edward Wortley Montagu Esq. and Theobold Taaffe Esq. London: 1752.

A Memorial to the Public in Behalf of the Roman Catholics of Edinburgh and Glasgow Containing an Account of the Late Riot Against them on the Second and Following Days of February, 1779. London: J. Coghlan, 1779.

Mendoza, Daniel. *The Memoirs of the Life of Daniel Mendoza.* Ed. Paul Magriel, 1951; rpt. New York: Arno Press, 1975.

A Modest Apology for the Citizens and Merchants of London, Who Petitioned the House of Commons Against Naturalizing the Jews. London: Printed for W. Webb, 1753.

Morgan, Thomas. *The Moral Philosopher in a Dialogue Between Philalethes a Christian Deist, and Theophanes a Christian Jew.* London: 1738.

_____ *The Moral Philosopher.* Vol. 2. London: 1739.

_____ *The Moral Philosopher* Vol. 3. London: 1740.

A New and True History of the Wandering Jew. London: n.d.

Nicholls, Benjamin, *A Sermon Preached on the Ocassion of the Present Rebellion at St. Anne's Church Manchester, October 13, 1745.* London: Printed for Henry Whitridge, 1745.

Paine, Thomas. *Age of Reason: Being an Investigation of True and Fabulous Theology.* New York, Wiley Book Co, n.d.

Parliamentary History, Vols. 14 and 15. London: Printed by T.L. Hansard, 1813.

Peckard, Peter. *The Popular Clamour Against the Jews Indefensible: A Sermon Preached at Huntington October 28, 1753.* Cambridge: 1753.

Penn, Thomas. *A Sermon Preach'd Before the Society for Reformation of Manners.* London: Printed for J. Humphreys, 1708.

Philanthropus, Thoughts *on the Jewish Sabbath Occasion'd By Some Gentile's Observation of That Day.* London: 1707.

Philo-Patriae, *Considerations on the Bill to Permit Persons Professing the Jewish Religion to be Naturalized by Parliament. In Several Letters from a Merchant in Town to his Friend in the Country.* Paul Radin, ed. *Sutro Branch California State Library Occasional Papers English Series No. 3.* San Francisco: California State Library, 1939.

A Political and Satirical History Displaying the Unhappy Influence of Scotch Prevalency in the Years 1761,1762, and 1763. London: Published by M. Darly, n.d.

Priestly, Joseph. *A Comparison of the Institutions of Moses with those of the Hindoos and Other Ancient Nations:.....and An Address to the Jews on the present state of the World and the Prophesies relating to it.* Northumberland: 1799.

_____ *Letters to The Jews; inviting them to An Amicable Discussion off the Evidences of Christianity.* Birmingham: Pearson and Rollason, 1786.

_____ *The Present State of Europe compared with Ancient Prophecies.* London: Printed for J. Johnson, 1794.

_____ *A Sermon on the Subject of the Slave Trade.* Birmingham: Pearson and Rollason, 1788.

The Quaker turn'd Jew being A true Relation, how an eminent Quaker in the Isle of Eli, on Monday the 18th of April 1675 Circumcised himself out of Zeal for a Certain Case of Conscience, Renounced his Religion, and Became a Prosolited Jew. London: Printed for W.L. 1675.

A Short Account of the Several Kinds of Societies Set Up of the Late Years for Carrying on the Reformation of Manners, and for the Propagation of Christian Knowledge. London: Printed by J. Brundell, 1700.

Some Queries, Relative to the Jews; Occasioned by a late Sermon: with Some other Papers, occasioned by the Queries. London: Printed for J. Payne, 1753.

Reasons Humbly Offer'd For a Law to enact the Castration or Gelding of Popish Ecclesiastics as the Best Way to Prevent the Growth of Popery in England. London: 1700.

A Representation of the Present State of Religion, With regard to the late excessive Growth of Infidelity, Heresy, and Profaneness.... London: Printed for John Bower, 1711.

Robertson, James. *The Resemblance of Jesus to Moses Considered, and the Extraordinary and Continued Punishment of the Jews Shown to be a Standing Evidence of the Truth of Christianity A Sermon February 25, 1765.* Edinburgh: Society For the Propagation of Christian Knowledge, 1765.

Robinson, John. *Proofs of a Conspiracy Against All the Religions and Governments of Europe, Carried on in the Secret meetings of Free Masons, Illumati and Reading Societies.* London: 1798.

Romaine, William. *An Answer to a Pamphlet Entitled Considerations on the Bill to Permit Persons Professing the Jewish Religion to be naturalized; Wherein the False Reasoning, Gross Misrepresentation of Facts and Perversion of Scripture, are Fully Laid Open and Detected......* London: H. Cooke, 1753.

St. John, Henry, Viscount Bolingbroke. *The Works of the Right Honourable Henry St. John, Lord Viscount Bolingbroke.* 5 vols. London: Published by David Mallet, 1754.

Sherlock, Thomas. *The Tryal of the Witnesses of the Resurrection of Jesus.* London: Printed for J. Roberts, 1729.

_____ *A Letter from the Lord Bishop of London to the clergy and people of London and Westminster on the occasion of the late earthquakes.* London: Printed for John Whiston, 1750.

A Short Account of the Several Kinds of Societies Set up of the Late Years for Carrying on the Reformation of Manners, and for the Propagation of Christian Knowledge. London: Printed by J. Brundell, 1700.

Skelton, Philip. *Deism Revealed.* Vol. 2. London: Printed for A. Millar, 1751.

The Snake in the Grass or Satan Transform'd into an Angel of Light. London: Printed for Charles Brome, 1697.

Some Remarks on the Quakers Address to His Majesty. London: 1701.

Stephens, Henry. *A True Representation of Popery as it Appears in Foreign Parts: Designed as a Preservative Against its Contagion; Particularly*

Recommended to British Protestants During Their Residence in Popish Countries. London: Printed for James and John Knapton, 1728.

Stillingfleet, J. *Seasonable Advice Concerning Quakerism.* London: Printed for Henry Mortlock, 1702.

Talbot, William. *A Sermon Preach'd Before the Queen at the Cathedral Church of St. Paul on May the first, 1707.* London: 1707.

Tawney Rachel; Or The Fortune Teller: With Some Account of Dreams, Omens, and Conjurers. London: S. Hazard, n.d.

Tillotson, John. *Several Discourses of the Truth and the Excellency of the Christian Religion.* London: 1703.

Tindal, Mathew. *Christianity as old as the Creation: or, the Gospel, a Republication of the Religion of Nature.* London: 1730.

Toland, John. *Appendix, Containing Two Problems Concerning the Jewish Nation and Religion.* London: 1718.

_____ *Christianity Not Mysterious.* London: Printed for Samuel Buckley, 1696.

_____ *Letters to Serena.* London: Printed for Bernard Lintot, 1704.

_____ *Tetradymus.* London: 1720.

Tovey, D'Blossiers. *Anglia Judaica: or the History and Antiquities of the Jews in England.* Oxford: 1738.

The Trials of all the Felon Prisoners, Tried, Cast, and Condemned, this Session at the Old Bailey. London: n.d.

The True Life of Eleanor Gwinn A Celebrated Courtezan in the Reign of King Charles II and Mistress to that Monarch. London: Printed by T. Bailey, n.d.

The Truth Found Out at Last or the Whig Prov'd Worse Than the Tory. London: W. Richardson, 1720.

Tucker, Josiah. *A Second Letter to a Friend Concerning Naturalizations.* London: Printed for Thomas Trye, 1753.

Twells, Leonard. *Twenty-Four Sermons.* 2 vols. London: 1743.

A View of London and Westminster: or the Town Spy. London: Printed for T. Warmer, 1725.

Voltaire, *Letters Concerning the English Nation.* London: 1733.

Warburton, William. *The Divine Legation of Moses Demonstrated.* Ed. Richard Hurd. London: Printed for Thomas Tegg, 1846.

Webber, Francis. *The Jewish Dispensation Consider'd and Vindicated, With a View to the Objections of Unbelievers, and Particularly of a Late Author called the Moral Philosopher A Sermon Preached before the University of Oxford Sunday October 23, 1737.* Oxford: 1738.

The Welsh Wedding. London: n.d.

Wesley, John. *The Journal of the Rev. John Wesley.* 4 vols. Ed. Ernest Rhys. London: J.M. Dent & Co. n.d.

_____ *A Reader.* Ed. John R. Tyson. Oxford: Oxford UP, 1989.

Whiston, William. *The Accomplishment of Scripture Prophesies.* London: 1708.

_____ *Friendly Address to the Baptists.* Stanford: 1748.

_____ *Six Dissertations.* London: Printed for John Whiston, 1734.

White, John. *The Protestant Englishman Guarded Against the Arts and the Arguments of Romish Priests and Emissaries.* London: 1753.

William, Lord Bishop of Chester. *A Sermon Preach'd before the Society for the Propagation of the Gospel in Foreign Parts, at the Parish Church of St. Mary-le -Bow, On Friday February 18, 1709.* London: Printed by Joseph Downing, 1709.

Winstanley, Thomas. *A Sermon Preach'd at the Parish-Church of St. George, Hanover -Square Sunday October 28, 1753.* London: 1753.

Secondary Sources

Aaron, Richard I. *John Locke.* Oxford: Clarendon, 1971.

Adler, Elkan Nathan. *London.* Philadelphia: J.P. S., 1930.

Allport, Gordon W. *The Nature of Prejudice.* New York: Doubleday, 1958.

Anderson, George K. *The Legend of the Wandering Jew.* Providence: Brown UP, 1965.

Ashton, T.S. *An Economic History of England: The 18th Century.* Methuen, 1955.

Atherton, Herbert M. *Political Prints in the Age of Hogarth: A Study of the Ideographic Representation of Politics.* Oxford: Oxford UP, 1974.

Bailey, Derrick Sherwin. *Homosexuality and the Western Christian Tradition.* Hamdon, Connecticut: Archon, 1975.

Barlow, Richard Burgess. *Citizenship and Conscience A Study of the Theory and Practice of Religious Toleration in England During the Eighteenth Century.* Philadelphia: University of Pennsylvania Press, 1962.

Bayne-Powell, Rosamond. *Eighteenth-Century London Life.* Dutton, 1938.

Becker, Carl L. *The Heavenly City of the Eighteenth-Century Philosophers.* New Haven: Yale UP, 1960.

Ball, Bryan W. *The Seventh-Day Men: Sabbatarians and Sabbatarianism in England and Wales, 1600 -1800.* Oxford: Clarendon Press, 1994.

Bell, Walter George. *The Great Fire of London in 1666.* London: John Lane, 1920.

Berger, David, ed. *History and Hate: The Dimensions of Anti-Semitism.* Philadelphia: J.P. S., 1986.

Berman, David. *A History of Atheism in Britain.* London: Routledge, 1990.

Bermant, Chaim. *The Cousinhood: The Anglo-Jewish Gentry.* London: Eyre & Spottiswoode, 1971.

Black, Eugene Charlton. *The Association: British Extraparliamentary Organization 1769-1793.* Cambridge, Massachusetts: Harvard UP, 1963.

Block, Martin. *Gypsies Their Life and Their Customs.* New York: Appleton-Century, 1939.

Bloom, Herbert I. *The Economic Activities of the Jews of Amsterdam in the Seventeenth and Eighteenth Centuries.* Williamsport, Pennsylvania: Bayard, 1937.

Brayshaw, A. Neave. *The Quakers: Their Story and Message.* New York: Macmillan, 1938.

Bready, J. Wesley. *England: Before and After Wesley.* London: Hodder and Staughton, 1939.

Briggs, Asa. *A Social History of England.* Middlesex, England: Penguin Books, 1985.

Brown, Philip Anthony. *The French Revolution in English History.* London: George Allen and Unwin, 1965.

Brown, Richard. *Church and State in Modern Britain 1700-1850.* London: Routledge, 1991.

_____ *Society and Economy in Modern Britain 1700-1850*. London: Routledge, 1991.

Browne, Alice. *The Eighteenth Century Feminist Mind*. Detroit: Wayne State UP, 1987.

Bruce, Donald. *Radical Doctor Smollett*. Boston: Houghton Mifflin, 1965.

Burford, E.J. *Wits, Wenchers and Wantons: London's Low Life: Covent Garden in the Eighteenth Century*. London: Robert Hale, 1986.

Bushnell, T.L. *The Sage of Salisbury: Thomas Chubb 1679-1747*. New York: Philosophical Library, 1967.

Capp, Bernard. *English Almanacs 1500-1800: Astrology and the Popular Press*. Ithaca, New York: Cornell UP, 1979.

Carswell, John. *From Revolution to Revolution: England 1688-1776*. New York: Scribner's, 1973.

Chapin, Chester F. *The Religious Thought of Samuel Johnson*. Ann Arbor: U of Michigan P, 1968.

Cohen, Abraham. *An Anglo-Jewish Scrapbook 1600-1840: The Jew Through English Eyes*. London: Cailingold, 1943.

Christie, Ian R. *Stress and Stability in Late Eighteenth-Century Britain*. Oxford: Clarendon, 1986.

_____ *Wars and Revolutions Britain, 1760-1815*. Cambridge, Massachusetts: Harvard UP, 1982.

Clapham, John. *The Bank of England: A History 1694-1797*. Vol. 1. Cambridge: Cambridge UP 1945.

Clark, J.C.D. *English Society 1688-1832: Ideology, Social Structure and Political Practice During the Ancient Regime*. Cambridge: Cambridge UP, 1985.

Clifford, James L. ed. *Man Versus Society in Eighteenth Century Britain*. Cambridge: Cambridge UP, 1968.

Colley, Linda. *Britons: Forging the Nation 1707-1837*. New Haven: Yale UP, 1992.

Commager. Henry Steele. *The Empire of Reason: How Europe Imagined and America Realized the Enlightenment*. rpt. Garden City, New York: Anchor Books, 1978.

Conder, Edward. *Records of the Hole Crafte and Fellowship of Masons*. London: Swan Sonnenschein & Co., 1894.

Cone, Carl B. *Burke and the Nature of Politics.* Lexington, Kentucky: U of Kentucky Press, 1964.

_____ *The English Jacobins: Reformers in Late 18th Century England.* New York: Scribner, 1968.

Cottret, Bernard. *The Huguenots in England: Immigration and Settlement c. 1550-1700.* trans. Peregrine and Adriana Stevenson. Cambridge: Cambridge UP, 1985.

Cragg, Gerald R. *The Church and the Age of Reason 1648-1789.* New York: Atheneum, 1961.

_____ *From Puritanism to the Age of Reason.* Cambridge: Cambridge UP, 1950.

_____ *Reason and Authority in the Eighteenth Century.* Cambridge: Cambridge UP, 1964.

Cranfield, G.A. *The Development of the Provincial Newspaper 1700- 1760.* Oxford: Clarendon, 1962.

Creed, John Martin, and John Sandwith Smith. *Religious Thought in the Eighteenth Century.* Cambridge: Cambridge UP, 1934.

Crompton, Louis. *Byron and Greek Love: Homophobia in 19th Century England.* Berkley: U of California P, 1985.

Cunningham, W. *Alien Immigrants to England.* London: Swan Sonnenschien & Co., 1897.

Curry, Patrick. *Prophesy and Power: Astrology in Early Modern England.* Princeton, Princeton UP, 1989.

Damrosch, Leo. *Fictions of Reality in the Age of Hume and Johnson.* Madison: U of Wisconsin P, 1989.

Davies, Horton. *The English Free Churches.* London: Oxford UP, 1963.

_____ *Worship and Theology in England From Watts and Wesley to Maurice, 1690-1850.* Princeton: Princeton UP, 1961.

Deane, Seamus. *The French Revolution and Enlightenment in England 1789-1832.* Cambridge, Massachusetts: Harvard UP, 1988.

de Castro, J. Paul. *The Gordon Riots.* London: Oxford UP, 1926.

Deporte, Michael V., *Nightmares and Hobbyhorses: Swift, Sterne, and Augustan Ideas of Madness.* San Marino, California: Huntington Library, 1974.

Derry, John W. *Charles James Fox.* New York: St. Martin's Press, 1972.

Dickinson, H.T., *British Radicalism and the French Revolution.* Oxford, Basic Blackwell, 1985.

Dickson, P. G.M. *The Financial Revolution in England: A Study in the Development of Public Credit 1688-1756.* New York: Macmillan, 1967.

Downey, James. *The Eighteenth Century Pulpit: A Study of the Sermons of Butler, Berkeley, Secker, Sterne, Whitefield and Wesley.* Oxford: Clarendon, 1969.

Duschinsky, C. *The Rabbinate of the Great Synagogue, London From 1756-1842.* London: Humphrey Milford, 1921.

Dykes, Eva Beatrice, *The Negro in English Romantic Thought.* Washington, D.C.: Associated Publishers, 1942.

Ellis, Aytoun. *The Penny Universities: A History of the Coffee-Houses.* London: Secker & Warburg, 1956.

Emanuel, Charles. *A Century and a Half of Jewish History: Extracted From the Minute Book of the London Committee of Deputies of the British Jews.* London: Routledge, 1910.

Endelman, Todd M. *The Jews of Georgian England 1714-1830: Tradition and Change in a Liberal Society.* Philadelphia: J.P. S., 1979.

_____ *Radical Assimilation in English Jewish History.* Bloomington and Indianapolis: Indiana UP, 1990.

Evans, A.W. *Warburton and the Warburtonians: A Study in Some Eighteenth -Century Controversies.* London: Oxford University Press, 1932.

Fay, Bernard. *Revolution and Freemasonary 1680-1800.* Boston: Little Brown, 1935.

Felsenstein, Frank. *Anti-Semitic Stereotypes: A Paradign of Otherness in English Popular Culture, 1660-1830.* Baltimore: Johns Hopkins UP, 1995.

Francis, John. *Chronicles and Characters of the Stock Exchange.* Boston: Crosby & Nichols, 1850.

Fraser, Angus. *The Gypsies.* Oxford: Blackwell, 1992.

Fuglum, Per. *Edward Gibbon: His View of Life and Conception of history.* Oslo: Akademisk Forlag, 1953.

Garrett, Clarke. *Respectable Folly: Millenarians and the French Revolution in France and England.* Baltimore: John Hopkins UP, 1975.

Gaster, Moses. *History of the Ancient Synagogue of the Spanish and Portuguese Jews.* London: 1901.

Gay, Peter. *The Party of Humanity: Studies in the French Enlightenment.* London: Weidenfeld & Nicholson.

_____ *The Enlightenment: An Interpretation The Rise of Modern Paganism.* New York: Vintage Books, 1968.

George, Dorothy M. *London Life in the XVIIIth Century.* New York: Knoff, 1925.

Gerzina, Gretchen. *Black London: Life Before Emancipation.* New Brunswick, New Jersey: Rutgers UP, 1995.

Gilmour, Ian. *Riot, Risings and Revolution: Governance and Violence in Eighteenth Century England.* London: Pimlico, 1993.

Girard, René, *The Scapegoat.* Trans. Yvonne Freccero. Baltimore: Johns Hopkins UP, 1986.

Glassman, Bernard. *Anti-Semitic Stereotypes Without Jews: Images of the Jews in England 1290-1700.* Detroit: Wayne State UP, 1975.

Goodwin, Albert. *The Friends of Liberty: The English Democratic Movement in the Age of the French Revolution.* Cambridge, Massachusetts: Harvard UP, 1979.

Grean, Stanley. *Shaftesbury's Philosophy of Religion and Ethics.* Athens, Ohio: Ohio UP, 1967.

Greene, Donald. *The Age of Exuberance: Backgrounds to Eighteenth-Century English Literature.* New York: Random House, 1970.

Gwynn, Robin D. *Huguenot Heritage: The history and contribution of the Huguenots in Britain.* London: Routledge & Kegan Paul, 1985.

Haggar, Betty. *Jewish Peddlers and Hawkers 1740-90.* Surrey: Porphyrogenitus, 1992.

Hampson, Norman. *A Cultural History of the Enlightenment.* New York: Random House, 1968.

Hancock, Ian. *The Pariah Syndrome,* Ann Arbor: Karona Publications, 1987.

Harris, R. W. *Reason and Nature in the Eighteenth Century.* London: Blanford Press, 1968.

Hay, Douglas, et al. *Albion's Fatal Tree: Crime and Society in Eighteenth-Century England.* New York: Pantheon, 1975.

Haydon, Colin. *Anti-Catholicism in Eighteenth-Century England 1714-80.* Manchester: Manchester UP, 1993.

Hempton, David. *Methodism and Politics in British Society 1750-1850.* London: Hutchinson, 1987.

_____ *Religion and Political Culture in Britain and Ireland: From the Glorious Revolution to the decline of empire.* Cambridge: Cambridge UP, 1996

Henriques, Henry Straus Quixano. *The Jews and the English Law.* Oxford: Oxford UP, 1908.

Henriques, Ursula. *Religious Toleration in England 1787-1833.* Toronto: U of Toronto P, 1961.

Hertz, Gerald Berkeley. *British Imperialism in the Eighteenth Century.* London: Archibald Constable, 1908.

Hibbert, Christopher. *King Mob: The Story of Lord George Gordon and the London Riots of 1780.* Cleveland: World Publishing, 1958..

Hill, Christopher. *Antichrist in Seventeenth Century England.* London: Oxford UP, 1971.

_____ *Change and Continuity in Seventeenth Century England.* Cambridge, Massachusetts: Harvard UP, 1975.

Hoecker, James J. *Joseph Priestly and the Idea of Progress.* New York: Garland, 1977.

Holmes, Colin. *Anti-Semitism in British Society 1876-1939.* New York: Holmes and Meier,.

Horne, Thomas A. *The Social Thought of Bernard Mandeville: Virtue and Commerce in Early Eighteenth Century England.* New York: Columbia UP, 1978.

Humphreys, A.R. *The Augustan World: Life and Letters in Eighteenth-Century England.* London: Methuen, 1954.

Hunt, John B. *Religious Thought in England, From the Reformation to the End of the Last Century; A Contribution to the History of Theology,* Vol. 3, 1870-73; rpt. New York: AMS Press, 1973.

Hunt, N.C. *Two Early Political Associations: The Quakers and the Dissenting Deputies in the Age of Sir Robert Walpole.* Oxford: Oxford UP, 1961.

Hyamson, Albert M. *The Sephardim of England: A History of the Spanish and Portuguese Jewish Community 1492-1951.* London: Methuen, 1951.

Jackman, Sydney Wayne. *Man of Mercury: An Appreciation of the Mind of Henry St. John, Viscount Bolingbroke.* London: Pall Mall, 1965.

Jacob, Margaret C. *The Newtonians and the English Revolution 1689-1720.* Ithaca, New York: Cornell UP, 1976.

Jarrett, Derek, *England in the Age of Hogarth.* London: Hart-Davis, Macgibbon, 1974.

Jones, James Rees. *Country and Court: England 1658-1714.* Cambridge, Massachusetts: Harvard UP, 1978.

Katz, David S. *The Jews in the History of England 1485-1850.* Oxford: Clarendon, 1994.

_____ *Sabbath and Sectarianism in Seventeenth-Century England.* Leiden: E.J. Brill, 1988.

Katz, Jacob. *Jews and Free Masons in Europe 1723-1939.* Cambridge, Massachusetts: Harvard UP, 1970.

_____ *From Prejudice to Destruction: Anti-Semitism, 1700-1933.* Cambridge, Massachusetts, Harvard UP, 1980.

_____ *Out of the Ghetto; The Social Background of Jewish Emancipation, 1770-1870.* Cambridge, Massachusetts: Harvard UP, 1973.

Kenyon, John. *The Popish Plot.* London: William Heineman, 1972.

Kindleberger, Charles. *A Financial History of Western Europe.* London: Allen & Unwin, 1984.

Kobler, Franz. *Napoleon and the Jews.* New York: Schocken, 1984.

Lavender, Abraham D. *French Huguenots: From Mediterranean Catholics to White Anglo-Saxon Protestants.* New York: Peter Lang, 1990.

Langford, Paul. *A Polite and Commercial People: England 1727-1783.* Oxford: Oxford UP, 1992.

Langmuir, Gavin I. *Toward a Definition of Anti-Semitism.* Berkley: U of California P, 1990.

Lessenich, Rolf P. *Elements of Pulpit Oratory in Eighteenth Century England (1660-1800).* Vienna: Bohlau- Verlag, Koln, 1972.

Leys, Mary Dorathy Rose, *Catholics in England 1559-1829: A Social History.* New York: Sheed and Ward, 1961.

Linebaugh, Peter, *The London Hanged: Crime and Civil Society in the Eighteenth Century.* Cambridge: Cambridge UP, 1992.

Lindsay, Jack. *Hogarth: His Art and His World.* New York: Taplinger, 1979.

Lloyd, Arnold. *Quaker Social History 1669-1738.* Westport, Connecticut: Greenwood, 1979.

Low, D.M. *Edward Gibbon 1737-1794.* New York: Random House, 1937.

Lyons, John O. *The Invention of the Self: The Hinge of Consciousness in the Eighteenth Century.* Carbondale: Southern Illinois UP, 1978.

Maccoby, Hyman. *Judas Iscariot and the Myth of Jewish Evil.* New York: Free Press, 1992.

Mac Dougall, Hugh. *Racial Myth in English History: Trojans, Teutons, and Anglo-Saxons.* Montreal: Harvest House, 1982.

Machen, Arthur. *The Canning Wonder.* London: Chatto & Windus, 1925.

Mackay, Charles. *Extraordinary Popular Delusions and the Madness of the Crowds.* London: Richard Bentley, 1841; rpt. New York: Harmony Books, 1980.

Manuel, Frank E. *The Eighteenth Century Confronts the Gods.* Cambridge, Massachusetts, Harvard UP, 1959.

_____ *Issac Newton Historian.* Cambridge, Massachusetts: Harvard UP, 1963.

_____ *The Religion of Issac Newton.* Oxford: Clarendon Press, 1974.

Margoliouth, Moses. *The History of the Jews in Great Britain.* Vol. 2. London: Richard Bentley, 1851.

Marshall, P. J., and Glyndwr Williams. *The Great Map of Mankind: British Perceptions of the World in the Age of Enlightenment.* London: Dent, 1982.

Mathew, David. *Catholicism in England: The Portrait of a Minority; Its Culture and Tradition.* London: Eyre & Spottiswoode, 1955.

Mayhew, Henry. *London Labour and the London Poor.* Vol. 2. London: Griffin, 1851.

McCloy, Shelby T. *Gibbon's Antagonism to Christianity.* London: Williams and Norgate, 1933.

McLynn, Frank. *The Jacobites.* London: Routledge and Kegan Paul, 1988.

Melville, Lewis. *The South Sea Bubble.* London: Daniel O' Connor, 1921.

Mossner, Earnest Campbell. *Bishop Butler and the Age of Reason.* New York: Macmillan, 1936.

Myers, Norma. *Reconstructing the Black Past: Blacks in Britain 1780-1830.* London and Portland, Oregon: Frank Cass, 1996.

Naggar, Betty. *Jewish Pedlars and Hawkers.* Surrey: Porphyrogenitus, 1992.

Newman, Gerald. *The Rise of English Nationalism: A Cultural History.* New York: St. Martin's, 1987.

Nicolson, Harold. *The Age of Reason (1700-1789).* London: Constable, 1960.

Norman, E.R. *Church and Society in England 1770 -1970:A Historical Study.* Oxford: Clarendon, 1976.

Norton, Rictor. *Mother Clap's Molly House: The Gay Subculture in England 1700-1830.* London: GMP Publishers, 1992.

O'Higgins, James. *Anthony Collins: The Man and his Works.* The Hague, Netherlands: Martinus Nijhoff, 1970.

Paston, George. *Social Caricature in the Eighteenth Century.* 1905; rpt. New York: Benjamin Bloom, 1968

Perry, Thomas W. *Public Opinion, Propaganda, and Politics in Eighteenth Century England: A Study of the Jew Bill of 1753.* Cambridge, Massachusetts: Harvard UP, 1962.

Peters, John. *A Family From Flanders.* London: Collins, 1985.

Petrie, Sir Charles. *The Jacobite Movement.* London: Eyre and Spottiswoode, 1958.

Petuchowski, Jacob J. *The Theology of Haham David Nieto: An Eighteenth Century Defense of the Jewish Tradition.* New York: Bloch, 1954.

Philipson, Nicholas. *Hume,* New York: St. Martin's, 1989.

Piccioto, James. *Sketches of Anglo-Jewish History.* London: Soncino, 1961.

Poliakov, Leon. *The Aryan Myth: A History of Racist and Nationalist Ideas in Europe.* New York: Basic Books, 1974.

_____ *The History of Anti-Semitism: From Voltaire to Wagner* Vol. 3. New York: Vanguard Press, 1975.

Pollins, Harold. *Economic History of the Jews in England.* Rutherford, New Jersey: Fairleigh Dickenson UP, 1982.

Priestly, Joseph. *Adventurer in Science and Champion of Truth.* London: Thomas Nelson, 1965.

Redwood, John. *Reason, Ridicule and Religion: The Age of Enlightenment in England 1660-1750.* Cambridge, Massachusetts: Harvard UP, 1976.

Rhys, John and David Brynmore-Jones. *The Welsh People.* 1906; rpt., New York: Haskell House Publishers, 1969.

Roberts, J.M. *The Mythology of the Secret Societies.* London: Secker & Warburg, 1974.

Rosenberg, Edgar. *From Shylock to Svengali: Jewish Stereotypes in English Fiction.* Stanford, California: Stanford UP, 1960.

_____ *Tabloid Jews and Fungoid Scribblers.* Hoboken, New Jersey: KTAV, 1973.

Roth, Cecil. *Anglo-Jewish Letters.* London: Soncino Press, 1938.

_____ *The Great Synagogue London 1690-1940.* London: Edward Goldston & Son, 1950.

_____ *A History of the Jews in England.* Oxford: Clarendon, 1964.

Rowdan, Aldred W. *The Primates Of The Four Georges.* London: John Murray, 1916.

Rude, George. *Hanoverian London: 1714-1808.* London: Secker and Warburg, 1971.

_____ *Paris and London in the Eighteenth Century.* New York: Viking, 1973.

Rupp, Gordon. *Religion in England.* Oxford: Clarendon, 1986.

Salbstein, Michael C.N. *The Emancipation of the Jews in Britain: The Question of the Admission of the Jews to Parliament, 1828-1860.* Rutherford, New Jersey: Fairleigh Dickenson UP, 1982.

Schilling, Bernard N. *Conservative England and the Case Against Voltaire.* New York: Octagon Books, 1976.

Schwartz, Hillel. *The French Prophets: The History of a Millenarian Group in Eighteenth -Century England.* Berkley: U of California P, 1980.

Scobie, Edward. *Black Britannia: A History of Blacks in Britain.* Chicago: Johnson Publishing Co., 1972.

Scult, Mel. *Millennial Expectations and Jewish Liberties: A Study of the Efforts to Convert the Jews in Britain, Up to the Mid Nineteenth Century.* Leiden: Brill, 1978.

Shachar, Isaiah. *The Judensau: A Medieval Anti-Jewish Motif and its History.* London: Warburg Institute, 1974.

Shesgreen, Sean, ed. *Engravings by Hogarth.* New York: Dover Publications, 1973.

Shulvass, Moses A. *From East to West: The Westward Migration of Jews from Eastern Europe During the Seventeenth and Eighteenth Centuries.* Detroit: Wayne State UP, 1971.

Shyllon, Folarin. *Black people in Britain 1555-1833.* London: Oxford UP, 1977.

Siebert, Donald T. *The Moral Animus of David Hume.* Newark: U of Delaware P, 1990.

Sisson, C.H., ed. *The English Sermon 1650-1750.* Vol. 2. Surrey, England: Cancanet, Press, 1976.

Smith, Joseph. *Bibliotheca Anti-Quakeriana.* London: Joseph Smith, 1873.

Speck, W.A. *Stability and Strife: England 1714-1760.* Cambridge, Massachusetts: Harvard UP, 1977.

Spencer, Christopher, ed. *Five Restoration Adaptations of Shakespeare.* Urbana: U of Illinois P, 1965.

Starkie, Walter. *In Sara's Tents.* New York: Dutton, 1953.

Statt, Daniel. *Foreigners and Englishmen: The Controversy over Immigration and Population, 1660-1760.* Newark: U of Delaware Press, 1995.

Stephen, Sir Leslie. *History of English Thought in the Eighteenth Century.* 2 vols. New York: Putnam, 1927.

Stevenson, John. *Popular Disturbances in England 1700- 1870.* New York: Longman, 1979.

Stromberg, Roland N. *Religious Liberalism in Eighteenth Century England.* London: Oxford UP, 1954.

Sullivan, Robert E. *John Toland and the Deist Controversy.* Cambridge, Massachusetts: Harvard University Press, 1982.

Sway, Marlene. *Familiar Strangers: Gypsy Life in America.* Urbana: U of Illinois Press, 1988.

Sykes, Norman. *Church and State in England in the Eighteenth Century.* Hamden, Connecticut: Archon, 1962.

_____ *From Seldon to Secker: Aspects of English Church History 1660-1768,* Cambridge: Cambridge UP, 1959.

Sypher, Wylie. *Guinea's Captive Kings: British Anti-Slavery Literature of the Eighteenth Century.* Chapel Hill: The U of North Carolina P, 1942.

Thompson, E.P. *The Making of the English Working Class.* New York: Random House, 1966.

Treherne, John. *The Canning Enigma.* London: Jonathan Cape, 1989.

Trigg, Elwood B. *Gypsy Demons and Divinities: The Magic and Religion of the Gypsies.* Secaucus, New Jersey: Citadel Press, 1973.

Turberville, A.S. *The House of Lords in the XVIII th Century.* Oxford: Clarendon, 1927.

Turner, John Munsey. *Conflict and Reconciliation: Studies in Methodism and Ecumenism in England 1740-1982.* London: Epworth Press, 1985.

Walvin, James. *The Black Presence: A Documented History of the Negro in England, 1555-1860.* New York: Schoken, 1972.

Warne. Arthur. *Church and Society in Eighteenth Century Devon.* New York: Augustus Kelley, 1969.

Watt, Ian. *The Rise of the Novel: Studies in Defoe, Richardson and Fielding.* Berkeley, California, U of California P, 1971.

Watts, Michael R. *The Dissenters: From the Reformation to the French Revolution.* Vol. 1, Oxford: Clarendon, 1978.

Westfall, Richard S. *Never At Rest; A Biography of Isaac Newton.* Cambridge: Cambridge UP, 1980.

White, T.H. *The Age of Scandal.* Oxford: Oxford UP, 1986.

Wiley, Basil. *The Eighteenth Century Background: Studies on the Idea of Nature in the Thought of the Period.* London: Chatto & Windus, 1940.

Williams, Bill. *The Making of Manchester Jewry 1740-1875.* Manchester: Manchester UP, 1976.

Wistrich, Robert S. *Antisemitism: The longest Hatred.* New York: Partheon Books, 1991.

Wooton, Graham. *Pressure Groups in Britain.* London: Allen Lane, 1975.

Yogev, Gedalia. *Diamonds and Coral: Anglo-Dutch Jews and Eighteenth-Century Trade.* Leicester: Leicester UP, 1978.

Essays And Articles

Abrahams, Dudley. "Jew Brokers of the City of London." *M.J.H.S.E.* 3 (1937): 80-94.

Altmann, Alexander. "William Wollaston (1659-1724): English Deist and Rabbinic Scholar." *T.J.H.S.E.* 16 (1945-51): 185-211.

Anderson, G.K. "Popular Survivals of the Wandering Jew in England." *The Wandering Jew: Essays in the Interpretation of a Christian Legend.* Ed. Galit Hasan-Rokem and Alan Dundes, Bloomington: Indiana UP, 1986. pp. 76-104.

Arnold, Arthur P. "Apprentices of Great Britain 1710-1773." *M.J.H.S.E.* 22 (1970): 145-57.

Austin, William H. "Issac Newton on Science and Religion." *Journal of the History of Ideas* 31 (October-December): 521-42.

Barnett, R.D. "The Correspondence of the Mahamad of the Spanish and Portuguese Congregation of London during the Seventeenth and Eighteenth Centuries." *T.J.H.S.E.* 20 (1959-61): 1-50.

Baron, Salo W. "Changing Patterns of Antisemitism: A Survey." *Jewish Social Studies* 38 (1976): 6-37.

Bartley, J.O. "The Development of a Stock Character II. The Stage Scotsman; III. The Stage Welshman (to 1800)," *The Modern Language Review* 38 (October, 1943): 279-288.

Booth, Alan. "Liberty or Slavery' Irish Radicalism in England in the 1790s." *Irish Studies Review* 2 (Winter, 1992):26-28.

Bosher, J.F. "The Franco-Catholic Danger, 1660-1715." *History: The Journal of the Historical Association* 79 (February, 1994):5-30.

Bowan, H.V. "The Pests of Human Society': Stock Brokers, Jobbers and Speculators in Mid-Eighteenth-Century Britain." *History: The Journal of the Historical Association* 78 (1993): 38-53.

Brewer, John. "The Misfortune of Lord Bute: A Case Study in Eighteenth-Century Political Argument and Public Opinion." *The Historical Journal* 16 (1973): 3-43.

Bryant, G.J. "Scots in India in the Eighteenth Century." *The Scottish Historical Review.* 64 (April, 1985): 22-41.

Canny, Nicholas. "The Marginal Kingdom: Ireland as a Problem in the First British Empire." *Strangers Within the Realm: Cultural Margins of the First British Empire.* Ed. Bernard Bailyn and Philip D. Morgan. Chapel Hill and London: U of North Carolina Press, 1991. pp. 35-66.

Chanes, Jerome A. "Antisemitism and Jewish Security." *Antisemitism in America Today: Outspoken Experts Explode the Myths.* Ed. Jerome A. Chanes. New York: Birch Lane Press, 1995. pp. 3-29.

Clark, J.C.D. "Reconceptualizing Eighteenth-Century England." *British Journal for Eighteenth Century Studies.* 15 (Autumn, 1992):135-39.

Cohen, Stuart A. "Anglo-Jewish Responses to Antisemitism: Suggestions for a Framework of Analysis." *Living With Antisemitism: Modern Jewish Responses.* Ed. Jehuda Reinharz, Hanover and London: Brandeis UP and UP of New England, 1987. pp. 84-103.

Connolly, S.J. "Varieties of Britishness: Ireland, Scotland and Wales in the Hanoverian state." *Uniting the Kingdom? The making of British History.* Ed. Alexander Grant and Keith J. Stringer, London and New York: Routledge, 1995. pp. 193-207.

Cranfield, G.A. "The 'London Evening-Post' And The Jew Bill Of 1753." *The Historical Journal* 8 (no. 1, 1965):16-30.

Crouzet, F.M. "Walloons, Huguenots and the Bank of England." *Proceedings of the Huguenot Society* 25 (1990): 167-78.

Dabydeen, David. "References to Blacks in William Hogarth's Analysis of Beauty." *British Journal for Eighteenth-Century Studies* 5 (Spring, 1982): 93-103.

Daiches- Dubens, Rachel. "Eighteenth Century Anglo-Jewry in and around Richmond, Surrey." *T.J.H.S.E.* 18 (1953-55): 143-69.

Davies, R.R. "Buchedd A Moes Cymry." ("The Manners and Morals of the Welsh.") *The Welsh History Review* 12 (December, 1984): 155-179.

Diamond, A.S. "The Community of the Resettlement, 1656-1684: A Social Survey." *T.J.H.S.E.* 29 (1970-73): 134-50.

_____ "Problems of the London Sephardi Community, 1720-1733- Philip Carteret Webb's Notebooks." *T.J.H.S.E.* 21 (1968): 39-63.

Ditchfield, G.M. "The Priestly Riots in Historical Perspective." *Transactions of the Unitarian Historical Society* 20 (April, 1991): 3-16.

Eck, Diana L. "Neighboring Faiths: How Will Americans Cope With Increasing Religious Diversity?" *Harvard Magazine* 99 (no. 1 October, 1996): 38-44.

Edelmann, R. "Ahasuerus, the Wandering Jew Origin and Background." *The Wandering Jew: Essays in the Interpretation of a Christian Legend.* Ed. Galit Hasan-Rokem and Alan Dundes, Bloomington: Indiana UP, 1986. pp. 1-10.

Edwards. Lewis. "Daniel Mendoza." *T.J.H.S.E.* 15 (1939-45): 73-92.

Endelman, Todd M. "The Checkered Career of Jew King: A Study in Anglo-Jewish Social History." *Association for Jewish Social Studies* 7-8 (1982-83): 69-100.

_____ "Comparative Perspectives on Modern Anti-Semitism in the West." *History and Hate: The Dimensions of Anti-Semitism.* Ed. David Berger. Philadelphia: Jewish Publication Society, 1986. pp. 95-114.

Ettinger, Samuel. "Yehudim Ve-Yahadut B'einei Ha Deistim Haangliyim Be Meah Ha-18." *Zion* 29 (1964):182-207.

Finberg, Hilda F. "Jewish Residents in Eighteenth-Century Twickenham." *T.J.H.S.E.* 16 (1945-51): 129-35.

Fisher, H.E.S. "Review Article: Jews in England and the 18th-Century English Economy." *T.J.H.S.E.* 27 (1978-80):156-64.

Flory, Wendy Stallard. "The Psychology of Anti-Semitism: Conscience-Proof Rationalization and the Deferring of Moral Choice." *Anti-Semitism in the Contemporary World.* Ed. Michael Curtis. Boulder Colorado: Westview Press, 1986. pp. 238-250.

Gartner, Lloyd. "Emancipation, Social Change and Communal Reconstruction in Anglo-Jewry 1789-1881." *Proceedings of the American Academy for Jewish Research* 44 (1987):73-116.

Gibbs, Graham C. "Huguenot Contributions to England's Intellectual Life and England's Intellectual Commerce With Europe 1680-1720." *Huguenots in Britain and their French Background, 1550-1800.* Ed. Irene Scouloudi, Totowa, New Jersey: Barnes and Noble, 1987. pp. 20-41.

Gilley, Sheridan. "Roman Catholicism" in *Nineteenth Century English Religious Traditions Retrospect and Prospect.* Ed. D.G. Paz, Westport, Connecticut: Greenwood Press, 1945. pp. 33-56.

Gilbert, Arthur N. "Buggery and the British Navy, 1700-1861" in *History of Homosexuality in Europe and America.* Ed. Wayne R. Dynes and

Stephen Donaldson, New York & London: Garland, 1992. pp. 132-158.

Giuseppi, J.A. "Sephardi Jews and the Early Years of the Bank of England." *T.J.H.S.E.* 19 (1955-59):53-63.

Green, Geoffrey. "Anglo-Jewish trading connections with officers and seamen of the Royal Navy, 1740-1820." *T.J.H.S.E.* 29 (1982-86):97-133

Green, Ian. "Anglicanism in Stuart and Hanoverian England." *A History of Religion in Britain: Practice and Belief from Pre-Roman Times to the Present.* Eds. Sheridan Gilley and W.J. Shells. Cambridge, Massachusetts: Blackwell, 1994. pp. 168-188.

Greene, Donald. "Augustinianism and Empiricism: A Note on Eighteenth Century English Intellectual History." *Eighteenth-Century Studies* 1 (1967): 33-68.

Gwynn, Robin D. "Patterns in the Study of Huguenot Refugees in Britain: Past Present and Future," in *Huguenots in Britain and Their French Background, 1550-1800.* Ed. Irene Scouloudi, Totowa, New Jersey: Barnes and Noble, 1987. pp. 217-35.

Hawksworth, John. "On the Trades of London." *The Adventurer* 57 (June 26, 1753):

Heinemann, F.H. "John Toland and the Age of Enlightenment." *Review of English Studies* 20 (April, 1964): 125-46.

Horowitz, Irving Louis. "Philo-Semitism and Anti-Semitism: Jewish Conspiracies and Totalitarian Sentiments." *Midstream* 36 (May, 1990): 17-22.

Hyamson, Albert M. "The Jew Bill of 1753." *T.J.H.S.E.* 6 (1908-10): 156-88.

Jacob, Alex M. "The Jews of Falmouth." *T.J.H.S.E.* 17 (1951-52): 63-72.

Jessop, T.E. "The Misunderstood Hume." *Hume and the Enlightenment.* Ed. William B. Todd, Edinburgh: Edinburgh UP, 1974. pp. 1-12.

Jenkins, Geraint H. "Horrid Unintelligible Jargon: The Case of Dr. Thomas Bowls." *The Welsh History Review* 15 (December, 1991): 494-523.

_____" A Rank Republican (and) a Leveller." *The Welsh History Review* 17 (June, 1995): 365-86

Jones, Emry. "The Welsh in London in the Seventeenth and Eighteenth Centuries." *Welsh Historical Review* 10 (December, 1981):461-79.

Jordan, Winthrop D. "First impressions: initial English confrontations with Africans." in *"Race 'in Britain: Continuity and change.* Ed. Charles Husband, London: Hutchinson, 1987. pp. 42-72.

Katz, David, "The Jews of England and 1688," *Persecution and Toleration.* Ed. W.J. Shells, Oxford: Published for the Ecclesiastical History Society by B. Blackwell, 1984.

Katz, Jacob. "Free masons and Jews." in *Jacob Katz, Studies in Modern Jewish History.* Westhead, Farnborough, Hants, England: Gregg International Publishers, 1972, pp. 147-58.

_____ "Misreading of Anti-Semitism." *Commentary* 76 (July, 1983): 39-44.

Kellenbenz, Hermann. "German Immigrants in England." *Immigrants and Minorities in British Society.* London: George Allen & Unwin, 1978, pp. 63-80.

Lemire, Beverly. "Consumerism in Preindustrial and Early Industrial England: The Trade in Secondhand Clothes." *Journal of British Studies* 27 (January, 1988): 1-24.

Maccoby, Hyam. "The Wandering Jew as a Sacred Executioner." *The Wandering Jew: Essays in the Interpretation of a Christian Legend.* Ed. Galit Hassan-Rokem and Alan Dundes. Bloomington: Indiana UP, 1986. pp. 236-59.

Maxfield, Ezra Kempton. "The Quakers in English Stage Plays before 1800." *P. M.L.A.* 45 (March, 1930): 256-73.

Morgan, Philip D. "British Encounters with Africans and African-Americans, circa 1600-1780." *Strangers within the realm: Cultural Margins of the First British Empire.* Eds. Bernard Bailyn and Philip D. Morgan. Chapel Hill and London: U of North Carolina Press, 1991. pp. 157-219.

Naggar, Betty. "Old Clothes Men: Eighteenth and Nineteenth Centuries." *T.J.H.S.E.* 31 (1988-90): 171-91.

Newman, Aubrey. "Anglo-Jewry in the Eighteenth Century: A Presidential Address." *T.J.H.S.E.* 27 (1978-80): 1-10.

Nokes, David. "The Radical Conservatism of Swift's Irish Pamphlets." *British Journal for Eighteenth-Century Studies* 7 (Autumn, 1984): 169-76.

Payne, Harry C. "Elite Versus Popular Mentality in the Eighteenth Century." *Studies in Eighteenth Century Culture.* Ed. Roseann Runte.

Madison: Published for the American Society for Eighteenth Century Studies U of Wisconsin P, 1979. pp. 3-32.

Peskin, Allan. "England's Jewish Naturalization Bill of 1753" *Historia Judaica* 19 (1957): 3-32.

Pettegree, Andrew. "The French and Walloon Communities in London, 1550-1688." *From Persecution to Toleration: The Glorious Revolution and Religion in England*. Eds. Ole Peter Grell, et al. Oxford: Clarendon, 1991. pp. 77-127.

Popkin, Richard H. "Hume and Isaac de Pinto." *Texas Studies in Literature and Language* 12 (1970): 417-30.

_____ "The Philosophical Basis of Eighteenth-Century Racism." *Studies in Eighteenth-Century Culture: Racism in the Eighteenth-Century.* Ed. Harold E. Pagliaro. Cleveland: Case Western Reserve U Press, 1973. pp. 245-62.

Reitlinger, Gerald. "The Changed Face of English Jewry at the end of the Eighteenth Century." *T.J.H.S.E.* 23 (1969-70): 34-43.

Reuther, Rosemary. "The Theological Roots of Anti-Semitism." *The Persisting Question: Sociological Perspectives and Social Contexts of Modern Anti-Semitism*. Ed. Helen Fein. Berlin, New York: De Gruyter, 1987. (Vol. 1 in the series Current Research in Antisemitism) pp. 23-45.

Richards, Eric. "Scotland and the Uses of the Atlantic Empire." *Strangers Within the realm: Cultural Margins of the First British Empire*. Eds. Bernard Bailyn and Philip D. Morgan. Chapel Hill and London: U of North Carolina Press, 1991. pp. 67-114.

Rokeah, Zefira Entin. "The State, the Church, and the Jews in Medieval England." *Antisemitism Through the Ages*. Ed. Shmuel Almog. Oxford: Peragamon Press, 1988. pp. 99-125.

Rogal, Samuel J. "Enlightenment Enthusiasm: Anti-Methodism in the Literature of the Mid and Late Eighteenth Century." *Enlightenment Essays* 5 (Spring, 1974): 3-13.

Ross, J.M. "Naturalization of the Jews in England." *T.J.H.S.E.* 29 (1970-73): 59-72.

Roth, Cecil. "The Jewish Peddler-An 18th Century Rural Character." *In Essays and Portraits in Anglo-Jewish History*. Philadelphia: J.P. S., 1962. pp. 130-38.

Rubens, Alfred. "Anglo-Jewish Caricature 1780-1850." *T.J.H.S.E.* 23 (1969-70): 96-101.

_____ "Portrait of Anglo-Jewry 1656-1836." *T.J.H.S.E.* 19 (1955-59):13-52.

Rude, George. "Popular Protest in 18th Century Europe." *The Triumph of Culture* Ed. Paul Fritz and David Williams. Toronto: A.M. Hakkert, 1972. pp. 277-97.

Rumney, J. "Anglo-Jewry as seen through Foreign Eyes (1730-1830)." *T.J.H.S.E.* 13 (1932-35):323-40.

Samuel, Edger R. "Dr. Meyer Schomberg's Attack on the Jews of London." *T.J.H.S.E.* 20 (1959-61): 83-111.

Senelick, Lawrence. "Mollies or Men of Mode? Sodomy and the Eighteenth-Century Stage." *History of Homosexuality in Europe and America*, Vol. 5. Eds. Wayne R. Dynes and Stephen Donaldson, New York and London: Garland, 1992. Reprint from *Journal of the History of Sexuality* 1 (1990):33-67.

Snyder, Edward D. "The Wild Irish: A Study Of Some English Satires Against The Irish, Scots, And Welsh." *Modern Philology* 17 (April, 1920):147-185.

Shaftesley, John M. "Jews in Regular Freemasonary, 1717-1860." *T.J.H.S.E.* 25 (1973- 5):150-209.

Solomons, Israel. "Lord George Gordon's Conversion to Judaism." *T.J.H.S.E.* 7 (1911-14): 222-71.

_____ "Satirical and Political Prints on the Jews' Naturalization Bill, 1753." *T. J.H.S.E.* 7 (1908-10):205-33.

Spector, David. "The Jews of Brighton, 1770-1900." *T.J.H.S.E.* 22 (1970): 42-52.

Sutherland, Lucy Stuart. "Samson Gideon: Eighteenth Century Jewish Financier." *T.J.H.S.E.* 17 (1951-52): 79-90.

_____ "Sampson Gideon and the Reduction of Interest 1749-50." *Economic History Review* 16 (No. 1, 1946):15-29.

Tait, Hugh. "London Huguenot Silver." *Huguenots in Britain and Their French Background, 1550-1800* Ed. Irene Scouloudi. Totowa, New Jersey: Barnes and Noble, 1987, pp. 89-112.

Thompson, E.P. "The Moral Economy of the English Crowd in the Eighteenth Century." *Past and Present* 50 (February, 1971): 76-136.

Trevor-Roper, Hugh. "The Sephardim in England." *Historical Essays.* 1957; rpt. New York: Harper Torchbooks, 1966. pp. 151-55.

Trumbach, Randolf. Sodomical Subcultures, Sodomical Roles and the Gender Revolution of the Eighteenth Century: The Recent Historiography" *History of Homosexuality in Europe and America.* Eds. Wayne R. Dynes and Steven Donaldson. New York & London: Garland, 1992. pp. 387-99.

Walvin, James. "Black Caricature: The Roots of Racism." *Race in Britain: Continuity and Change* Ed. Charles Husband. London: Hutchinson, 1987. pp. 59-72.

Wiener, Max. "John Toland and Judaism." *H.U.C.A.* 16 (1941):215-42.

Wykes, David L. "The Spirit of Persecutors exemplified the Priestly Riots and the victims of Church and King mobs." *Transactions of the Unitarian Historical Society* 20 (April, 1991): 17-39.

Yardeni, Myriam. "Huguenots and Jews in Seventeenth and Eighteenth Century Brandenburg and Prussia." in *Studies in Judaism: Anti-Jewish Mentalities in Early Modern Europe.* Lanham, Maryland: U P of America, 1990. pp. 241-53.

Index

Bernard Glassman is a visiting professor in the history department at UMass Dartmouth and a faculty member of the Harvard-Radcliffe Hillel Institute of Jewish Studies. Currently, he is also the Book Review Editor for *Conservative Judaism Quarterly*. He holds a B.A. in philosophy from Brooklyn College (1957), an M.A. in history from Old Dominion University (1969), and a B.H.L.(1958), M.H.L. (1961), and D.H.L. (1971) from the Jewish Theological Seminary of America. He has served as the rabbi of Gomley Chesed in Portsmouth Virginia and Tifereth Israel in New Bedford. He was also the co-founder and co-director of the Center For Jewish Culture at U Mass Dartmouth.

South Florida Studies in the History of Judaism

South Florida Academic Commentary Series

South Florida International Studies in Formative Christianity and Judaism

South Florida-Rochester-Saint Louis
Studies on Religion and the Social Order

DATE DUE

			Printed in USA

HIGHSMITH #45230